DISTURBANCES IN THE FIELD

ESSAYS IN HONOR OF

DAVID L. MILLER

EDITED BY
CHRISTINE DOWNING

Spring Journal Books
New Orleans, Louisiana

Published by
Spring Journal, Inc.;
627 Ursulines Street;
New Orleans, Louisiana 70116
www. springjournalandbooks.com

Printed in Canada.
Text printed on acidfree paper.

Cover Art by Elizabeth Fergus-Jean
Photograph of David L. Miller by BillyconCarne

Library in Congress Cataloging in Publication Data Pending

DAVID L. MILLER

David L. Miller is the Watson-Ledden Professor of Religion, Emeritus, at Syracuse University, where he taught in the areas of myth, depth psychology, literary theory, and continental philosophy. In his research and writing, he works at the intersections of religion and mythology, literature and literary theory, depth psychology, and theology.

Dr. Miller received a B.A. from Bridgewater College in 1957 and a B. Div. from Bethany Theological Seminary in 1960. His Ph.D., awarded in 1963, was in the field of Theology and Culture at Drew University.

Dr. Miller taught from 1967-2001 at Syracuse University, where he was appointed Watson-Ledden Professor of Religion in 1983. He was the first to hold the William P. Tolley Distinguished Teaching Professorship in the Humanities (1996-99), and the first to be named University Scholar-Teacher of the Year (1980-81). He also received the Outstanding Teacher Award from the Alumni Society of University College of Syracuse University (1979-80) as well as the Graduate School Alumni of the Year Award from Drew University (1990). In 1994, Dr. Miller was awarded the Syracuse University Chancellor's Citation for Exceptional Academic Achievement.

In addition to his career at Syracuse University, Dr. Miller served as a Core Faculty Person in the Mythological Studies Program at Pacifica Graduate Institute in Santa Barbara, California from 1993-2004. He has also been involved in the training of psychotherapists at the C.G. Jung Institute in Zürich, Switzerland, as well as at Jung Institutes in the United States. A sought-after lecturer both nationally and internationally, Dr. Miller was a member of the Eranos Circle in Switzerland from 1975-88. He has also been active in scholarly associations, having served as President of the Society for the Arts, Religion, and Contemporary Culture, Chair of the Publications Committee of the American Academy of Religion, and as a member of the Boards of Directors of Scholars Press, the American Academy of Religion, and the Joseph Campbell Foundation.

Dr. Miller has written more than sixty articles and book chapters, as well as five books. The books include *Gods and Games: Toward a Theology of Play, The New Polytheism: Rebirth of the Gods and Goddesses, Christs: Archetypal Images in Christian Theology, Three Faces of God*, and *Hells and Holy Ghosts*. He is also the editor of two books: *Interpretation: The Poetry of Meaning* and *Jung and the Interpretation of the Bible*.

CONTENTS

FOREWORD

Spring 2006 will be a big year for birthdays: David Miller's 70th, my own 75th, Jim Hillman's 80th—and Freud's 150th. I intend to celebrate all of these—but David's comes first—and this is our gift!

I woke up one morning last summer knowing I wanted to mark David's birthday by putting together a *Festschrift* in his honor—a celebration in writing! I woke up just a few days later with a title in mind, "Disturbances in the Field," a title meant to evoke David's often-voiced conviction that his aim, as teacher, as writer, was dérangement. Almost every year at Pacifica Graduate Institute's fall orientations he told us that he had earlier that morning noticed a placard inscribed "Do Not Disturb, *Ne Pas Déranger*" hanging on the doorknob of his hotel room and how that led him to realize that his wish for us was an openness to being deranged. Some of us may have begun to wonder how often he could be surprised by finding that same placard once again!—but none of us questioned his commitment to the project of disturbing us and challenging us to become disturbers in our turn.

After putting together my other two anthologies, I swore I would *never* undertake such a project again—but working on this one has been sheer delight from that first morning's inspiration to today's sending it off to *Spring Journal* for publication. Everyone invited to contribute responded with such delight, wrote wonderful pieces, and got them in on time!

The day the idea first came to me I wrote Nancy Cater at *Spring Journal* to ask whether she might be willing to publish such a volume and to David's wife, Patricia, as to whether she thought David would welcome it. Both responded immediately with enthusiastic "yes"es, and Patricia Miller been enormously supportive and encouraging at every step of the way. She helped me put together the list of contributors and told me where to find many of them; she supplied the photo of David and the biographical sketch. When I sent her a list of all those who had agreed to write for the volume, she wrote me: "I'd break out into song if it wouldn't make David suspicious!"

She couldn't then, but now we may:

HAPPY BIRTHDAY, DAVID!

CHRISTINE DOWNING
ORCAS ISLAND, WASHINGTON
DECEMBER 2005

WHO IS THE POET?

STANLEY ROMAINE HOPPER

Who is the Poet?

He
whose heart
hath known

the vigils of
the wilderness
who
fed with ravens

knows
the bliss
of fire and storm
and thence
the forms, the norms
of gentleness

Who is the Poet?

He
in whom the vision
does not die

Whose eye
is open, and whose ear
is blest
with silences and song

The rest
he waits for
as the sky
lies still
at dawn[1]

—from *Why Persimmons and Other Poems* (Atlanta: Scholars Press, 1987), pp. 149, 151.

On the Etymology of "Festschrift" and Other Imaginal Realities: An Essay In Honor of David Miller

STAN AND JAN MARLAN

Worship is a kind of holy play in which the soul,
with utter abandonment, learns how to waste time
for the sake of God. —*Romano Guardini*[1]

Festschrift is defined as "a volume of learned articles or essays by colleagues and admirers, serving as a tribute ... especially to a scholar."[2] But hidden below words are paths to an archetypal depth, circuitous and profound.

Etymology is an attempt "to understand words in their fullest implications and subtleties, in their nuances and most delicate modifications..."[3] Partridge, for example, notes that most of the innumerable learned words—e.g. scientific, technical, philosophical, psychological, sociological and literary ones—are missing from the dictionary. "These," he notes, "are specialist terms."[4] He sites the word *Calyptorhynchus*, a genus of dark-colored cockatoos, and notes:

> Such a word has no right to appear in an etymological dictionary and no privilege to appear in any 'straight' dictionary ... yet the list of elements will reveal that the word is compounded of *calypto-*, meaning 'covered', hence 'hidden', and *–rhynchus*, 'beak'.[5]

1

It would seem that even these kinds of obscure words have deep occult reference, and so it is important to both respect and deviate from the well-worn paths of scholars such as C.T. Onions, in his classic *Oxford Dictionary of English Etymology*, where—among a myriad of standard, scholarly etymological elaborations of always interesting words—*festschrift* (with its obvious Germanic roots) remains notably absent.[6]

For our purposes with the word *festschrift*, we must also consider etymology as an archetypal and psychological operation. Turning from Onions to *Dragonflies* (the journal), enter imaginal psychology. "Psychologists seek soul when they etymologize," says Kugelman. "Psychological etymology is an operation on language that raises psyche into presence. ... Etymologizing is a poesis with words."[7]

Likewise, David Miller's work, in the spirit of psychological etymology, has inspired researchers to seek below the surface and to probe the shadows and nuances of our beliefs, to uncover the unconscious roots, and to find the important dark and sacred images that animate our daily lives. In this spirit we believe looking at the etymology of *festschrift* will help us to understand Miller's work and his contribution to the fields of both depth psychology and theology.

If *festschrift* as we have noted is a volume of learned articles, it is also a festival, an occasion for feasting, revelry, conviviality and celebration. It is especially a day or time of religious significance. The Latin *festivus,* from *festus,* also alludes to a time of pleasure, joy and gaiety. Schrift can be traced to Middle High German *schrift,* from Old High German *scrift,* from *scriban,* to write, from Latin, *scribere.*[8] *Fest,* festival, plus *schrift,* writing—a celebration of written words. Likewise from the root *skribh* we find important derivatives such as scribble, scribe, script, ascribe, circumscribe, conscript, describe, inscribe, prescribe, subscribe, transcribe, manuscript, postscript—all of which most importantly in Miller's case lead to *scripture.*

With scripture and from the Latin *scribere* we find some essential meanings with regard to Miller's work. *Scribere* means to scratch, incise, write and, from the Greek, *to scarify.* Here in the roots of *festschrift* we begin to find a hint of the deep meaning of etymology and a way from it to Miller's contribution: the scarification of scripture. Scratching below the surface, for instance, of the sacred hero mythology of the Christ figure, Miller de-scribes the clown and the drunk. "When life goes drunk," says Miller, "things seem transitory and extreme, flowing here and there, like time's Heraclitean river."[9] One cannot step in the same Miller twice.

This work is part of what Miller has recently called "skiopoiesus" in his twenty-year project to "identify a problematic idea, [and] probe its depth to uncover its unconscious image…"[10] We might say: to scarify it, to mark its surface with a cross, that is, to 'x' it out in postmodern fashion, to reveal its uncomfortable underbelly. Miller moves from peaks to pits as he continues to deepen his exposé of the shadow of religious ideas. He concludes that religion has a psychopathogenic nature, or—to put it more graphically—that religion makes us sick. Miller, a-theist, notes that Christian images are dangerous and quotes Kierkegaard as having said: "Christianity is the invention of Satan calculated to make human beings unhappy."[11]

Here is Miller as master of scarification, placing 'negation' in our face; but Miller is no simple preacher of darkness. He is also a *fun-da-mentalist* (duh!), a mentalist who descends into laughter, a master of *theologia ludens*.[12] Consider:

> Laughter may be the key for understanding this odd and obnoxious fantasy of Western religion because there has existed since Aristotle, which is to say, since well before the time of Christian thinking, a curious correspondence between theories of laughter and comedy, on the one hand, and the notion that the bliss of the blessed consists in taking delight at the eternal suffering of the damned, on the other hand.[13]

In another place he has shown us that laughter is one of his own aims: "not literal laughter so much as liberation that comes from comic release, or, in a Shakespearean tragedy, from comic relief."[14] We are moving to fest as feast, meaning scrumptious meal or entertainment, related to religious festival. Middle English, *feste*, from Old French, from Vulgar Latin, *festa*, festal (not vestal), meaning joyous. When you have fun, you are mental; when you are mental, you have fun. With Miller we revel in mental fun—a joyous feast, a celebration.

In *Gods and Games*, he quotes Nietzsche: "The trick is not to arrange a festival. The trick is to find people who can enjoy it."[15] Not an easy task, and so it is our contention that this early recognition continues throughout Miller's work and is perhaps the most significant strand of his multi-faceted oeuvre. To demonstrate this requires further inquiry and etymological exposition to a polytheistic etymological inquiry (from the words to the letters to the spaces between them).

David Miller is a man of letters and, to give his work a strong misreading, it is important to turn back to the letters themselves, even to displace them for their hidden ill-usions. Let's take the word itself.

F-e-s-t-s-c-h-r-i-f-t.

Ahh, good cheer.

F is for fun, feast, frivolity—not to mention fool, foolish, and foolhardy. Let alone, for Firemaker.[16] F is linked to fest-er and jester, and by extension, to its shadow side, fest-evil (cf: Faamiti (Samoan): to make a squeaking noise by sucking air past the lips in order to gain the attention of a dog or a child[17]...or a colleague.)

E is for the evil, the evil that follows fest. Not to mention: Easter, Eagle Scout, effort, edges, and egregious errors.

S is for Shepherds, schlep-herds, raising Miller's work to a missionary zeal (cf: sherry and sapphire [Bombay], raising Miller to a missionary zeal; also, S is the third letter, the Trinitarian letter, the purloined Q turns fest to quest and thus to Quatrinity.)

T is for theopoesis—not to mention, tennis (Miller's rackets).

S again. More shepherds, following the star by night (the star of David, after all... have we mentioned that he was a tennis star?)

C. Ah, then....C. C is for Christianity, Clowns, and C'ers. (Miller is visionary.)

H is for Hells, Holy Ghosts, and wholes.

R is for ontology (i.e. we R).

I is for the eye of God, and for ego. (If you notice that the I is in the word, it's because the ego is still present, and God is not. Until D.)

4

D is for the death of the ego, for Deity, drunkenness, dumb, and dumber. For those of you who bothered to notice that there is no D in festschrift, well, then you are looking in the wrong place. The D is in the empty space between letters, the Holy Ghost of letters, and the D appears in the nothingness between the I (ego) and the F (fool)....very iffy. [Similar analytical achievements in psychological etymology brought Miller to the attention of the IAAP. Better to have the man on the inside, sublated, than running around on the loose...]

F and T, already accounted for... End of cheer.

Notice, too, that festschrift and David Miller have the same number of letters: eleven. We are not sure of the exact significance of this, but you never know, and that's the subject for another paper.

As we draw our reflection on etymology to a close and make our professional exit, we turn again to festschrift itself,

FESTSCHRIFT

trying to sublate it, bracket it, perform the *sous rapture,* actively imagine it, passively imagine it, alchemically calcine it, mortify it, drive it to the nigredo, let it rot, sing it, play with it, speak to it, put it in touch with its lost objects, sublimate it, torture, scratch and scarify it, à la Miller. But alas, none of our scholarly apparatus worked. Then: a gift, an epiphany, a resurrection, a revivification, the word simply rolled over, mirrorlike, looked back at us, and revealed its secret meaning:

ꞭE2ꓕ2CH𐐒ꞮEꝆ

[BESTSCHPIEL.] ....i.e., best schpiel!

All along, Miller has been known for his fine lectures and rich tapestries. A typical example of Millerschpiel is as follows:

> Could it be that when King James' translators rendered *der Heilige Geist* and *to pneuma to hagion* with the English phrase "Holy Ghost," they were, wittingly or unwittingly, implying an intimacy of meanings, a complex of theological sense, in whose perspective God

> is Guest as well as Host when God is a Ghost? That is, God is God when being a Ghost, and God is Ghost when being Ghastly, the Ghastly Anger which haunts, being at the same time the Host of the human and its strange Guest—wounded and torn, shade and shadow, presence and absence, in life and death, forever. The Divine Host is Ghost which is at the same time Ghastly Guest. In this odd sense that which is implied by an improper translation, one which is somehow correct just the same? Can it be that "ghost" and "spirit," "ghost" and "host" in fact do belong together in the fantasia of the eternal mystery sustained by the word?—the Lord of Hosts a Ghost; the Ghost our Host![18]

Through such ghastly schpiels, we get a clearer view of the holy fool, the drunken teacher, the iconoclast, descent into the underworld, ghosts and disappearing angels.[19] For such as this, Miller has received many awards and re-cognitions, including the Outstanding Scholar-Teacher of the Year, and a Chancellor's Citation for Exceptional Academic Achievement, and—our favorite, though not as well-known award—the I-con-a-class't Award for Tricksterish Behavior and Theological Revisioning.

Last but not least, we note that David once quoted Kierkegaard: "It is always good to be distinguished by something. I ask nothing better than to be pointed out as the only one in our serious age who is not serious." We hope that our reflections have paid tribute to David in this spirit.

The only serious thing we must add is an endnote, remarking that it is an honor to honor David Miller, to be considered his friends, and to share our appreciation for his profound contribution, subtle humor and *joie de vivre* which have inspired and touched us over the many years we have known him.

NOTES

[1] Romano Guardini, *The Church and the Catholic and the Spirit of the Liturgy* (New York: Sheed and Ward, 1935), 179.

[2] *The American Heritage Dictionary of the English Language: Third Edition* (Boston: Houghton Mifflin, 1992), 674.

³ Eric Partridge, *Origins: The Encyclopedia of Words—their meanings, etymology, and use throughout history* (New York: The Macmillan Company, 1958), xiii.

⁴ *Ibid.*, xiii.

⁵ *Ibid.*, xiii.

⁶ The authors note that, while it would have been beneficial to consult a Germanic etymological dictionary as well, we did not have that book. We did consult Eric Partridge's *A Classical Dictionary of the Vulgar Tongue*, however, and noted that—between 'ferret' and 'fetch'—festschrift is noticeably absent from it, as well.

⁷ Robert Kugelman, "Etymology as a Psychological Operation," *Dragonflies: Studies in Imaginal Psychology* (Fall 1978): 45, 52.

⁸ *The American Heritage Dictionary of the English Language: Third Edition* (Boston: Houghton Mifflin, 1992), 674.

⁹ David Miller, *Christs: Meditations on Archetypal Images in Christian Theology* (New York: The Seabury Press, 1981), 140 [repr. ed. New Orleans: Spring Journal Books, 2005].

¹⁰ David Miller, "Theology after Jung: Holy and Not So Holy Ghosts! Psychopathogenic Shadows in Religious Images and Ideas," *Journal of Jungian Theory and Practice Vol. 8 No. 1* (2006—in press).

¹¹ Søren Kierkegaard, *Journals XI.I.A487.*

¹² David Miller, *Gods and Games: Toward a Theology of Play* (New York: The World Publishing Co., 1970), 158.

¹³ David Miller, *Hells and Holy Ghosts: A Theopoetics of Christian Belief* (New Orleans: Spring Journal Books, 2004), 61-62.

¹⁴ David Miller, *The New Polytheism: Rebirth of the Gods and Goddesses* (New York: Harper & Row, 1974), 78.

¹⁵ David Miller, *Gods and Games: Toward a Theology of Play* (New York: The World Publishing Co., 1970), 135.

¹⁶ Synchronistically, we note that the first letter of Festschrift corresponds to that of Firemaker, the patch that Miller never received as a Boy Scout. Oddly, this missing F may be at the psychological root of the fires Miller now sets in the intellectual world.

¹⁷ Internet reference from the Holy Ghost, not traceable.

[18] David Miller, *Hells and Holy Ghosts: A Theopoetics of Christian Belief* (New Orleans: Spring Journal Books, 2004), 106.

[19] See the internet, http://web.syr.edu/~dlmiller/dlmcv.htm, where David himself or someone else says something very similar.

The Thunderbolt Stitches

LYNDA SEXSON

When I entered the Ph.D. program at Syracuse University, David Miller immediately sent me in search of frogs, fairy tales, and grandmothers. Ever since he has graciously opened conversation: presenting together in church basements, sitting on my dissertation committee, writing a meditation on angels for our journal, *Corona*, delivering a luminous essay on my book at a session of the American Academy of Religion. Above all those gifts, David Miller introduced me to Heraclitus. In gratitude, I offer seventy little fragments, one for each year. Happy Birthday, David.

1. Change hangs loose. Everyone else has fled. How is it, then, that there's a fragment we call memory?

2. *Hen Panta*, I remember my teacher saying: *One. All.* Fragment as wholeness. *Panta pei*, eternal flux, he told us, and Heraclitus shifted the shapes.

3. The splinters and slivers of the world look random as a broken mirror. But stand back far enough, and all is one. This must be why Archimedes, with lever in hand, asked for a place to stand. I have my pencil, with no room of my own.

9

4. The gods are myriad; their quarrels are one.

5. This is why the gods laugh at the limp of Hephaestus and the thousand wounds of Indra. The limp of Hephaestus is the jagged lightning. The wounds of Indra are eyes; the eyes are vulvas. Divine disgrace is human grace.

6. Heidegger said that *language plays with us*; is that why we are thunderstruck?

7. Teaching, Miller says, gets us *not what one desires or expects*. I became his student.

8. He sent me looking for frogs. When I came to love the work too much and accidentally turned the frogs to princes, he sent me out again for more frogs.

9. The frog's ransom for the golden ball ameliorates the bloody ransom designed by Tertullian. Transmutation preserves all the beastly parts; salvation discards the earth.

10. Clinging to the clock's hands, dangling from the tower, anachronism is necessary.

11. The children set fire to the sacred books and cups. When they sifted through all the ashes they found only one little stone that was engraved, *Ahimsa*, Do No Harm. It got lost. The kids sifted again, and discovered another stone. It was carved with, *Madhu*, Honey. It got lost. The children made inadvertent letters with their smudgy fingers.

12. Laughter is the thunderbolt of all things.

13. Freud liked Goethe saying, *The best of what you know, you must not tell the boys.* This is called teaching.

14. What goes on four in the morning, two in the afternoon, three in the evening? Insomnia.

15. At night the sheep count me. They cannot learn to count to two, thus we never get to sleep.

16. Didn't Jesus say in some lost gospel that sin is the failure to recognize the on-going miracle, to give thanks for the sustained rather than the surprise? This was called turning water to wine. *Metanoia.*

17. Miller said, *To put a story or explanation on an image is like putting a biography on an angel. It makes the angel an alternator. No lightning.* How many stories can be pinned on one angel?

18. What is the difference between angels on the head of a pin and a moth impaled on a pin? Freud dreamed of a moth flying with a pin through its thorax. A moth dreamed he was Freud, pinned to the couch.

19. Chuang Tzu went to sleep with a skull for a pillow. The skull talked to him about death, which is what we expect from skulls. But the skull smiled, which is uncanny, even given the skull's constant grin.

20. After the blackbird whistled, or just before ceasing, another took up the song. *A man, a woman, a blackbird are one.* The blackbird sings, *Anitya.*

21. Logocentrism's circumference is just around the corner.

22. The David Miller Effect we call it. Bricoleur and magus, he has the last word, weaving the longwinded, the obscure, the pedestrian, the pedant, into his response—he spins straw into sunlight.

23. The forestry department hires villagers to drive away the elephants. When the money runs out, the villagers drive the elephants back to the crops. The forestry department repeatedly hires the villagers. Finally, the elephants pay no attention to drums and firecrackers. The ceremony declines.

24. Another part of the forest. The elk are bugling. A man walks between bull and cow to get the picture. The elk charges. The forest rangers

tranquilize the elk and saw off his antlers. The man goes free. The ceremony declines.

25. They forgot to put out dishes for the leopards. Amnesia became the ceremony.

26. We know what a mind is: that which can be lost; we know what a soul is: that which can be lost; we know what time is: what a tooth is: what a shirt is: that which can be .... [Here the text breaks off.]

27. We know by absences rather than presences. The Garden of Eden. God. My old blue glass beads. One of the hairs of the old dog still clings to the couch.

28. The earth is indifferent, yet so willing to take us back at any moment.

29. Joan Crawford, *Possessed*, wearing the mask of the weeping philosopher, crosses the *noir* street. From one take to the next, in the same scene, Joan Crawford's shoes change. It's the Movies. They are made of light.

30. The self is an imaginary island in which our ravaged shores of familiarity are constantly eroded into the borders of unknowing. Each day we awaken to an unfamiliar map of the self.

31. Each of us is alone in her thoughts, yet we all turn at once, like a flight of birds, toward the fruit. But the fruit thinks the thoughts of tree, sky, water, even of birds.

32. The mind is a wanderer.

33. The mind is an out-of-body experience. But neither Descartes nor St. Paul should rely on the split.

34. *Mind the gap.* Missionaries insert a compressed Sanskrit word, *Sachitananada*, into the Christian liturgy so that the concept of the Trinity will sound familiar. So the heathen will recognize the Three Faces of God. *Sat, chit, ananda* are three emptied words (being,

knowing, bliss) for that which is *nirguna,* beyond attributes. The insertion of the word widens the gap.

35. Stevens asked of Eden, *Does ripe fruit never fall?* In the Garden, the fruits, which will become Nature (as postlapsarian consequence) are already ripe (as prelapsarian desire): Gravity knocks the apple to the earth, levity slips on the banana peel. The laws of Nature are cast out of Paradise.

36. Logos is both the moment and momentum of psyche. These are what Heraclitus called change.

37. Between thin*g* and thin*k* is a small hedge (*hij*), or a long pilgrimage.

38. Miller told three hundred students that Hermes tied sandals on all the cattle. And the students, with three hundred pencils, wrote it all down. It was as true as walking backwards.

39. Voyaging Darwin, catching up with Heraclitus, captured a drop of the luminous sea and wrote, *When the water was put into a bottle, it gave out sparks.*

40. Psyche plays at persona *like a child moving counters in a game.* The child held up a spoon and said, Pretend this is a spoon.

41. History is psyche's pageant. Emerson whispers of *an occult relation between man and the vegetable.*

42. Gigantic shards of granite fall decorously and continuously from the sky. The dreamer runs a labyrinth amid falling stones to rescue Mother, and awakens to the relief that they are mere dream stones. Then, she grieves, in the dream it was merely a rain of sharp stones between the quick and the dead.

43. Ovid is the changer of minds. Trees are reluctant girls; birds are regrets; echoes are as close as it comes to love.

44. Coyote looked everywhere for his eyes. Blind Coyote had to learn to see without them, and that is how he invented writing.

45. If a whole room becomes visible at once, the house collapses.

46. Sarah lies to the angels about laughing. Then gives birth to Pleasure. *Isaac.* Psyche listens to her sisters' lies and peeks into the darkness. Then gives birth to Pleasure. *Volupta.*

47. Eggs dress up in feathers and go disguised as chickens. Chickens fold up their suits and pack them into tiny oval trunks. The question is hatched over and over.

48. Which came first: the masquerade.

49. *A coil of rope is mistaken for a snake.* What if Eve had asked, instead of only for three, for the fourth? She hungered for fruit, for beauty, for wisdom. If she had hungered for likeness, she would have rolled back the nakedness, *arom,* of the snake, and uncovered the slickness, *arum,* of the rope. The story might not be about salvation, but simulation.

50. The rope, so weary of being taken for a snake, begins to hiss.

51. Miller said, *There is no unironic situation because there is always an other side, an unsaid. It's threshold all the way down.* We are all Schrödinger's not-yet cat, and always on the wrong side of the door.

52. History of religions: A man tries to squeeze blood from a stone. He had heard the stone's heartbeat. Other men trample over the stones searching for the man who squeezed blood from bread. When they find him, they pierce him, lapping from the wounds. Then they hear about the turnip and run to find it.

53. I dreamed of water reflecting Mt. Rainier. *The way up and the way down are the same.*

54. Prospero drowned his book. Rabbi Nachman burned his. What will it matter if we don't know the alphabet?

55. Plato wanted to burn the writings of the Laughing Philosopher. Who would laugh, if the soul is fire?

56. The bell rings for dinner and for death. The dog salivates, with no ambiguity. Pavlov counts seizures until the dog reaches the fatal one. Dinner bell. Death knell.

57. The dog barks at the mailman, one of his closest friends. Heraclitus received no letters, so his dogs had to bark at strangers.

58. Despite unique hexagonal crystals, snow sticks together. Despite its hexagonal, crystalline perfections, snow has the grace to melt.

59. A rainbow is an optical collusion between water and fire.

60. A man went to the stationmaster and presented his ticket to claim his soul. You want to give up this ticket? The stationmaster was incredulous. Give me my soul, the man said. The ticket's non-refundable, shrugged the stationmaster, handing him a wrinkled brown paper bag twisted at the top. Just then the train pulled into the station. Suddenly giraffes, gods, bats, lions, bristlecone pines, painters, spiders, and pearls all rushed to board the train. The man longed to jump on the train. You have no ticket, said the stationmaster. I'll give it up, said the man, trying to give back the little bag. The stationmaster laughed. Non-refundable. Where are they all going? They are going on the train, said the stationmaster.

61. Bottom had been loved by a fairy and still desired to play all the parts.

62. Longing casts a shadow, which is mistaken for the beloved.

63. While a man slept loaves became calendar pages. The decay of bread. While a man slept a serpent ate the thorny plant. The sloughing of skin. These are the dreams the world has while the sleeper dreams of immortality. The earth dreams in time.

64. *Nature loves to hide*, said the philosopher. Yet, bread falls butter side down and cats feet first. So if bread defies the rules and falls butter side up, then falling cats beware.

65. Miller said, *Gratification and closure are infinitely deferred.* Thus, the wise centipede drops another shoe. And we listen.

66. If the question has an answer, Ask again later.

67. The self is the one who calls herself into question.

68. The self: Buster Keaton, as movie projectionist, falls asleep, and by means of his dreaming body he leaves his sleeping body, walks past the audience and up over the piano, onto the proscenium and into the screen. He is thrown out of the movie by other celluloid characters, but picks himself up and re-enters. He is an imperfect fit, buffeted by continual scene changes. He approaches a door to find himself falling from a stone garden bench, suddenly in a busy street fleeing cars, he nearly runs off a cliff. Avoiding the precipice, he finds himself in a den of lions, but as they are about to taste him, he's in a desert. And then before he can be run over by a train, he's stranded on a rock in the ocean, diving off into a snow bank and finding himself back on that stone garden bench. *C'est moi.*

69. Images of soul shatter images.

70. Body, embodiment, theory, acting self, sleeping self, dreaming self, screen self, all made of light.

David L. Miller:
Scholar, Gentleman, Friend

JAMES B. WIGGINS

D avid L. Miller and I met in September 1960 when with some other students we walked into a room at Drew University to sit for a German language proficiency examination. Reading ability in German and French was a requirement for qualifying for admission to Ph.D. candidacy. In short order we began to have regular social contact as well as finding ourselves in some graduate courses together.

In some ways we were unlikely to have become such close friends as happened quickly. He is the son of a minister father and a mother, a high schoolteacher. From and with them he was involved in important educational, ecclesiastical and travel opportunities. David grew up in the Washington, D.C. area and had the benefit of regular exposure to the cultural and major sporting events of living in one of the country's leading metropolitan areas. By contrast, I grew up in a small town in central Texas. My parents were working people, my father a laborer in the oil fields of Texas and my mother a saleslady for Avon products. Although I had as good an education as a small town school system could provide with dedicated teachers, my cultural education was limited during those early years, certainly in comparison with living in metropolitan Washington.

David and I did share a similar undergraduate educational experience in that both of us attended small church-related colleges, he Bridgewater College, a Brethren institution in Virginia, and I Texas Wesleyan College (since then having been renamed Texas Wesleyan University), a Methodist school in Fort Worth, Texas.

After college, he attended Bethany Theological Seminary in Chicago for his Bachelor of Divinity, and I graduated from Perkins School of Theology at Southern Methodist University in Dallas. I rehearse our pre-Drew educational backgrounds because, although in different institutions, we came over the years to share a conviction about some of the things we gained from having had those years in higher education before starting our Ph.D. studies. The obvious possible benefits of intellectual and psychological maturation that were provided by three years of theological study after our undergraduate work, and also the benefit of formal participation in the structure and content of the theological curriculum—we gained much from both of those. We came to understand something of what is involved substantively in scriptural, theological and philosophical thinking. And we were taught the importance of rhetorical work through courses in homiletics and practical organizational administration through courses in "practical theology" that included how to organize and manage church institutions. We often pondered what analogous arrangements might have been provided to graduate students who did not have the benefit of a theological school background. But I am getting ahead of the story.

Not only did David and I begin Ph.D. studies on the same day in the same institution. We received our degrees and graduated on the same day three years later. In the meantime we shared many things. With our wives we spent many a wonderful evening playing bridge together. We sometimes ventured into Manhattan from Madison, New Jersey, to attend plays together. We played handball and tennis together. We took courses together. We made enduring common connections and friendships with graduate student colleagues that have lasted in many cases until today. We became junior colleagues with many professors who in subsequent years became close friends and peers in the field. Our study offices in the university library were close to each other. We endured the challenges of qualifying examination preparation and dissertation writing within the same time frame. We each experienced the birth of a daughter only a few weeks prior to our graduation. Such were some of the bases for friendship that has continued uninterrupted for forty-five years, and will continue, I trust for yet more years to come.

I had the good fortune to be appointed to the faculty of the Religion Department of Syracuse University after graduation from Drew in 1963. After three years during which he stayed on at Drew as a faculty member, David went to Syracuse University as my colleague. We had maintained a close connection during those three years, and his decision to join us was greeted gladly. (I fully acknowledge that I exerted as much influence on my colleagues at Syracuse and upon David personally as I could muster to accomplish his coming.) From fall 1967 when he went to Syracuse until May 2001 we were colleagues on the Syracuse faculty; as we had begun graduate school together and graduated together, so we retired together on the same day. I am unaware of many other instances of such close relationships in the academic world marked by such common significant events. And I have been the beneficiary of his friendship and collegial relationship through it all.

Those were exciting times for many reasons. The Supreme Court decisions of that year opened the field of the academic study of religion to be incorporated in the curriculum of many tax-supported institutions of higher education where it had never been included before. Rehearsing the history of that expansion in the period from the mid-1960's until the early 1980's is a project worthy of doing in its own right, but for another day. I will confine these remarks to but a few of the highlights to indicate why I value having been David's colleague for all those years.

David has been a celebrated and renowned teacher throughout his career. He is gifted with an extraordinary ability to engage audiences large and small, young and older when he lectures. In a department blessed with many other colleagues who were fine teachers, David stood out. His courses were always over-subscribed in enrollment, regardless of the subject. I had the opportunity on a few occasions to team-teach with

19

David. And I was deeply impressed first hand and up close with his imaginative, provocative, sometimes profane, and always profound thinking and presentations. That is not to say that he was always understood clearly by all audiences, but for those with ears to hear, he provided what has come to be called "transformative education." One of the clearest instances of the regard in which students held him was his course on mythology taught to undergraduates over many years. Regardless of the capacity of the room in which it was scheduled, and it always exceeded 200 seats, it was over subscribed with a waiting list. He brought a world populated by gods, goddesses, ogres, demons, archetypes, and animal images, etc. to life and to contemporary importance for thousands of undergraduates in that single course. And it was typical of his work in the many other courses he provided.

David has thought deeply and creatively about normative issues involved in designing and delivering graduate education. He was extensively involved in 1967-1969 in designing and inaugurating a revised MA curriculum and new Ph.D. program. Professor Gabriel Vahanian was then the director of Graduate Studies and the program was innovative in many ways. It established a trajectory for graduate studies that has marked Syracuse University from that inception as a distinctive place to study religion. In the broadest possible terms the words "Religion and Culture" have been enduring descriptors of the graduate program at Syracuse. Great emphasis has been placed over the decades in enabling students to become familiar with a variety of approaches to the study of the phenomena that fall under the rubric of the "academic study of religion." Each student has been required to generate a very tailored and concrete array of content or subject areas to which she or he would apply different approaches. Thus, deep study of content with broad familiarity with diverse approaches to those studies has prepared students capable of creativity and flexibility in responding to opportunities to teach in a wide variety of academic institutions and settings. And, no less important, in a time of the over production of people graduating with preparation in the academic study of religion combined with fewer teaching opportunities, many of the SU graduates have found distinguished careers outside the academic world. Through every permutation and assessment of graduate studies in religion at SU from the time he arrived on the faculty until the time of his retirement, David has played an integral role in the process.

In addition to being a theoretician of graduate studies, David has been an exemplary teacher of graduate students. Throughout his service at Syracuse and in the subsequent years during which he was an adjunct at the Pacifica Graduate Institute in Santa Barbara, California, he has directed well over 100 Ph.D. dissertations and participated in hundreds of qualifying examinations. His courses have repeatedly evoked accolades from students. In my estimation as a teacher and mentor, David is *nonpareil*.

David has been a very productive scholar with five books and dozens of journal articles and book chapters written over the decades. His interpretive skills range very far and his creative flair is deeply impressive. Others writing for this book will have delved into many of his writings, so I am foregoing that here. Rather, I want to remark that his exploring the mythological and depth psychological dimensions and resonances of remarkably diverse "religious" resources and others that are typically identified as "secular" materials, has resulted in a very distinctive body of work. It has been met with an equally distinctive reception of much of his work. I perceive him to have been disappointed, even to a degree disillusioned, by the lack of a broader response and engagement by and from scholars focused in the academic study of religion. To be sure he has been admired by and his work widely appreciated by some who work in very particular sub-fields in the study of religion. But many others in the field with whom he might have had a very interesting interaction have all too often ignored or ignorantly criticized his thinking. Too bad for them and for the field, in my estimation!

David, on the other hand, has a sterling reputation and very wide and appreciative audience and following in the worlds of mythological studies and of Jungian analytical psychology. Although I am aware of a few others trained in the study of religion who also participate in those circles, I am certain that virtually none has risen to such prominence therein. The formal evidence for that judgment is totally convincing, culminating in 2004 when he was made an honorary member of the International Association of Analytical Psychology, an honor rarely extended to anyone who is not a practicing therapist. Leading up to that honor, Dr. Miller has lectured extensively and internationally at gatherings of Jungian therapists and has been widely involved in training new therapists. Unfortunately his is by no means the only case in which a thinker has not been anywhere nearly sufficiently honored in his own country (in this case the field of the academic study of religion), but at least he is widely known and honored in other very significant arenas.

One other dimension of my appreciation for the person and professional work of David Miller lies in our shared involvement in the same department for all those years and concurrently in the American Academy of Religion. David was my personal advocate through the process of promotion in rank on the faculty of Syracuse University and, as an honored professor (he was named to the prestigious Watson-Ledden Professorship in 1983), he was instrumental in our university appointing me to a named professorship late in my own career at SU. I am grateful for that support.

From 1980 until 2000 I served as chairperson of the Department of Religion and from 1982 through 1991 I sandwiched in serving as Executive Director of the American Academy of Religion. Although we did not always agree (which two people ever do, and how boring it would be if it were the case), David was a constant ally and friend upon whose counsel and actions I depended heavily. When policy issues were considered, he was invariably thoughtful and participative in the process of arriving at the most equitable decision possible. In the intellectually challenging and emotionally laden tasks of evaluating colleagues for such things as contract renewal, tenure recommendation, promotion, and departmental roles, he was extremely thoughtful and insightful. As I already indicated, he contributed greatly to the design and content of the curriculum of the department. He did not relish the work, but when requested to serve as Director of Graduate Studies in the Department, he did so with commitment and aplomb.

DAVID L. MILLER: SCHOLAR, GENTLEMAN, FRIEND

In the larger university he was recognized and admired. He was selected as the first Tolley Distinguished Teaching Professor of the Humanities for a three-year appointment that revolves among professors across the university. The conversations he engendered across the university faculty during those years were stimulating and enriching to all of us who were able to participate.

During my years as administrator of the AAR I recruited David to service in a number of important roles. He was on the Board of Scholars Press for a three-year term and concurrently was chair of the AAR's Publications Committee and was thereby a member of the AAR Board of Directors *ex officio* during that same period. At one time he was nominated for but not elected to the position of Vice-President of the AAR. He served on the steering committee for some AAR program units and frequently made presentations at the annual national meetings, including a plenary address one year. Thus, he contributed widely and very significantly to the development and expansion of the scholarly and professional organization for the field of the academic study of religion. He is one of not many who were in attendance at the meeting of the National Association of Biblical Instructors (NABI) in 1963 at Union Theological Seminary in New York where the decision was taken by the members present and voting to change the name to the American Academy of Religion and to adopt a new constitution for the organization. It has been a rare year since then that he has missed being in attendance at the annual meetings.

With those few and in many ways quite superficial words of rehearsal and commendation for David as teacher, scholar, professional, I will conclude with some reflections of a more personal appreciation regarding David as a friend. We have shared many meals over the years, just the two of us and with our families. Our children grew up well acquainted with each other as we socialized in a variety of ways. We have shared the challenges of transitions in our respective families and been available to each other through some very difficult times. We continue to be together frequently. Invariably I experience David L. Miller as a friend for all seasons. After forty-five years' duration of our relationship, I look forward to many more years of connection and appreciation. I am forever profoundly indebted to and appreciative of sharing his friendship.

MATCHING THE HATCH

TED L. ESTESS

On the occasion of David Miller's retirement from Syracuse, a group of graduate students kindly invited me to come back for a special day to honor David. I was asked, of all things, to speak on "success," specifically, success in the field of religious studies, a subject about which I know nothing at all. But I was proud to have been asked to join with those fine students, who, like me, owe so very much to David. On that bright blue day in Upstate New York, I spoke as follows:

At the outset, I must tell you that I dislike the word "success." I avoid it whenever I can. But like many other words, it's the only one we have for its purpose, so we'll have to make do until a better one comes along.

The old-fashioned notion of success involves the process of setting out to achieve some goal, purpose, or intention, and then achieving that goal, purpose, or intention. If, for instance, my goal is to make hay, I am a success if I make hay. That seems simple enough, and barely worth remarking.

What, for example, is the goal of graduate study in the field of religion, the realization of which goal would justify us deeming a person a success, the frustration of which would lead us to deem that person a failure?

25

Well, in the old definition, you are successful if you have some work—some intellectual or pedagogic work that you distinctly, perhaps even uniquely, are prepared and compelled to do—and then are able to secure gainful academic employment that supports you in the doing of said work. Success means that you live a life of thinking and writing and teaching, and secure your future, ideally, as a tenured member of the professoriate.

To a graduate student in religious studies, achieving such a goal is not as improbable as winning the lottery: it only seems so.

Now, there certainly are other goals attendant upon one's undertaking graduate study, particularly in the field of religion, but the goal of an academic career organizes, even justifies, the entire project of graduate study as we know it.

Now what is the secret to success understood in this way? There is, I notice, a recent book on the topic by a young observer of corporate America by the name of Rachel A. Seff. The book is entitled *60 Minutes to Success: The Ultimate Guide to Power Lunching.* Ms. Seff would, for success, have us go to lunch, which, one must admit, is seldom a bad idea.

But it is better, I think, to heed John D. Rockefeller's advice: for success, you must get up early; work hard; and, strike oil. Rockefeller thus suggests that success is inexorably linked to both hard work *and* good fortune. Better, then, to think of success as most likely to come to those, who, as William Stafford has suggested, work and act over a long period of time so as to enhance the possibility that good fortune will, in due season, come their way.

But we might pause simply to ask, Why is success so important to us? And why is it all the more important if one has not yet achieved success, and is thus left on the outside looking in? Success, in some ways, is like money, even like food: it is rightly treasured precisely to the extent that one does not have it. Moreover, we value success to the extent that societal structures or prejudices diminish the likelihood that we shall be able to achieve it—which leads me to say that it is rude at best and insulting at worst for someone who, like myself, has had a modicum of old-fashioned success to belittle or diminish it, particularly in the presence of persons who earnestly yearn for it.

Still, the question merits asking: Why is success important to us? To get at this question, let me do as my teacher David Miller used to do. Years ago, whenever David was stuck, he would commit an etymology. Sometimes I suspected that he was just making things up, as I shall now proceed to do.

Consider, first, our two syllables, *succ* and *ess*. We might surmise that *ess* is a diminutive of the Latin *esse*, as in Bishop Berkeley's *esse ist percipii*, to be is to be perceived; and *succ* we might take to be a diminutive of *succor*, to be nurtured or fed.

So *success* is related to our being *succored*, and maybe that's why we love it so. Success feeds, nurtures, succors us. It is the very milk of life.

But we shouldn't miss the pun. *Succored* puns the colloquial verb *suckered*, to be duped or cheated. We see, then, how quickly success runs into its opposite. In being a success, one is not only *succored*—fed—one is *suckered*—duped, cheated. Hence it is not uncommon for old-fashioned successful persons to arrive at a point when they say, *It sucks*.

Success—and the activities by which one realizes success—thus promises one thing and delivers another. Instead of succoring, success sucks the very life out of us. Instead of nurturing and feeding, it enervates and impoverishes. It is this duplicity of success that led someone—William James, it was—to speak of "that bitch goddess success."

Sometimes it seems that we live under an inexorable law: gaining something in one arena, we invariably lose in another. We make straight As and flunk life; star in public and shrivel in private; inflate in the boardroom and deflate in the bedroom.

Having now committed an etymology, which might in this context be called a Millerism—and surely without David's immense influence on my sensibility, it would never have occurred for me to play in this way—I take another tack to remember, honor, and thank him. I turn to stories, stories from my days as a graduate student at Syracuse when David became my teacher, dissertation advisor, and friend.

DISTURBANCES IN THE FIELD

Over the years, it has occurred to me that David Miller wanted his students at Syracuse to think like a good fly fisherman fishes. He wanted them to be nimble and playful, light of touch and quick to react, ready to move upstream to locate new sweet spots, and always able to match the hatch.

When I arrived in Syracuse in the fall of 1968, I was as far from being a fly fisherman as a tadpole is from a swan. As far as thinking was concerned, I was more like one of those folks who sit on the side of bridges in Mississippi, where I come from. Some folks there just sit on the bridge all day, waiting for something to grab the grub worm on the end of the line. There is not much style in grub worm fishing.

The first indication that my new teacher was different from anything I had previously known occurred during registration my first semester at Syracuse. Two saucy undergraduates sidled up to the table where I was sitting. One was advising the other what teachers to take. *Oh take Miller!* she said. *Miller can make crap sound good.*

At lunch, I told David what the student had said. He got a charge out of it, which was, I thought, a good sign.

One reason I decided to go to Syracuse was that David Miller chose me to be his teaching fellow, though I'll never understand why. I just walked in the door of his office, and it seemed as if he had already made up his mind about me.

And I was hooked.

If you are a fly fisherman, presentation is nearly everything, that, and what you have to present, and David was always thinking about presentation. He wanted to match the hatch.

A park ranger out in Colorado reminded me one day that Izaak Walton was the first to write about matching the hatch. When I went to college in 1960, I had never heard of Izaak Walton. Here he is, the author of perhaps the most widely published book in the western world, after the Bible and Shakespeare, from about 1650 to 1850, and I no more knew who he was than I knew Sacco and Vanzetti, two figures honored by a stunning mosaic by Ben Shahn on the wall of the building that housed the Syracuse Religion Department when I was there. I didn't know about

28

Sacco and Vanzetti until I arrived at Syracuse; and until I read a selection from *The Compleat Angler* in freshman English, I didn't know what an angler was. There are no anglers in Mississippi.

David Miller can do what Izaac Walton talks about. He can read the stream, see what the fish are taking, and match his presentation to the time and place. David is a master at it. It comes from having a nimble mind, but also from a practiced effort to stay unhooked, from a disciplined attempt to see from more than one perspective. David often alluded to that line from Wittgenstein: *A picture holds us captive*, thereby, I think, urging his students not to be captive to a picture, which means not taking any of them literally. David plays with and among various pictures, but he wants to be self-conscious about it. He will allow himself temporarily to be held by a picture in a stylish way, just to know what it's like to see the world that way, but he thinks that there is nothing uglier—or more dangerous, for that matter—than a person who is hooked, really hooked by a picture, and who doesn't know it. People who are hooked and don't know it are often unpleasant to be around, and some of them will kill you.

My second semester in Syracuse I made a presentation on Picasso in one of David's seminars. I started off at a disadvantage because I didn't know much about Picasso. That's one reason Syracuse was good for me: I spent a good deal of time talking about things I didn't know much about. There is no better preparation for a teacher than that.

My presentation was on the child figure in a series of etchings that Picasso made in the late 1920s and 1930s. *Here we see the child and the Minotaur,* I said to David and my fellow students, pointing them to the slide on the screen. *Notice the young girl on the ladder and the Minotaur below. The child is going up the ladder with her light, in flight from the threatening Minotaur at the foot of the ladder.* And I went on to associate the Minotaur with sexual energy and the young girl with innocence and vulnerability, and to talk about flight and so forth.

Why do you think that the child is going up the ladder? was David's first question. *You could as easily say the child is going down the ladder.*

29

I was undone, speechless. To hide my panic, I turned to look at the slide on the screen. He was right. Any fool could see it. The child could as easily be going down the ladder as up the ladder. Why hadn't I seen that? I had been looking at those etchings for three months. I had read everything there was to read about those etchings. None of the experts had said anything about the child going down the ladder. That would change everything. It would be like Daniel's stepping into the lion's den. Who would have thought that Daniel would stand down a lion? Who would think a child would go toward a Minotaur? Picasso's child holds the light in her hand, and could be taking light into the labyrinth and toward the great bull.

Turning back to the seminar, I was face to face with a Great Bull. I was the child, and my light was nearly out. I wanted to flee, and would have if I had been near the door and there had been a ladder. I was exposed. They were on to me: I didn't know what I was talking about, and they knew it. I had fooled my teachers for twenty-five years, in every school I had ever attended, and now the truth was out. From Mississippi to Texas to Kentucky to New York, I had kept my secret. Now my teacher David Miller and all my fellow graduate students knew: Estess doesn't know shit. That is why I had kept on going to school year after year, from 1948 to 1971, twenty-four fricking years of school. I kept going, going, going, until it was established beyond a reasonable doubt, and brought out in the open for the whole fricking world to see: Estess don't know rat shit.

What makes you think the child is a young girl? David's second question followed like a death knell on the first. He added, *Picasso could be dealing with androgyny, you know.*

I didn't half know what androgyny was, and I sure didn't have anything to say about it that afternoon. I wanted to go home. But I did have sense enough to see that if I had learned anything, it had little to do with Picasso and that series of etchings I had been looking at for three months. A picture of a set of pictures had held me captive, and I couldn't see what was before my nose. I could see only the picture that had me hooked. To see the pictures before me, I needed to get unhooked.

As much as anything, that is what I got out of studying with David Miller and out of graduate study at Syracuse University: I got unhooked. I was released, at least in part, from a few of the pictures that had held me captive.

But to tell the truth, getting unhooked is not altogether a good thing, and it took the best part of twenty-five years to recover. I am glad it happened to me when I was young. It is not good for one never to have been unhooked; neither is it good forever to remain so—even if one cultivates that rare capacity, knowingly, playfully, to be hooked on being unhooked.

For a while, I tried to imitate David Miller and do things as he does them—and not do things as he does not do them. That's what a student is supposed to do. But I quickly learned that I never would have the style of David Miller, a fact that does not elude those who know me best, such as my son. Some years back when he and I were doing some skiing out in New Mexico, my then adolescent son took a look at my attire and told me that I had the style of a walrus in pantaloons. I don't know where he learned to talk like that. I didn't teach him.

So I am not a stylish fly fisherman. But neither do I sit all day on a bridge with a grub worm on a hook. That's not exactly true either. David Miller taught me that it's sometimes a good thing to try something different, so sometimes I *choose* to sit on a bridge with a grub worm on a hook. And it's true, you can catch some good eating catfish with grub worms. As skillful fishermen always say, there is more than one good way to catch a fish.

Another thing that came out of Syracuse is that I met a passel of interesting people, some pretty famous ones too. I stood around at David Miller's house talking to Joseph Campbell and Rollo May, Alan Watts and Huston Smith, Sam Keen and Norman O. Brown, Hans George Gadamer and Amos Wilder, and the likes. Getting to know people like that teaches you pretty quick that they are about as messed up as everybody else.

One day I was able to have lunch with Alan Watts. Watts was an Episcopalian who turned Zen Buddhist back in the 1950s and wrote a book. Over the next twenty-five years he wrote about twenty-five more books, but it was always the same book, with a different title. Like I said: Watts turned Zen Buddhist and wrote a book, a pretty good one, too. That semester, David and Jim Wiggins and a fellow named Doug Gunn and I were teaching some Buddhism to a big lecture class, and we decided to show an Alan Watts film. As a climax to the course, Watts himself would come to town and lecture for us.

Our first problem was which Watts film to show. The university film library had three, so David and I screened all three. We couldn't choose among them. They were like Watt's books: the same film with a different title. Fly fisherman that he was, Miller suggested that we show all three at the same time. We would have three projectors sitting in the middle of the lecture hall, with one showing one film toward the front, and the other two projecting on the walls to the side. One sound track would be heard. Perhaps we thought that would unhook those students.

It was crazy, but it worked. In front and to the sides, the room was suffused with images of autumn leaves falling into mountain streams, and birds sitting on snowy branches, and clouds scuttling across mountain peaks, and all the while we heard Alan Watts' sonorous voice intoning something like, *All is turning and drifting, through endless time, as one thing flows into another, becomes another, is another, as snow falls and leaves drift, across and down into the ocean at the foot of the mountain, and at the center of all that is, you see, you suddenly see the light turn to shadow, become the shadow, as day gives way to night, and night to day,* and all the while, David and Jim and Doug and I sat with two hundred anxious undergraduates as images flickered all around, images of leaves and snow and birds on frosty branches, with Watts' droning on, *and you see, you suddenly see what you knew all the time, the light turn to shadow, become the shadow, as day gives way to night, and night to day.*

Leaving the lecture hall that day and turning on to sidewalks covered with the sludge of a late March snowfall, the undergraduates were chirping like birds on a frosty branch. *That is the best class I have ever been to,* one young fellow opined to another, his scruffy vest festooned with peace signs and various other symbols of counter cultural neglect. *Nothing like it, man, nothing like it,* came the reply. I felt pretty good myself, walking along with my friend Doug Gunn.

One day that spring Gunn and I walked after class over to the Commons in front of Hendricks Chapel there in the heart of the Syracuse campus to watch an anti-war rally going on. It was an early spring day in 1970, and Dick Gregory was there to talk about ending the war and eating right. After he gave up being a comedian, Dick Gregory spent his time on two things: war and eating right.

Let me read what I've got in my wallet, Dick shouted. *I carry it with me all the time.* Doug Gunn and I were sitting on the top step of the stately chapel, a good seventy-five yards away from Dick and his crowd, but we could hear every word, even as we chatted away.

That was years before Dick Gregory went into eating right full time. On one occasion, Dick took special interest in a young man on Long Island named Walter Hudson. It seems that, one day, Walter went to the bathroom in his house and got stuck coming out the door. Walter weighed 1158 pounds. His mother called in the carpenters, and they came and took out the door so Walter could get back to bed and eat some more hamburgers. He was exhausted by it all.

Dick Gregory heard about Walter and flew in from his home down on an island off of Cuba to help out if he could. Dick went on TV with Walter, and Walter said that all he wanted to do in life was to lose enough weight to be able to get out the front door. Walter said he appreciated Mr. Gregory coming up from his island to help him and he was going to do what Mr. Gregory said. He wasn't going to eat three dozen Twinkies a day any more. He was going to eat sprouts and drink Mr. Gregory's tea.

And he did. After six months on sprouts and Dick's tea, Walter lost 247 pounds. He got out the front door of his house for the first time in six years. For that very special day, Dick Gregory came up from his island again and went back on TV with Walter. I watched the two of them standing on the front porch, Dick and Walter, busting their buttons with pride. Dick said it was quite an accomplishment, Walter's being able to get out the front door for the first time in six years.

But it didn't last. Walter went back to hamburgers and Twinkies. Dick made the long trek up to Long Island to see what he could do. Dick said to Walter, *Look, man, you already lost 247 pounds! Can't you hold out, man?*

But now that I think about it, what is 247 pounds to an 1158 pound man?

Finally, Dick went on TV, this time by himself. He said that he reluctantly was withdrawing his help from Mr. Hudson. Mr. Hudson, he said, would not follow his advice on eating right. Yes, it was true, he said to the reporters, Mr. Hudson was now back up to two dozen hamburgers and three dozen Twinkies a day and he wasn't drinking the tea. Dick said he was just going to go on back down to his island and hope that Mr. Hudson could make it on his own. He had done what he could. I always appreciated that about Dick: he did what he could.

But all that was a long time after Doug Gunn and I heard Dick Gregory admonishing the crowd in front of Hendricks Chapel that spring day of 1970. There must have been a thousand students in scruffy jeans out there, taking in Dick's words about the war like they were Twinkies and hamburgers.

I want you to carry a copy with you all the time, like I do, Dick shouted. *Here it is. Folded up, right here.* And Dick held up a frayed piece of paper and began to read to the cheers of the crowd. He read, *When in the course of human events, it becomes necessary for one people to dissolve the political bonds,* and the way cheers erupted across the Commons, it crossed my mind that perhaps these students had never heard these words before.

See all these buildings, Doug Gunn said to me.

What about them?

We hold these truths to be self-evident, that all men are created equal. . . . Take a good look at those buildings, Doug said, moving his arm around and pointing to the mottled collection of buildings surrounding the Commons at Syracuse University. Doug was an assistant professor with a Ph.D. from Yale. He was what I have come to call an *eschatophile,* a lover of the end, an *eschatophiliac.* In that, he was not much different from Dick Gregory. Doug set out to study New Testament at Yale, but got interested, as I recall, in Coptic and Ugaritic and Egyptian hieroglyphics and some other things of the ancient world. He felt good that three students at Syracuse University were interested in what he was interested in.

But when a long train of abuses and usurpations, pursuing invariably the same object, evinces a design to reduce them under absolute despotism. . . . The roar of the students made it hard for me to hear Doug.

Take a good look at these buildings, he said. *They won't be standing long. Stone by stone, brick by brick, they will come tumbling down. It will happen in our lifetime, well within our lifetime, like Joshua and Jericho.*

It is their right, it is their duty, to throw off such government, and to provide new guards for their future security. In the distance, the crowd went into a frenzy, and I looked around at the buildings surrounding the Commons, wondering when the stones might come tumbling down.

A few weeks later Alan Watts came to town to lecture to the class, but before the lecture, David Miller and Jim Wiggins and I and a couple of other faculty members met him for lunch at a country club near the campus. Watts had had a bad night in Pittsburgh, where he had stopped over to try to get his son out of jail. As I recall, Watts had been up all night talking to the cops and to lawyers and to his son. All this was revealed as Alan ordered his second double martini, Beefeater's, straight up, with a twist, while the rest of us sipped away at Michelob. We all commiserated with him over our Reuben sandwiches. He, I'm afraid, didn't eat a bite.

Back in the lecture hall, which had not yet tumbled down, the students waited to hear Alan Watts. A hush fell over the room as we walked in from the club. I felt proud, striding down behind Alan Watts and David Miller to take a seat in the front. David did the introduction; and as with many of his introductions, that one was an insurance policy against a bad lecture: in case Watts turned out not to have anything to say, the audience wouldn't leave empty-handed.

And please join me, David finally came to say, *in welcoming a person whom I have known for many years, someone whom we have all been looking forward to hearing, my friend, Alan Watts.* With that, David turned toward Alan Watts, who sat partially hidden behind the lectern. But from my seat, I had been watching it all. During the introduction, Watts the Zen practitioner had closed his eyes and started to meditate, composing himself for the words of wisdom he was about to speak, centering himself, listening to the silence within so that he could speak to the silent ones without. I admired him, sitting there, meditating, focused, the centered one amid the decentering distractions of the day.

I present to you, Alan Watts, David repeated, *my good friend, Alan Watts.* By then a meditative calm held poor Watts captive. The martinis and the all-nighter in Pittsburgh had done their work: he was sound asleep. *Alan! Alan!* David said off-mike. And Alan Watts jerked to attention and took the mike from David; and as he began to speak, familiar sonorous tones suffused the room, *All is turning, all is drifting, through endless time, and one thing flows into another, becomes another, is another,* and within the mind's eye of each person in the lecture hall, pictures of drifting snow and falling leaves and flowing water and floating birds moved toward the sea.

As I walked out of the lecture room, the students were chirping like birds on a snowy branch. *Wasn't that wonderful?* one girl from Poughkeepsie asked me. *Yes,* I said, *I suppose it was.* And, it was.

Good Bean Paste Ethics

ERNEST WALLWORK

"Bean paste that smells like bean paste is not good bean paste" might have been the motto of the seminar on Freud and Jung that David Miller and I co-taught during the 1998-99 academic year, just before his retirement from the Department of Religion at Syracuse University. David used this Zen saying in his 1986 article "'Attack Upon Christendom!' The Anti-Christianism of Depth Psychology" to make the point that the alleged "anti-Christianism" that permeates depth psychology from Freud to Lacan and Jung to Hillman is not a threat to theology or faith, but, rather, part of a valid iconoclastic critique of bad religion and bad piety, congruent with the very best of the Western religious tradition it attacks.[1] Like Amos, Jesus, Paul, Luther, the Buddha, Lao Tzu and Dogen, Freud and Jung open fresh possibilities for religion and ethics, at a time when the official versions seem lacking in vitality.[2] As with bean paste, David writes, "religion that smells like religion is not good religion."[3]

David finds in depth psychology a way of deconstructing the kind of totalistic thinking found in mainstream theology, ethics, piety and science, a thinking that is attributable to the monotheistic desire to "get it all together," to possess some definitive universal truth or truths.[4] The totalistic thinking that pervades much modern theory in all fields of thought takes a single-minded, one-dimensional exclusionary, tyrannical single angle of vision on things. Writing and teaching against this legacy of monotheism, David has long sought to open the minds of his students, readers and colleagues to the possibility of new ways of seeing that acknowledge "the multiple dimension of everything," teaching us "a new tolerance—even more, an acceptance of the variousness of ourselves and others."[5] Depth psychology, David writes, is one of these deconstructive openings that invites us to "listen closely...to the moods, emotions, unusual behaviors, dreams, and fantasies of ourselves and our societies" so that we may reach "an expanding consciousness, a new sensibility, a new polytheism...."[6]

It is this ambition to deconstruct in ways that open up unexpected creative possibilities that lies behind David's insistence that the usual interpretations of Freud and Jung on religion are overly simplified, even wrongheaded. It is not that Freud is hostile towards religion, and Jung soft on it. Freud attacks the childish, psychopathological and social destructiveness of religion, but he does not give religion up. "...[I]ts *fascinosum* did not let go of him," David writes.[7] *Moses and Monotheism* is scarcely resistant to religion's symbols and images and there is also Freud's fascination with the uncanny and the mysterious depths of psychic life.[8] Jung is ostensibly more positive about religious images and symbols, but Jung's Christianity is scarcely favorable towards mainstream orthodoxy. His Christ is that of 'gnostic' (i.e., heretical) Christianity. Jung interprets the eucharist from the point of view of pagan rites (the Aztec Teoqualo) and through the lens of Gnostic alchemy.[9] In David's reading of Jung's critique of Christianity, Western theism is responsible for a great deal of the psychopathology we see around us, which focuses on blaming evil on sinful people. David writes:

> A religious viewpoint, logically necessitated by a monotheistic God who is *Summum Bonum*, is responsible for human feelings of shame, guilt and anxiety, not to mention inferiority, worthlessness, and depression. At least in part, Jung's clients suffer from an unconscious Christian theology rather than from a conscious personal history.[10]

GOOD BEAN PASTE ETHICS

I can think of no more fitting tribute to David than to engage one of his concerns, namely, the concern for "therapeutic ideas" with which to counter the psychopathological ideas that have such a pernicious effect on our collective and personal lives. One of these therapeutic ideas is Jung's concept of the shadow, which David sees as introducing a deconstructive element into thought. In David's take on the shadow, it haunts every thought, every ideology, every religion, every religious perspective, so what we need is to always look for that which is "otherwise". Although the shadow is consciously experienced as a threatening negative, it conceals a constructive positive. It is by acknowledging and wrestling with the shadow that the complexity of life emerges—whether in our intrapsychic lives, our interpersonal relations or politics.

What interests me, as an ethicist who is also a practicing psychoanalyst, is how ethical thinking, speaking and acting is haunted by unacknowledged negatives. It was Freud, of course, who first drew attention to how moral behavior masks and, at the same time, gives expression to unseemly meanings and motivations. For Freud, it is not that genuine moral behavior is psychologically impossible; to the contrary, he goes to some length to preserve the integrity of morality against his own deconstructive insights.[11] Freud's point about morality is, rather, that the immoral affects and actions that hide underneath and partially propel purportedly moral behavior undermine it in varying degrees, so that the good that we would do is often bad, sometimes, even evil. Jung uses the concept of the shadow to make an analogous point.

A good example is the way moral language itself typically overrides other discourses. There is a superior, controlling power-play at work in the use of moral language, even for good purposes, that often subordinates the Other, making him or her inferior to the speaker, in ways that surreptitiously harm and/or hurt the Other while serving the speaker's hidden narcissistic aims. Paraphrasing what David says about religion, "ethics that smells like ethics is not good ethics." It needs another critical layer or dimension.

Clearly, if morality masks silently immoral conduct, we need to do ethics differently. In David's terminology, we need "therapeutic ideas" in ethics with which to counter the pathological ideals that inhabit our moral discourse and that end up doing so much harm in our lives, both private and public.

How do we develop an ethic that encourages the kind of self-interrogation that leads to the acknowledgement of unpalatable unconscious affects? My proposal is that we need an ethic that retrieves the *askesis* tradition in classical Greco-Roman ethics. What this tradition has to offer is the fundamental idea that moral agents need self-reflective mental "exercises" and "practices" focused on bringing hidden meanings and motivations to consciousness and, then, on "working through" the new insights achieved through self-examination. As Pierre Hadot points out in his groundbreaking study of *askesis* in antiquity, ancient moral philosophers like Marcus Aurelius sought to acquire more than the purely abstract knowledge of ethical standards, which has been the focus of so much modern moral philosophy.[12] They sought mental exercises, equivalent to an athlete's physical training program, that would prepare them for thinking and acting morally in the practical world of the agora. *Askesis* was a kind of depth therapy for the soul that involved meditation, reading, and therapies of the passions that directed the practitioner's whole way of being—the '*habitus*' of his/her soul. To have this result, the exercises had to link reason with the passions and volition in the service of self-reflective moral practices.[13]

What the several depth psychologies offer ethics today are resources for recovering and updating the *askesis* tradition—for what else are the talk therapies than forms of self-examination that aim, with the help of an experienced coach, at altering for the better the way patients conduct themselves in the world. My patient, Emily, for example, learned during the course of her analysis not only why she abused her children verbally, but, more importantly, how to "work through" the motivations behind her outbursts of rage so as to avoid the serious psychic harms she was inflicting, against her best intentions, on her young children and spouse. Max started analysis unaware of how narcissistic and morally self-righteous he was; he had simply taken it for granted that he was better than most men. The most painful moments of his analysis came when he realized that his passive aggression was not so innocent and that he actually often "set up" his wife, children, and business partner by behaving in ways that drove them crazy. When they reacted with rage to his extraordinary provocative actions, he felt himself unfairly accused and justified in retaliating. In this way, he justified lying to or cheating those closest to him under the guise of rationalizations that barely concealed his unconscious hostile, aggressive and self-serving motivations. As with Emily, the 'working through' phase of Max's analysis provided an opportunity for him to own his unacceptable motivations, to try out more constructive ways of behaving, to fail, to learn from his mistakes and to try again. Max put it well, towards the end of his analysis, when he observed how much mental effort and practice it took to train himself not to fall into the "old ruts" and, then, to develop the skills that worked in channeling constructively his formerly repressed anger and in helping him live more honestly in his relationships—with himself as well as with those around him.

A major obstacle to reviving the *askesis* tradition in ethics by drawing on clinical insights lies with the lack of genuine interest among ethicists in depth psychology and the reciprocal neglect of ethics by most therapists, at least until recently.[14] One might have expected the recent "turn" toward virtue theory and moral psychology in ethics to have generated a great deal of philosophical interest in depth psychology, but issues like character, emotions, empathy, character, flourishing and care seldom stimulate attention to therapeutic insights and practices among philosophical and religious ethicists. On the depth psychology side, only a few authors have ventured into the relationship between the two fields and these authors have yet to take up the application of self-reflective practices to moral decision-making.[15]

In the trenches of clinical work, however, patients continue to draw heavily upon what they learn about themselves to facilitate their everyday moral decisions. One of my patients recently spelled this out explicitly during the termination phase of his analysis. Reflecting on how analysis enters into his daily decision-making, after having managed to solve a particularly difficult moral problem at work the previous day, he had this to say:

> Boy, analysis is amazing. The way we look at what's going on, inside and out. It affects everything I do now. At work, I used to be paralyzed by the decisions that my job requires. I was perpetually: "on the one hand this, on the other hand that." I couldn't make up my mind, because, as we've come to see, I wanted to please everyone, like I did as a kid, when my two angry parents argued. If I couldn't figure out a resolution that all parties would applaud, I couldn't decide at all. I used to be so hungry for approval. But, as you said at the beginning, that made me really vulnerable to what others thought. I couldn't get into my own mind enough to figure out what I thought. For awhile I substituted you for my own mind. I tried to figure out what you'd do, which was at least better than not deciding at all or taking a risky leap in the dark. But it wasn't my way of thinking, and that's what I'm finally doing—finding the solution in myself.
>
> I hope it lasts, this increased awareness and the adjustments I'm constantly making. As you know better than anyone, those old patterns go so very deep. It's not easy to change them. But I'm doing so much better and I have so many ways of thinking about things now. I think I'll be all right, though I'll miss you and coming here. I wish we didn't have to stop. If I had the money, I'd keep going for the rest of my life. I used to hate coming here, but now I love it. There's nothing like it, anywhere! This quiet time away from the frantic pace of daily life at the office and home. This time to just sink into my own mind and figure out what's in there, without the distractions.
>
> I didn't realize I was this complex, convoluted. It's given me a whole new way of thinking about how complicated other people are, too. It's amazing when you think about it, just how multi-layered life is for everyone and how complex it is to make a decision that's right on many levels simultaneously. I know, I sound like I'm repeating the old pattern by again setting up an impossible task for myself. I still do that sometimes. But I notice it now, take stock of that and find a way around it or through it. What I'm trying to say is that life is complex and decisions are complex and that's just the

way things are. And my decisions don't have to be perfect. It's enough if they're good enough for the circumstances, and they usually are that.

Yesterday, I had a disagreement with L (a business colleague). She said....[the contents are unimportant]. And I said... She thought what I said was...., but that's not what I meant. So, I explained it again. Once, she understood where I was coming from, she agreed with me. Imagine! So, instead of the old battles that had me arguing that there was only one right way that had yet to be discovered or passively going along to get along with something I disagreed with, she and I reached a quick easy solution. For the first part of the disagreement, it was hard, though. I was in two places at once. I was starting to get into the old pattern and, then, I was trying to analyze it and to come up with different responses. It's how I feel a lot these days. I'm in two places at once. I'm in life. And I'm looking at it and trying out something new.

What we have here is an example of good bean paste ethics that doesn't smell like the old ethics. It is open, curious, empathic, tolerant and reflective. In place of acting without thinking to implement an *a priori* principle, the narrator thinks reflectively as he takes other views into account in trying to craft unique solutions to the complex moral dilemmas that life brings his way. What we need today is to link self-examination of this sort, which our culture too readily denigrates as narcissistic self- preoccupation,[16] with compatible ethical guidelines and virtues.

In concluding this essay in honor of David Miller, I want to express my deep thanks to David and his wife Pat for playing such a crucial role in my decision to join the Syracuse Religion faculty and for their friendship over the past 23 years. In the Fall of 1982, while sitting on a plane on my way to Syracuse for the job interview that led to my joining the faculty, I wondered what I was doing making the trip, since there was no way, I thought, that I would leave the Kennedy Institute of Ethics at Georgetown to begin a commute to Syracuse from Washington, D.C.. Commuting would be too much of a strain on me and my wife's job precluded a move to upstate New York. Yet, by the end of that day, after a very long evening of bracing conversation with David and Pat that ranged shamelessly across the fields of depth psychology, religion, theology, ethics, literature, early Christianity and Greco-Roman antiquity, I had come to a profound appreciation of the truly unique academic environment that existed, and continues to exist, at Syracuse, one in which I could pursue my idiosyncratic interests in depth psychology, religion and ethics with like-minded colleagues.

NOTES

[1] David L. Miller, "'Attack Upon Christendom!' The Anti-Christianism of Depth Psychology," *Thought (Fordham University Quarterly), LXI* (1986), 56-67.

[2] I argue similarly in "The Psychoanalytic Diagnosis: Infantile Illusion," in Roger Johnson, Ernest Wallwork, *et al.*, *Critical Issues in Modern Religion* (Englewood, NJ: Prentice-Hall, 1973), 275-76.

[3] "'Attack Upon Christendom!'"

[4] David L. Miller, *The New Polytheism: Rebirth of the Gods and Goddesses* (Dallas, Texas: Spring Publications, 1981), 98, see also .

[5] *Ibid.*, 98.

[6] *Ibid.*, 99-100.

[7] "'Attack Upon Christendom!'"

[8] Ernest Wallwork with Anne Wallwork, "A Psychoanalytic Perspective on Religion," in Joseph E. Smith, ed., *Psychoanalysis and Religion, Psychiatry and the Humanities Series, Vol. 11* (Baltimore: Johns Hopkins University Press, 1989), chapter 9, 160-173.

[9] David Miller, "Attack Upon Christendom!'", 59.

[10] *Ibid.*, 59-60.

[11] Ernest Wallwork, *Psychoanalysis and Ethics* (New Haven, CT: Yale University Press, 1991).

[12] Pierre Hadot, *What Is Ancient Philosophy?* (Cambridge, Mass.: The Belknap Press of Harvard University Press, 2002); "Reconfiguring Askesis," *Annual of the Society of Christian Ethics* (1999), 19: 167-189.

[13] See Ernest Wallwork, *Psychoanalysis and Ethics* (New Haven: CT: Yale University Press, 1991).

[14] Writing about the lack of interest among moral philosophers in psychoanalysis, Jonathan Lear observes that "if the question is, 'What influence did psychoanalysis have on philosophy in Britain [the United States and Australia] over the past century?' the simple answer is none whatsoever." Jonathan Lear, "The Idea of a Moral Psychology: the Impact of Psychoanalysis on Philosophy in Britain," *International Journal of Psychoanalysis* (2003) 84: 1351.

[15] I have sought to highlight the implications of psychoanalysis for ethics and ethics for psychoanalysis in "A Constructive Freudian Alternative to Psychotherapeutic Egoism," in *Soundings, Vol. LXIX* (1986, Fall), 145-164; *Psychoanalysis and Ethics*; "Psychodynamics Contributions to Religious Ethics: Toward Reconfiguring Askesis;" "What Psychiatry Can Offer Ethics: Psychodynamic Contributions," *Psychiatric Annals Vol. 31, Number 2* (2001, February), 105-112; "Ethics in Psychoanalysis," in *The American Psychiatric Publishing Textbook of Psychoanalysis*, edited by G. Gabbard, E. Person and A. Cooper (New York: International Universities Press, 2005), Chapter 19, 281-297.

[16] See Christopher Lasch, *The Culture of Narcissism* (New York: W.W. Norton, 1979); Robert N. Bellah *et al.*, *Habits of the Heart* (Berkeley and Los Angeles: University of California Press, 1985); Ernest Wallwork, "A Constructive Freudian Alternative to Psychotherapeutic Egoism."

THE MANY FACE(T)S OF DAVID MILLER

WILLIAM DRAKE

Listening to David Miller is Theatre.

Knowing David Miller is "flesh," in the sense of Merleau-Ponty's "chiasmic flesh," to be thought and lived as an element of Being in the world.

Being with David is to experience Eros and Pozzo; the Hunter/ Gatherer, AND the Farmer.

David has the gift of teaching an idea and making it seem an integral part of oneself; something you have always known; something anciently familiar, and something excitingly new.

Sitting with David and his very chilled, straight-up, two-olive martini, telling an hilarious joke in deadpan, HE is the consummate "Subject" of Being merging with the intertextual "Object," the mirror in the *abyme*, the Dancer and the Dance.

THE MANY FACE(T)S OF DAVID MILLER

David is the Chinese waiter, palming a tiny, folded, origami menu of concepts which he magically juggles, and then, transforming to Chinese Chef, inscrutably blends the "Raw" and the "Cooked" into a gourmet meal which feeds our Soul.

David is both Cartographer and Geographer who charts the garden's map and then leads us through it, expertly describing each flower.

David is Boundary; deceptively aloof, enigmatic, charismatic; Deleuzianly "Rhizomic;" a multi-dimensional Trickster. He runs on high-Octane Honey from the Gods.

David is Zen Master and Poet who mesmerizes us with images of the chrysanthemum's shadow cast by the full moon on the window sill, which segues to Wallace Stevens's "Snowman" and the "nothing that is there."

David is both image and text, sign and symbol, visible and invisible; a POSTCARD, with a "program always running in the background."

David tantalizes us with tales of Russian farm boys and dancing pigs; Hanuwele's magical gifts, and his personal friendship with clowns. He can be poignantly sad, moving us to great emotion and tears, as in his farewell lecture invoking Fellini's final scene of the trumpet exchange in "Clowns" as the Big Top Show closes down and moves on.

David is Myth, Reality, and Imagination. He has the Power and the Gift of giving us Ideas as our own, to laugh as if We had made the joke, and cry as if we are losing our dearest friend, all at the same moment, and, in doing so, we Love the Wonderful, Bright-Shining, Multi-Face(te)d, Complex Man.

MILLER AND THE BUTTERFLY

GLEN SLATER

In the quiet and repose of the humors, the
soul attains understanding and prudence.
—*Albert Magnus*[1]

In September 1992 David Miller traveled to Santa Barbara to present
a graduate seminar on psychology and humor. The topic has been an
enduring one for David and remains to this day a point of entry into
his approach to the psyche. Present at this seminar was a rather enthusiastic
and earnest student in his late twenties. He had come halfway around
the world to learn from the likes of this esteemed professor of religion
and maverick Jungian scholar from Syracuse University. Little did the
student know he was about to undergo an unplanned initiation into
academic life, one in which his equal parts of conviction and uncertainty
would be blended into the kind of Miller martini that soul imbibes with
satisfaction just as the ego leaves the scene with a hangover.

For this seminar, David had assigned his 1973 paper, "Achelous and
the Butterfly: Toward an Archetypal Psychology of Humor,"[2] in the middle
of which is a riff on Jung's typology that returns the four functions to

48

their roots in fantasy and mythos. The soon to be unwittingly initiated student, whose classical Jungian worldview had not yet been loosened by either archetypal perspective or postmodern thought, started to take issue with this apparent dissolution of his identity as an introverted thinker (or feeler, or something). So he sat carefully plotting his strategy, waiting for the right moment to fire off a tightly wound critique. Ironically, as it turned out, the student was just as motivated by a need to dilute his introverted inclination to sit quietly in the back row as by a concern with the ideas at hand. What he really wanted was to enter the fray. In David's world, irony is golden; humor was already infiltrating the situation.

In terms of keeping typology in its rarified place, the young guy didn't stand a chance. David's article lined up one heavy-hitter after another— from Aristotle to Nietzsche, Barfield to Bachelard, Levi-Strauss to Heidegger. All aided him in injecting serious doses of "humor" (read moisture and flow) into dry, rigid psychological theorizing. In addition to the decades of scholarly contests under his belt, including bouts with the likes of Corbin and Gadamer, David had his old friend, James Hillman, riding shotgun (super-soaker at least) in the footnotes. When this pair approaches, Jungian reductionism starts to appear caught in its own inertness—like a deer in the headlights.

I don't remember exactly what I said when the moment came to deliver my tightly wound critique (maybe this was the deer factor), but I recall the sensation of it rapidly unraveling. I also vividly recall what happened next. David did something I've not seen him do since, despite my having spent considerable time in the classroom with him. He told me to stand up and say my name. I did. Then he asked me to repeat what I said. I did. At this moment, though it must have seemed mostly unremarkable for everyone else there that day, right in front of me, just visible through the threads of my argument, appeared the crossroads of a fledgling academic career.

Typology is not actually a sizable part of "Achelous and the Butterfly." It is in there to illustrate a larger point: What happens when a sense of humor is remembered in psychological discourse? First David traces the etymological back-roads of "humor," leading us straight to that which is moist, "humid." He then goes on, amplifying the term through its ties to the four humors, those fundamental fluids of old physiognomy—blood, phlegm, choler (yellow bile) and melancholer (black bile), which are thoroughly imbued with psychic images. This move fleshes out the situation and starts to locate the character of the psyche-humor relationship. Via reflections on the humors as temperaments—sanguine, phlegmatic, choleric, melancholic—David shows how psyche is predisposed to bring together the airy mind (spirit) and the moist matter of experience. Psyche's presence in conceptual thinking is revealed when we see the degree to which our theories recapitulate our most nascent images of body and earth. Jungian typological thinking, for example, echoes not only the four humors but also creation mythology's tree of life and the four rivers that feed it. Typology can then be recognized as a new bud on a long branch of that rather old tree.

To punctuate the overall of point of seeing the humor in psychology, David returns us to that enduring image of psyche's essence, *the butterfly*. The butterfly transforms from wet cocoon to flying insect, from fluid worm to rider of the breeze. As he points out, "moths and butterflies are called *lepidoptera*, a name indicating that they have *scales* likes fish but also *wings* like birds."[3] Psyche, in its own self-imaging, moves continually from the wet to the dry, from unconscious immersion to conscious flight and back again. Our attempt to make meaning and create discourse in psychology—to open psyche—is thereby called to follow this spirit-soul, dry-moist confluence.

I sketch out David's thinking in this paper not only to describe the context of my first encounter with him but also to underscore what he does. "Achelous and the Butterfly" shows us how psyche incubates ideas and it simultaneously conveys David's approach to being psychological: He moistens theory on the one hand and unearths insights on the other. He returns concepts to images and experiences and places the instinctual ground of being within the lofty and fiery reaches of intellectual discourse. He knows when to hold the cocoon and when to release the butterfly. He follows psyche's dance and can convey her nature, bringing "levity to moisture," as he says of the butterfly.[4] Those who've attended a Miller lecture have experienced this archetypal *sense of humor*—high humidity with the possibility of *solutio* never far away. One thus finds in "Achelous and the Butterfly" something of the heart of his project—the talk he has also walked these past thirty years or so.

What happened after I stood up and repeated my comment was an experience of David's humor. While I had clearly taken issue with his point of view, he found a way to bring my perspective (or at least some of its remaining threads) into a meaning-making process. My "crossroads" turned into a threshold. Instead of keeping me out, he invited me in. Instead of showing where I had gone astray, he allowed my view to illuminate the issue from another side. Most of all, he sensed my passion for this kind of thing and he essentially said, "OK, you get to do this too, welcome into the academy."

A few years after this encounter I became David's teaching assistant in one of the early mythological studies classes at Pacifica Graduate Institute. On breaks and in class we continued our dialogues, very often with me trying to pin him down or establish some firmer ground for the topic at hand. He would refer to this as our "Laurel and Hardy act"—a compliment given David's dedication to clowns. More recently and up until his retirement from teaching, I worked with David as a colleague in the mythology department at Pacifica. I saw him last at a conference on sacrifice in Portland, Oregon, where we had a friendly spar on the panel discussion over the archetypal status of the subject: Is sacrifice an archetype? As usual, it was a rich exchange and I found myself once again taking a page from David's sketchbook on the way one works with meaning and interpretation without falling into the traps that come with a term like "archetype."

Just like Achelous, the ruler of rivers, "the underground of humors,"[5] David has brought moisture and fluidity to Jungian and religious discourse. He has presided over the *flow* of ideas, allowed different disciplines to eddy around each other and released the rarified, the inflated and the fixed back into the water. This work has not been easy. It has involved an on-going showdown with Heracles—a battle with utilitarianism, literalism and reductive thinking, in psychology and beyond it. Among other allies in this battle, David has joined with postmodern philosophy, a sometimes misunderstood embrace that has always been about serving the vicissitudes of soul: "Religion is impossible without uncertainty" and "wisdom is knowing what we don't know so that we can keep the future open," writes Mark C. Taylor in a recent remembering of Derrida.[6] These notions also describe the Miller philosophy, so evident in pieces like "The 'Stone' which is not a Stone: C. G. Jung and the Post-Modern Meaning of 'Meaning,'" "Nothing Almost Sees Miracles! Self and No-Self in Psychology and Religion" and "An Other Jung and an Other . . ." among numerous others.[7] In these contributions and in David's disposition toward anything worth understanding, knowing and not knowing may be recognized as the most elemental of his beloved binarisms: David knows a lot, but he knows what he doesn't know better than anyone I know.

Although Achelous's battle with Heracles is difficult to overcome, myth itself always returns to undo things and offer another way. So we may take some refuge in the moment when, at the height of the battle, Heracles breaks off one of Achelous's horns and the nymphs gather to turn it into the Cornucopia. "Cornucopia" needs no interpretation in this context. Nevertheless, this image invokes another, one I cannot overlook: The mythic moment reminds me of how nymphs would indeed gather around David, after class at the bar, where one could wet the whistle and let spirits and humor flow. One must now see that these gatherings were more reflective of David's work than we might have suspected . . . A punctuation point at the end of the day becomes an exclamation mark for a manner of discourse— or maybe a colon: He always liked playing jazz with the ideas . . . "Serious play," I hear him say . . .

The term "a gentleman and a scholar" was made for David. In his lectures and his writing he is always a step ahead of you, forcing a game of catch-up, never departing the scene without having created the necessary gaps of comprehension. But when the lecture is done, he walks beside you and adjusts himself to your pace. I've experienced this in many moments and am deeply grateful for each and every one of them.

David, I salute you.

NOTES

[1] David L. Miller, "Achelous and the Butterfly: Toward an Archetypal Psychology of Humor," *Spring*, 1973 (Zürich/New York), 1-23.

[2] Miller, "Achelous."

[3] Miller, "Achelous,"17.

[4] Miller, "Achelous," 19.

[5] Miller, "Achelous," 19.

[6] M. C. Taylor, "What Derrida Really Meant," *The New York Times*, October 14, 2004.

[7] David L. Miller, "The 'Stone' which is not a Stone: C. G. Jung and the Post-Modern Meaning of 'Meaning'," *Spring 49* (Dallas: Spring Publications, 1989), 110-122; David L. Miller, "Nothing Almost Sees Miracles! Self and No-Self in Psychology and Religion," *Journal of Psychology of Religion*, 4-5, 1995, 1-25. David L. Miller, "An Other Jung and an Other …" , in Karin Barnaby and Pellegrino D'Acierno eds., *C. G. Jung and the Humanities* (Princeton: Princeton University Press, 1990), 325-340.

I Have Learned "Nothing"
from David Miller

GINETTE PARIS

When my colleagues and I, at Pacifica Graduate Institute, were planning David's retirement party, I went to a store that prints T-shirts and asked if they could print one that read:

> Hi! My name is Ginette.
> I am a David Miller fan.
> I have learned "nothing" from him.

It turned out that the party was not a t-shirt-and-barbecue-on-the-beach kind of gathering, but rather a silk-and-pearls formal party. We all wanted a really grand celebration, because David has been the most influential and admired professor ever to teach at Pacifica, and one of our most loved colleagues.

I am grateful to Christine Downing to give me more space than the front of a T-shirt to express my reasons for thinking that David Miller's work should be part of every Humanities curriculum. It has to do with how Miller presents and uses the philosophical insights about "nothing."

The history of the concept of "nothingness" fills tons of tomes that explore the argument through Hegel, Sartre, Heidegger and almost every philosopher worth his salt. Not being a philosopher, but rather a depth psychologist, it was in reading Miller's interpretation of the Holy Ghost (the Spirit) that I became convinced of the importance of the concept of "nothing" for understanding psychic events. Take for example, depression.

DEPRESSION DEFINED AS ABSENCE OF JOY

Depression has reached epidemic proportions and is the cause of more medical prescriptions than any other condition, ever. It is a cause of immense suffering, personal as well as societal. For depression to be recognized in the *DSM*, clinicians had to make depression into a positive thing. A philosopher would say that clinicians had to "posit" or "positivize" depression.

In contrast to the medical definition, philosophy suggests a negative approach. It starts with a consideration of the depressed person as somebody impacted by something that is *not* there. This negative definition might be described thus:

> Depression is a psychic state in which the experience of love is missing (no love of self, no love of work, no love of others, or of the world). The body is not yet dead but the person has no experience of the feeling of aliveness. Feelings have no intensity. There is an absence of psychic movement, a laziness of imagination. Succinctly, depression is the absence of joy.

The invisible qualities that are absent—love, joy, imagination, vitality, intensity—are themselves not "things." They are similar to what David Miller defines as the Spirit, the Holy Ghost, which does not exist either. What is missing is a quality of presence to oneself and to the world that is hard to define positively. By contract, the distress of hunger is easy to define—sharp pangs, that may or may not be accompanied by fear of dying of famine. The suffering of a depressed person is not that easily described. It is rather like a lack of appetite when presented with a banquet, which explains the annoyance of the entourage. (Why don't you cheer up? Don't you see you have everything you need to be happy?) Something is missing and that "something" is not some *thing* as literal as food. David Miller might say that the person is de-spirited.

DISTURBANCES IN THE FIELD

The medical approach begins with a positive definition of depression (You *have* depressive symptoms. You *are* depressed.) and seeks a cure. By contrast, a negative definition (*depression as absence of joy*) sends one on a philosophical pursuit. That philosophical adventure is essentially similar to a depth psychological analysis, essentially similar to an experience of the Holy Ghost, if one is able, like Miller, to consider a de-literalized version of the spiritual quest.

I EXIST, BUT MY EGO IS NOTHING

The distinction between "I" and "ego" is one that helps clarify the usefulness of a negative approach to depression. Someone suffering from amnesia can still order a cappuccino by saying "*I* would like a cappuccino, please." That person's sense of being a body, with an objective physical presence, is intact. What the amnesia has destroyed are the memories, dreams and reflections that gave that person a sense of what Jungians call the Self. It has also destroyed the capacity to orient oneself in terms of goals and projects, a faculty that psychologists have traditionally referred to as *ego*, another concept that refers to something invisible, intangible, not positively existing.

One of the basic feelings expressed by depressed patients is a sense that one is of little importance to others, neither seen nor heard, not valued or mirrored. One has no weight, no impact and no value even in one's own eyes. The ego has lost its capacity to orient, motivate, lead, to build persona, to win, to strive, to perform. The captain won't steer the ship; the hero won't show up. One becomes a "loser," narcissistically obsessed with one's own emptiness.

Here is where the negative approach becomes interesting. If "ego" is nothing, purely a construction of the mind, like all the other nothings (Joy, Love, Holy Ghost, Unconscious, God, Self, Nation, Race, Gender, and so forth), then, through awareness, I can de-literalize it. I can see through its nothingness. I can de-identify from all previous definitions of "me" and re-invent "me" (ego) all over again. The severity of my depression is the measure of my identification with one definition of "me," one that was rigidly maintained. The good news that the philosopher brings to me is that my ego is not a positive concrete reality. Since it is a construction, it can be de-constructed. The task of analysis (a philosopher might say "awareness") is to deny the ego its habitual posture of domination.

The idea that I am free, always, at all times, to re-invent another definition of *me*, was one of the main arguments of Jean Paul Sartre's *Being and Nothingness.*[1] It became a core idea of existential psychoanalysis. I believe it is also a core idea, although formulated in very different terms, of archetypal psychology, which affirms the dramatic basis of the psyche. The ego always tends to interpret facts as having a fixed meaning. It tends to positivize. ("I *am* depressed.") An archetypal approach suggests that one can *see through* to the archetype that organizes my perception. (Who, in me is depressed? What I am looking for in the Underworld?)

What theses perspectives may have in common, beyond their many differences, is a strategy that reverses common sense. Instead of re-assuring the depressed person ("You are a wonderful person. Your depression will eventually lift. It is treatable."), a negative approach suggests the opposite. "Of course you are nothing. Of course you have no weight, no importance, no impact on the world. Who does?" The acceptation that my ego is "nothing" can be a pivotal point because it frees the imagination and brings psychic movement. It is no coincidence that a person coming out of a depression does surprising things. S/he quits old attitudes, makes unpredictable choices, looks and feels different, even irrational, to the eyes of those who were accustomed to the old ego structure. The imagination has invented new meaning for objective reality and now has a fresh interpretation of what that reality allows one to be. The presence of a Holy Ghost can be felt again.

NOTES

[1] Both Sartre and Jung use the word 'conversion' although Sartre insists on the conscious aspect of the choice of new values while Jung tends to see the epiphanic aspect of the experience. Nevertheless, both

Sartre and Jung see that a conversion is a move that deconstructs the ego, an expression of one's essential freedom to change.

Iconoclastic Idolatry *or* There's Something About David

SOPHIA HELLER

It seems a risky business to profess an unequivocal adoration for one's teacher. Especially when one is a student of depth psychology and therefore supposed to know about projection and infantile longings for authority figures. And especially when the teacher resists worship through the very method and content of his teaching. But my devotion to David Miller is not in defiance of maturity or out of an unwillingness to take his teachings seriously. No, it is his iconoclastic method itself that seems to call for the opposite. It's as if his drive to see through the theories driving us (what he sometimes calls a computer program running in the background) demands *something* that adheres and coheres. For me, (and, I suspect, many of my classmates) that something has come to be an unapologetic love of David as a teacher, no less than his teachings.

Perhaps David might protest a little here. In his writings he repeatedly defers to a postmodern logic that can only be suspicious of the reverence I am applying to him. Readers of his work will be familiar with his frequent return to no-thingness over a some-thingness that all too often gets wrapped in an egoic, prohibitively literalistic perspective. Such a something, like religion read dogmatically or myth brandished politically—one could say language stripped of its poetry—functions repressively, restrictively, unconsciously. It becomes an arrogant claim to knowing that tries to pin down what ultimately cannot be pinned down. But the refusal to turn what is not a thing, whether God, truth, meaning, beauty, or even David Miller as Teacher, into something concrete is one way of acknowledging the limitations of our knowledge. David calls this epistemological humility. We cannot escape our theories; we can never *not* have a program running in the background. Thus, there is only so much we can perceive in its nakedness—and all the more that we cannot.

Whatever one feels moved to objectify or worship therefore reflects a partial, subjective, and all-too-human perspective. And any foundation of knowledge that is built on all-too-human theories and beliefs is no more or less stable than that which we are seeking to know, like our notions of God, truth, meaning, or even my imagination of the person that is David Miller. So then in the attempt to know God, for example, what one essentially has is a foundation of knowledge that is far from immutable or stable, built to support something that is neither ontologically or logically a thing. The something that I fervently attach myself to, such as a cherished teacher, becomes in the moment of attachment a reflection of my own needs and desires. The teacher or idea, or even God, that I revere is just a faint but frozen trace of the original, something I wrap my mind or my heart around to keep close, while forgetting that this beloved object (whether a person or an idea) is not an object and cannot be so easily contained and compartmentalized.

Why worship, then? Why go through all the trouble of attempting to know these subject matters (truth, beauty, God) that compel such maniacal devotion? Does this not create the temptation for the false idolization and reification of our God-images? Is this not the source of much current political conflict in the world, where literal interpretations of religious texts assume a rigidity incommensurate to the nuances and paradoxes, even the banality, of language? Wouldn't it be wiser to remain quiet and settle into the Nothing that so many philosophers and poets have long declared to be the ground of existence? Meister Eckhart prayed to God to be free from God, but what if we just skip the prayer and assume the freedom?

For one thing, a preemptive assumption of nothingness carries the danger of being a death wish disguised as spiritual superiority. But we are human beings, not gods, and to follow David following Samuel Beckett (among others), we speak in our attempts to know truth, beauty, God, or even ourselves, knowing precisely as we speak that we are failing at the task before us. The effort to turn nothing into something and its subsequent failure keeps our epistemological humility in check. Our failure prevents us from objectifying what ultimately is not an object. It prevents us from worshipping false idols, whether the idol is a particular notion of God, an inflated vision of the self, or an unconscious ideology masquerading as objective truth. The point *is* to fail. The failure to posit God or the self, for example, becomes in and of itself truthful and meaningful. It we did not try and subsequently fail, we (and our ideas) would be like permanently unhatched and uncooked eggs—stuck in the infinite possibilities of potential while denying the obligation to live a messy, all-too-human, and limited life.

There is the possibility, to be sure, that "nothing" becomes the next God-term, the next thing to worship. But, as David has written, as soon as this happens, then one is no longer talking about nothing. Depression and low self-esteem, for example, those personal experiences of nothingness, can become even more insufferable when regarded as something negative that must be medicated and sanitized into something positive, a healthy sense of self. Yet depression and feelings of emptiness can also serve as an opening into the deep nothing within, the "no-self" of Eastern religion or its analog, the Self of depth psychology. The becoming of one's self, of individuation, is by definition an invitation to allow nothingness inside, to penetrate the ego's certitude, including the belief that one is nothing, that is, bound to one's depression. One could only be excessively attached to or depressed about being nothing if one had the underlying desire to avoid it or change it into something. The moment that "nothingness" becomes the next God-term thus is the moment, one could say, that one has forsaken God. It would be the moment that one refused to admit the fallibility and partiality of an ego-centered perspective.

As we cannot be completely devoid of our theories, we cannot reach an absolute nothingness. We cannot get to a "no" that is entirely independent of the self (ego). But we can detect hints of nothingness, like when one repeats the same word over and over again until the word becomes nothing, non-sense. We can, as archetypal psychology advocates, repeatedly "see through" or psychologize our literalisms into an imaginal, poetic way of seeing that refuses to land on what anything *is*, only what it is like, what it evokes. We cannot relinquish entirely our ego strongholds, but we can dig through to our "ontological commitments" (Kugler) into deeper layers of meaning and truth. Seeing through or digging for a deeper psychological meaning is an act of iconoclasm; thus iconoclasm itself becomes the only tenable act of worship in a world that knows that objective truth has become epistemologically problematic and for the empirical personality that senses the underlying nothingness but cannot ever fully belong to it.

So if one feels the obligation to speak about such notions as the self, meaning, God, and so forth, what can one possibly say? There is the possibility of saying you have nothing to say, which is something David did in his lecture at a Pacifica conference on archetypal activism: "I am committed to speak and I have nothing to say." He was troubled by the concept of "archetypal activism" which to him is oxymoronic. "Archetypal" refers to a metaphorical, pluralistic, and often ambiguous, noncommittal manner of viewing the world, whereas "activism" depends on a literal, singular, and outer driven, goal-oriented stance. I do feel the need to state the obvious: although David said he had nothing to say, he did, of course, manage to say quite a bit. But I think it's fair to suggest, following the spirit of his thinking, that what he said was not any *thing* at all. Rather, he poked a few holes in the whole idea of archetypal activism.

Short of remaining mute, one can at least take back one's words after they have been spoken. Wittgenstein said this was what made discourse meaningful (this from another lecture where David says, again, that he has nothing to say [this time about teaching] but an obligation to speak).

This disavowing or negating of one's words and ideas turns up regularly in David's work. It shows up in his discussions of Joseph Campbell's 1957 Eranos lecture, "The Symbol without Meaning," where Campbell said that symbolic meaning exists, that is, is meaningful, only when it has purposely disengaged from the symbol itself, like a bow releasing its arrow from itself. Or in a lecture David gave at the conference, "Psychology at the Threshold," held at the University of California, Santa Barbara in 2000, where he (again) somewhat subverted the title of the conference when he refused to give credence to the notion that psyche is *at* the threshold (which implies an imminent crossing) and instead argued that psyche *is* the threshold; there is "always another side, an unsaid. It's threshold all the way down."

It remains to be asked, is this line of thinking any more substantive than mental gymnastics? The determination to remain in a threshold state, constantly flitting back and forth between one side and another, between false somethings and deep nothings, calls to mind a seesaw that ultimately goes nowhere. If one is committed to speaking without saying anything, then these playground gymnastics are necessary and perfectly adequate. It's not unlike Mark C. Taylor, a theologian David often cites, who instead of writing an introduction to his book, *Tears*, submits a letter to his publisher saying he will not write an introduction. "No! No, I will not write the introduction you request. You want a book and I have struggled—perhaps vainly—not to write a book." Of course, the letter becomes the introduction, but a rejected one, and there is, in fact, a book, despite Taylor's admitted attempt not to write one.

I do not think, however, that David's writing is mere word play, as much as he clearly loves playing with words. A more appropriate trope for his work (and for Taylor's) would be that of *mise en abyme*, that infinite regression of one image (or word) to another that always refers back to itself. Like the image on Morton's Salt, where there is a picture of someone holding a box of salt on which there is a picture of someone holding a box of salt on which there is a picture of someone holding a box of salt, *ad infinitum*. The image on the box of salt is always the same. Or, if one wants to think in terms of talking about "nothing" and "something," the words always come back to themselves: one imagines one is talking about something (God) that on deeper examination turns out to be nothing, that is, not a thing. Like the Buddhist call to examine any object and find its inherent emptiness: for example, the paper on which these words are written is empty because it does not exist separately from the myriad of elements that give rise to it (trees, soil, sunshine, the logger). Since we personally cannot ever reach absolute nothingness nor escape language, what we have to use to describe this sense of nothing is in fact, another something that we hope can at least *imply* the nothing through negating our words. We can try to "do nothing with words" as Taylor, Lacan, Derrida and others do. Taylor submits an introduction, but it is a negated one; in his book the thing that one calls "introduction" loses some of its certainty or thing-ness.

It's like when David points out the axiomatic, that we are always in some sort of theory, dream, idea, program. In my first class with David, the first image he showed us was Pigpen, a character from the comic strip, *Peanuts*, who is always drawn with a cloud of dust above his head. We all are walking around in our own clouds of dust. Even as we may think we have broken free from a particular cloud or theory, we have only replaced it with another one. The statement "God is not a thing" is still a theory, even as I try to free the concept "God" from other, more opaque and restrictive theories.

As I said, I do not hold David's work to be shallow word games or an easy mimicry that shuns a deeper investigation into the nature or logic of any given concept (whether archetypal activism, teaching or God). Perhaps the image of Morton's Salt is inadequate, because there, the image is structurally identical, just infinitely smaller. But David's cycling around "theory" or "something/nothing" is really more a spiraling; a traveling that while seemingly going nowhere except back into itself, does return to itself—but it is a self that is no longer quite the same as it was before. The structure of the image changes, however minute the change may appear. It is a moving inward and downward, ever further (however futile) into the abyss. And with each subsequent spiraling, one chips away at the something to get to more of its underlying nothing. One reaches

64

another rung of truth, ripping away a new insight that perhaps before remained obscured. Because an introduction remains in Taylor's book, it is only partially negated. But even with a partial negation, the concept of what an introduction is unravels a bit. It questions our assumptions of what an introduction to a text should or even can be. David's subversion of "archetypal activism" does more than reveal its inner contradiction. He demonstrates the real life consequences that occur when what is metaphoric by nature is taken literally, and when literal actions have an excess of metaphor or imagination attached to them, like the Gothic-inspired shootings at Columbine High School in Littleton, Colorado in 1999.

In any endeavor concerned with the pursuit of knowledge, iconoclasm is a necessary method. It is necessary because by definition it cannot accept any assertion of truth without first checking for leaks (plumbing is another metaphor David likes). David once told me about a conversation he had with James Hillman. Hillman asked, "What do you believe in?" David's response was "Iconoclasm." (Being the faithful and devoted student that I am, I thought that was a good answer to adopt. Otherwise, if someone had asked me what I believed in, I probably would have said, "I don't know.") But what about idolatry? Is that equally necessary to a pursuit of knowledge? If we understand that idols (images, words) really point to an underlying truth that needs the image for its expression but is not to be conflated with the image itself, can we skip the middleman, those images, objects, and words that draw us in but are mere representations of something else?

The denial of our words and images would probably make life insufferably sterile: we would all remain quiet, silenced in the knowledge that our expressions were little more than inadequate approximations. I think there is also the danger that we would get stuck in the non-redeeming nothingness, the depressive stance that takes failure so personally and so much to heart. There would be no opening, however transient, to any experience of no-self, to an experience of negativity not inflated with the desire to be worth something. We need to create our images and write our texts precisely so that we can then see through them. Derrida said that nothing exists outside the text, but Stanley Romaine Hopper, one of David's teachers, said there would be nothing *inside* the text if the words did not already possess their own psycho-poetics. The instinct to take back one's words after speaking them does not suggest the need not to speak at all. We cannot avoid the middleman because the words and images themselves are the necessary gatekeepers, to truth, beauty, the soul, and everything else.

We need the icons, the words and images, so that we can have something to smash because they (the icon or symbol and its smashed or negated self) are two logically different forms of what is essentially the same psychic truth. To make a somewhat crude analogy: say one has a dream with an image of a house. In order to understand what "house" means to the dreamer, the image needs to be seen through, smashed, analyzed to reach its underlying meaning. The image of house no longer exists when it gives way to another one, perhaps "body," which may hit closer to the bone for the dreamer. Both of these images are saying the same thing, and in this example, both share a similar structure; both are concrete or physical representations. But one could say that a more thorough iconoclasm changes the form as well as the substance. The move from *mythos* to *logos* is just one historical and cultural example of this. The natural, concrete gods of myth eventually give way to the abstract, spiritualized God of monotheistic religions. Moreover, in light of depth psychology, one could then say that the spiritualized God becomes even further "smashed" into psychological insights into human nature, such as Freud's theory of God as an over-idealization of the father or Jung's correlation of God with the Self and the process of individuation. Without the icons, iconoclasm becomes little more than a temper tantrum.

It could follow, then, that iconoclastic idolatry is not a contradiction in terms but rather two different sides of a many-sided coin. And yet if I idolize David for imparting such liberating (in my mind) teachings, does this not somehow defeat his whole intention? It's almost as if I'm only partially listening to what he's saying, applying the teaching to abstract concepts like God, beauty, meaning, but not in the realm of daily life where the consequences of one's thinking scream out from newspaper headlines. But this is the beauty of loving a thinker like David, because you can't turn him into the next Big Thing. His work won't let you.

I already mentioned David's placement of the psyche *as* threshold rather than *at* a threshold. This metaphor turns up frequently in his writing, in various forms. He talks of edges, the liminal, the middle, the *tertium non datur*. He repeatedly situates his thinking in the in-between spaces, those gaps between the literal and metaphoric, identity and difference, sacred and profane, I and Thou, God and not God. He does not succumb to either term of a binary opposition that by definition constrains one's thinking to a monistic and ultimately egocentric "either/or" rather than a pluralistic "both/and" that makes room for opposing perspectives (or even better, the ironic "neither/nor" that takes nothing at face value). At the edges, in the threshold, there is little, if anything, to hold on to. Certainty, comfort, dogma, and perhaps even "reality" are abandoned for a penetrating and unceasing discernment into the psycho-poetic depths. In the in-between spaces, one chooses failure over and over again.

Of course, one can easily misconstrue David's work and still manage to reify it. But the adoration I am speaking of presupposes a faithfulness to his thinking. This, in turn, presupposes hanging out on the edges, too. So, then, what is this something about David? *Is* there even something? There are the ideas, some of which I have introduced in this essay. And then there are the multitudes of ordinary moments, in the classroom, at the conferences, in the bar, over lunch. These moments may on closer examination prove to be nothing more than approximations of some larger truth and an inherent emptiness, but taken together, they suffice in illuminating the abstract notions of love and devotion that David has inspired in his students. True to form, it is difficult to pin down what it is exactly about David. And as all papers cannot go on interminably, the silence after speaking is inevitable. I am running out of the space in which I can offer and then take back my words in the hope of saying something meaningful about my teacher and his work. But if there is one thing I do know about David, it is that it doesn't matter whether or not I have succeeded in saying what I wanted to because the attempt itself, however flawed and incomplete, includes what I cannot say.

ERANOS AND JUNGIAN PSYCHOLOGY: A PHOTOGRAPHIC HISTORY

PAUL KUGLER

ERANOS CONFERENCES: 1933-1988

The Eranos Conferences represent one of the most remarkable cultural and literary achievements in the history of analytical psychology. Intellectual traditions from the Far East, the Middle East, and the West came together at Eranos for over half a century: Max Knoll from Princeton lectured alongside Corbin from Tehran and Paris, Jung from Switzerland, and Suzuki from Japan. At its core, Eranos was interdisciplinary and multicultural, with speakers from various cultures presenting on religion, philosophy, literature, science, psychology, and medicine. Different cultures, different disciplines, and different languages came together at the Eranos Conferences for eight days each August for lectures and discussions over dinner.

69

The Eranos Round Table

Olga Froebe, the originator of the conferences, is seen in the photograph below standing on a garden walk just above Casa Eranos. The first floor of Casa Eranos is where the lecture hall is located, and on the second floor is an apartment in which Jung often stayed while attending the conferences.

Froebe above Casa Eranos

Olga Froebe expressed her vision of Eranos as a process of gradually building up a multidisciplinary picture of the inner transformations of the psyche. The photograph on the opposite page is of the Eranos round table at which speakers and invited guests would share meals and discuss lectures.

Casa Eranos, Casa Gabriella, and Casa Shanti

Olga Froebe was born in 1881 in London of Dutch parents and grew up in Blooms-bury. Her father, Albert Kapteyn, was an inventor, a photographer, and director of the London office of Westinghouse. Her mother, Gertrude, was a writer on social issues and a friend of George Bernard Shaw. Olga studied applied art in Zürich and later married Irwin Froebe, an Austrian musician. During World War I, Irwin died when his plane crashed while testing one of the first aerial cameras for the Austrian government.[1]

Froebe, 1920

Olga Froebe was pregnant at the time, and later that year gave birth to twin daughters.[2] This picture of Olga Froebe (above) was taken in 1920.

Around 1920, Olga Froebe and her father visited Ascona for a vacation. They enjoyed the setting and her father bought Casa Gabriella for his daughter.

The building seen in the middle of the photograph on the opposite page is Casa Gabriella, located on a narrow strip of terraced land once used as a vineyard. In 1928, Froebe built a guest house, seen here on the far right, called Casa Shanti. The same year, she also built Casa Eranos with a lecture hall on the first floor. Casa Eranos is the building on the far left.

Eranos Lecture Hall

The photograph above was taken inside the lecture hall. While the purpose of the lecture hall was, at the time, still unclear, Froebe was beginning to feel an urge to create some kind of public format to initiate a dialogue between East and West, especially around issues of spirituality, aesthetics, and inner transformation.

While Froebe had occasionally used the word "Eranos" on her letterhead in the early 1930s, it was not until she met Rudolf Otto in November 1932, that she permanently settled on the name "Eranos" for the conferences. Otto was a distinguished scholar of comparative religions and mysticism, particularly known for his book, *The Idea of the Holy*. Froebe described to him the lecture hall and her plan for an annual multidisciplinary conference bringing together leading scholars from the East and the West. Otto responded warmly to her plan and to the name "Eranos," which in ancient Greek means a "shared feast" or "picnic" to which each of the participants brings his or her own contribution. The original Greek meaning described well Froebe's underlying idea for the conference.[3]

The first lecturer Froebe sought out after speaking with Otto was Heinrich Zimmer, professor of Indology at Heidelberg. Zimmer accepted enthusiastically and lectured at Eranos from 1933 to 1939. The photograph of Zimmer shown below was taken at the 1935 conference.

Froebe initially met Jung in 1930 at Hermann Keyserling's School of Wisdom in Darmstadt. Following her conversation with Otto, she invited Jung to speak at the first Eranos Conference in August 1933. Jung accepted her invitation and delivered his lecture on "The Psychological Process of Individuation."

The conferences presented Jung's work in a new light, as a collaboration with world-renowned scholars from many different disciplines. During the 1930s, 40s, and early 50s, Eranos was a place where Jung often presented,

Rudolf Otto   Heinrich Zimmer, Eranos 1935

for the first time, his most important new work. Through Eranos, he brought his evolving ideas into a dialogue with different cultures, different disciplines, and different lines of research. The photograph below of Jung delivering his first Eranos lecture was taken in 1933.

Jung delivering his first Eranos lecture, 1933

In 1924, Froebe attended a seminar by Martin Buber at nearby Monté Verità and initiated a correspondence with him.[4] Ten years later, she invited Buber to lecture at the second conference. The photograph of Buber on the right was taken at Eranos in 1934.

Jolanda Jacobi was attending Eranos conferences long before she moved to Zürich in 1939.[5] In the 1935 photograph shown below, Jacobi is seen standing behind the speaker's podium just inside the lecture hall looking out of the window towards Gustav Heyer.

Born in Budapest, Jacobi underwent both Freudian and Adlerian

Buber at the 1934 conference

Jacobi and Heyer, 1935

77

Layard, 1936 Eranos

analysis in Vienna, before moving to Zürich in the late 1930s to train with Jung. In 1948, Jacobi took a leading role in founding the Zürich Jung Institute, where she served on the curatorium for 20 years.

The portrait of John Layard on the left was taken at Eranos in 1936. Layard was a distinguished Oxford anthropologist as well as a Jungian analyst. He wrote extensively on the interrelation between anthropology and analytical psychology. His most important book is *The Stonemen of Malakula*. Layard gave five Eranos lectures between 1937 and 1959.

Eranos Photo Archive, 1938

During the 1930s, Froebe had been busy traveling to various countries collecting pictures reflecting various archetypal themes. At the 1938 Eranos, Froebe introduced a new feature to the conference, an exhibition of enlarged photographs from the archives she had been compiling on archetypal symbolism.

The photograph below of Jung and Aniela Jaffé sitting on the wall outside of the Eranos lecture hall was taken at the 1938 conference. Jung's lecture that year was entitled "Psychological Aspects of the Mother Archetype."

Jung and Jaffé, 1938 Eranos

Jung gave his Terry lectures at Yale University in October of 1937. Following the lectures, he conducted a dream seminar for the Analytical Psychology Club of New York. Mary and Paul Mellon attended the seminar and were so touched by the experience that the following spring the family traveled to Zürich and Mary began attending Jung's English seminar. When the seminar concluded for the summer, the Mellons traveled to Ascona to meet Froebe and visit Eranos. Mary Mellon later wrote to Froebe about her visit in the following way: "The first thought that went through my mind when I stepped onto the terrace at Casa Gabriella was: "This is where I belong."[6]

Later that summer, Mary and Paul Mellon attended the 1938 Eranos Conference.

Mary Mellon and Louis Massignon, 1939 Eranos

The woman on the left in the 1939 photograph above is Mary Mellon. In the background, Jung can be seen talking to another conference participant. Mary Mellon was the motivating force behind the establishment of the Bollingen Foundation and its remarkable series of books. The man on the right in this photograph is Louis Massignon.

Louis Massignon, one of the most dynamic Eranos speakers, opened the 1939 conference with his talk on "Resurrection in the Mohammedan World." He lectured at Eranos from 1939 to 1955. The photograph of Massignon on the opposite page was taken at the 1939 conference.

Paul Mellon and Zimmer, 1939 Eranos

Massignon, 1939 Eranos

The photograph above of Paul Mellon and Zimmer was taken at the 1939 conference. That year Mary Mellon was 35 years old and just beginning to formulate her ideas about what would later become the Bollingen Foundation. Particularly moved by the lectures of Zimmer and Massignon, she would later publish their works in the Bollingen Series.

In 1940, Zimmer fled Germany with his family and eventually took up residence in New York City, where he secured a teaching position at Columbia University. In 1943, he gave a series of private seminars at the apartment of the anthropologist Maud Oakes. Part way through the seminar, Zimmer developed a severe cold, but instead of taking time off to rest, he continued to teach. The cold developed into pneumonia, and seven days later Zimmer died at the age of fifty-two.[7]

Joseph Campbell, then a graduate student at Columbia University, was one of those who attended the classes at Oakes's apartment. Zimmer became a major influence on Campbell's work. After Zimmer's death, Campbell spent many years preserving and publishing his lectures and supervising the translation of his books into English.

Jung and W. F. Otto, 1939 Eranos

The photograph above of Jung and W. F. Otto, the distinguished Greek scholar, was taken at the 1939 conference. Otto authored such classic texts as *The Homeric Gods* and *Dionysus*. He lectured at the 1939 conference and again in 1955.

In 1940, in view of the war and travel restrictions, Froebe arranged for a symbolic Eranos conference. Only one speaker, Andreas Speiser, a Swiss professor of mathematics at the University of Zürich, was scheduled

Jung and Speiser, 1940 Eranos

to give a lecture on "Plato's Unknown God." Forty people unexpectedly attended, including Jung, who gave an extemporaneous lecture on "The Psychology of the Trinity." Jung and Speiser appear together outside of the lecture hall in the 1940 photograph shown above.

Kerényi, 1941 Eranos

The photograph of Kerényi on the left was taken in 1941, the first year he appeared on the program. At the time, Kerényi was a professor of classical philology in Hungary. He had been a student of W. F. Otto and was earlier introduced to Jung by Jolanda Jacobi, a fellow Hungarian. In 1939, Kerényi collaborated with Jung on a book entitled "Introduction to a Science of Mythology."

Among the Eranos speakers, he was one of the most dramatic lecturers, with a mane of white hair, deep-set piercing eyes, and a charismatic presence. Kerényi lectured

Jung and Medard Boss, 1942 Eranos

at Eranos from 1940 to 1950 and was always very popular with the audience. In 1950, Froebe felt Kerényi had become too charasmatic a presence, and no longer invited him. After Froebe's death in 1962, Kerényi was asked to lecture again at the 1963 conference.[8]

The photograph of Jung and Medard Boss on the opposite page was taken at the 1942 Eranos conference. Boss studied with Freud in Vienna and under Bleuler at the Burgholzli Klinik in Zürich, before beginning a ten-year affiliation with Jung in 1938. During this time, Jung invited Boss to join a clinical seminar held at his home every fortnight to discuss clinical cases with a group of therapists of different theoretical orientations.[9]

Jung and Boss had a falling out in 1947 over the question of giving precedence to theory over clinical phenomena. Each accused the other of the same failing.[10] Boss went on to found existential psychoanalysis. In 1948, a year after his departure from Jung's seminar, Boss invited Martin Heidegger to participate in a new clinical seminar he was organizing at his home in Zollekon, just outside of Zürich. Boss's case seminar with Heidegger continued for ten years until 1958.

The 1943 Eranos Conference was the first in ten years at which Jung did appear on the regular program.[11] The portrait of Hugo Rahner on the right was taken at the 1943 conference. During the war and from 1942 to 1948, his Jesuit community from Innsbruck had taken refuge from the Nazis in Switzerland. Rahner lectured at Eranos on Christian mysticism.

Hugo Rahner, 1943 Eranos

Mary Mellon, 1938 Eranos

In May of 1943, just after her 39th birthday, Mary Mellon approved the establishment of the Bollingen Series. Later, she would write: "Bollingen is my Eranos."[12] The photograph of Mary Mellon shown above was taken during a visit to Eranos in 1938.

On October 11, six weeks after the conclusion of the 1946 conference, Mary Mellon died suddenly at the age of 42. At the time, she had been living at her home in Virginia overseeing the Bollingen Foundation.

Mary Mellon had gone horseback riding with her husband in the morning and suffered an asthma attack. The applicator containing her medication had broken during the ride and she was unable to receive immediate treatment. The asthma grew more severe and later that afternoon she died of a heart attack. Only a year before her death, Mary Mellon had begun talking about the possibility of buying Eranos to make it financially sound and to officially bring together Eranos and Bollingen. Several years after her death, Froebe approached Paul Mellon about Mary's offer to buy Eranos. Paul Mellon had by now remarried and was no longer inclined to pursue Mary's plan to purchase the property.[13]

Mary Mellon on horse, 1940's

Jung and Schrödinger, 1946 Eranos

The photograph of Jung and Erwin Schrödinger shown above was taken in a garden near the Round Table at the 1946 conference. The conference theme that year was "Spirit and Nature." Jung lectured on "The Spirit of Psychology" and Schrödinger spoke on "The Spirit of Natural Philosophy." A theoretical physicist, Schrödinger won the Nobel Prize in 1933 for his formulation of the Schrödinger wave equation.

The portrait of Adolf Portman on the right was taken at the 1949 conference. Portman was a distinguished professor of biology at the

Portman, 1949 Eranos

University of Basel. He lectured at Eranos from 1946 to 1977, a total of 31 years. Following Froebe's death in 1962, Portman became a guiding force at Eranos. Portman's lifelong project was to give biology an orientation that is both ethical and aesthetic. In 1946, he lectured at Eranos for the first time.

Jung and Baeck, 1947 Eranos

The photograph of Jung and Leo Baeck shown above was taken at the 1947 Eranos. Jung and Baeck had met many years before at Keyserling's "School of Wisdom" in Darmstadt. During World War II, Baeck, the Rabbi of Berlin, at age 69 had followed his congregation to the concentration camp at Theresienstadt. He had been one of only a few members to survive. Baeck lectured at the 1947 Eranos conference.[14]

Quispel and Portman, 1947 Eranos

Gilles Quispel is the man on the left next to Adolf Portman in this 1947 photograph. A Dutch Gnostic scholar, Quispel, in his early 30s, became one of the youngest persons ever invited to lecture at Eranos. He went on to deliver thirteen lectures between 1947 and 1971.

The year 1947 was a milestone in the history of Gnostic studies. In the winter of 1947, shortly after the discovery of 13 Gnostic codices in upper Egypt, one of the manuscripts was offered for sale to the Bollingen Foundation. Bollingen declined the offer. Quispel, a young Gymnasium teacher at the time, decided to intervene. Quispel eventually located the codex and, with the help of C. A. Meier, secured funding for the purchase. On May 10, 1952, Quispel acquired the codex for the Zürich Jung Institute. The manuscript later became known as the "Codex Jung" and has since played a significant role in our understanding of Gnosticism.[15]

In Casa Gabriella, on August 25, 1947, just after the completion of that year's conference, Jung signed the contract with Bollingen and Kegan Paul for the English translation of his collected works. Herbert Read, a senior editor at Kegan Paul, proposed R. F. C. Hull as the official translator. The photograph of Hull on the right was taken in Casa Gabriella in the 1950s.

Hull was a former medical student turned poet, journalist, and translator, who had worked as a cryptographer during the war. Within four months of the signing of the contract, Hull was admitted to a hospital in England. He had developed polio in all four limbs. Nevertheless, by January of that

Hull at Eranos, 1950s

year, while lying on his back in bed, Hull was busy dictating his translation of *Psychology and Alchemy* to his wife. Hull went on to translate nearly all of Jung's *Collected Works,* with the exception of *Volume Two, Experimental Studies.*[16]

Erich Neumann lectured at Eranos between 1948 and 1960. The photograph of Neumann on the left was taken at the 1948 conference. Born in Germany in 1905, Neumann was a student of literature and Jewish mysticism and had a Ph.D. in philosophy

Neumann, 1948 Eranos

91

prior to entering medical school. However, he had to leave Germany for Tel Aviv in 1934 before completing his medical degree.

In 1947, Neumann traveled to Europe to visit his old childhood friend, Gerhard Adler, vacationing in Ascona. Adler introduced him to Froebe and Eranos.[17] Impressed by Neumann, Froebe invited him to lecture at Eranos the following year. The title of his lecture was "Mystical Man." Froebe opened her picture archive to Neumann, hoping he might write on the various archetypal themes she had collected over the previous 10 years. Neumann started with a study of her collection of the archetypal feminine and the result was his book, *The Great Mother*, illustrated with over 250 pictures, mostly from the Eranos archive.

Jung and Corbin, 1951 Eranos

Henry Corbin, a world-renowned scholar of Sufism, appears with Jung in the 1951 photograph above. Several years earlier, Corbin had been introduced to Eranos by Louis Massignon, also a scholar of Islamic mysticism. Corbin lectured at Eranos for 27 years, between 1949 and 1976. During most of his academic life, he divided his teaching time between Paris and Tehran.

The portrait of Gershom Scholem on the left was taken in 1949, the first year he appeared on the conference schedule. One of the pre-eminent scholars of Jewish mysticism, Scholem was a gifted lecturer with a wonderful sense of humor. He spoke at Eranos for thirty years, from 1949 to 1979.

Gershom Scholem, 1949 Eranos

Corbin knew Eliade in Paris and introduced him to Eranos in 1949. The following year, Eliade was invited to lecture on "Psychology and the History of Religions." The portrait on the right was taken at the 1949 conference. Eliade lectured at Eranos from 1950 to 1967.

Eliade, 1949 Eranos

93

Jung speaking on veranda, 1951 Eranos

In addition to round table discussions, Jung started a tradition known as the "terrace-wall sessions." Immediately following a lecture or during intermission, Jung and friends, especially Neumann, would gather by the stone wall of the terrace and discuss the psychological significance of the lecture.[18] The photograph shown above of Jung in conversation with a small group of participants was taken at the 1951 conference.

Max Knoll, 1951 Eranos

Max Knoll, a professor of physics from Princeton University, lectured at Eranos between 1951 and 1965 on the history of science. The photograph of Knoll on the left was taken at the 1951 conference. In 1934 Knoll and Ernst Ruska, his graduate student, invented the electron microscope. Knoll died in 1969, seventeen years before his co-inventor, Ruska, would be awarded the Nobel Prize in physics for their invention.

Gerhard Adler, Neumann, and Quispel are seen in the photograph below, sitting just outside the lecture hall at the 1951 conference. When

Adler, Neumann and Quispel, 1951 Eranos

Bollingen and Kegan Paul prepared to translate and publish Jung's *Collected Works*, they appointed Herbert Read and Michael Fordham as editors. Jung requested that Gerhard Adler also be made a co-editor because of his understanding of the intricacies of the German language.[19]

Read and Scholem, 1958 Eranos

The photograph shown above of conference participants milling around outside the lecture hall was taken at the 1958 Eranos. Herbert Read, the tall man with white hair on the left, was an English poet, art historian, and publishing editor. As a director at Kegan Paul, Read oversaw the publication of Jung's *Collected Works*. For twelve years between 1952 and 1964, Herbert Read lectured at Eranos on literature and art history.

The photograph of Ernst Benz and D. T. Suzuki on the opposite page (top) was taken at the 1953 conference. Benz, on the left, is a world-renowned scholar of comparative religion, who lectured at Eranos between 1953 and 1978. The Zen Buddhist, D. T. Suzuki, was in his 80s when Max Knoll recommended he be invited to lecture at Eranos. Jung had

Benz and Suzuki, 1953 Eranos

earlier written an extensive foreword to Suzuki's book, "Introduction to Zen Buddhism."[20]

Ira Progoff, Suzuki, and Miroko Amura are seen in a photograph from 1953 shown below, sitting at the round table. Progoff, a professor at Drew

Progoff, Suzuki and Miroko Amura, 1953 Eranos

University Graduate School, spoke at Eranos between 1963 and 1966. As a Bollingen Fellow in the early 1950s, he studied with Jung in Zürich and went on to develop a workshop model known as "The Intensive Journal Process." Progoff's final lecture in 1966 was entitled "The Man who Transforms Consciousness: The Inner Myths of Martin Buber, Paul Tillich, and C. G. Jung."

Campbell, Erdman, Hull and his son Jeremy in Ascona, 1950s

The photograph above of Joseph Campbell, his wife Jean Erdman, Hull, and his son Jeremy was taken in 1953 in Ascona. Campbell began a project in 1949 for the Bollingen Foundation to publish a series of English translations of selected Eranos lectures. Six volumes of "Papers from the Eranos Yearbooks" were eventually published between 1954 and 1968, under such titles as *Man and Time, Spirit and Nature,* and *Man and Transformation.* In 1953, Campbell attended the Eranos Conference for the first time, and returned in 1957 and again in 1959 to lecture himself.

The photograph of Kurt Wolff on the right was taken at Eranos in the 1950s. The founder of Pantheon Books, Wolff was the Bollingen Foundation publisher for almost twenty-five years. While attending the 1956 Eranos conference, Wolff persuaded Jung to write his autobiography in collaboration with Aniela Jaffé. Immediately following the Eranos Conferences during the 1950s, Wolff, representing Pantheon Books, Herbert Read, representing Kegan Paul, and Vaun Gillmor, representing the Bollingen Foundation, would

Kurt Wolff, 1950s

meet with Jung to discuss the progress of the English translation of his *Collected Works*.

In 1956, Froebe donated the Eranos Picture Archive to the Warburg Institute in London and gave duplicates to the Jung Institute in Zürich and the C. G. Jung Foundation in New York. The Eranos Picture Archive in New York later grew into what we today know as the Archive for Research in Archetypal Symbolism (ARAS).

Froebe and the Ritsemas, 1958 Eranos

A Dutch couple, Rudolph and Catherine Ritsema, took over management of the Eranos Foundation after Froebe's death. In selecting the Ritsemas to succeed her at Eranos, Froebe ensured the continuation of a Dutch influence at Eranos. The photograph above of Froebe walking with the Ritsemas was taken at the 1958 conference.

Carved Stone in Garden of Casa Gabriella

Eranos has many beautiful terraced gardens, with multiple paths at different levels connecting the three buildings. This carved stone is located in the garden of Casa Gabriella. On it is a Latin dedication suggested by Jung and Quispel, which translates, "To the unknown genius of this place." When Froebe died on April 25, 1962, her ashes were interred beside this monument.

Kerényi and Gillmor, 1963 Eranos

In 1963, following Froebe's death, Kerényi was again asked to lecture at Eranos. Vaun Gillmor, seated next to Kerényi in the picture above, was one of the Bollingen representatives meeting yearly with Jung after the conference to oversee the publication of his *Collected Works*.

The photograph of Scholem and Quispel (opposite page, top) was taken at the 1965 conference. Each year, lectures were divided between French, English, German, and occasionally Italian. Quispel was the only speaker to lecture in three different languages: twice in French, seven times in German, and four in English.

While serving as Director of Studies at the Jung Institute in Zürich, James Hillman attended the 1964 conference with the hope of extending invitations to Eranos speakers to lecture at the Zürich Jung Institute. It was Hillman, however, who was to be extended an invitation to lecture at Eranos. During the 1966 conference, he gave his first Eranos lecture, entitled "On Psychological Creativity." The photograph of Rudolph Ritsema and Hillman (opposite page, bottom) was taken at the 1969 Conference.

Scholem and Quispel, 1965 Eranos

Hillman and Ritsema, 1969 Eranos

Miller and Ritsema, 1975 Eranos

In 1969, David Miller attended his first Eranos Conference and returned in 1975 to deliver his first lecture, entitled "Images of Happy Ending."[21] Miller studied with Owen Barfield and Stanley Hopper at Drew University before going on to hold the Watson-Ledden Chair in Religion at Syracuse University. His major work is a four-volume study of the Greek mythological, psychological, and literary expressions in images of Christ. The photograph above of Miller and Ritsema was taken in 1975.

Corbin, Scholem, and Eliade, all highly acclaimed scholars in their own right, came together at Eranos for almost three decades. Their combined efforts during those years played a significant role in moving the approach known as "The History of Religions" from the margins of academic life to center stage in Religious Studies.[22]

Henry Corbin presented at Eranos for over twenty-five years between 1949 and 1976. The photograph of Corbin sitting on the bench behind the round table (opposiste page, top) is from 1976, the year he delivered his final Eranos lecture.

Corbin behind round table, 1976 Eranos

In the photograph on the left, David Miller is seen delivering his 1980 lecture, entitled "Between God and the Gods—Trinity." The conference theme that year was "Extremes and Borders." Miller delivered nine Eranos lectures between 1975 and 1988.

Miller, 1980 Eranos

Durand, 1980 Eranos

A distinguished French philosopher of the imagination, Gilbert Durand spoke at Eranos between 1964 and 1988. Durand was awarded the Legion of Honor Metal for his covert activity during World War II in the French resistance movement. The photograph above of Durand lecturing is from the 1980 conference.

*   *   *

The seating at lunch and dinner during the conferences was always carefully arranged in advance according to which language each person spoke. Often French and Italian speakers were grouped at one round table, with German and English speakers at the other. The photograph at the top of the opposite page is of the 1982 round table. David Miller and Eric Hornung can be seen in the back left and center of this photograph. On the right front is Patricia Berry.

106

Round Table, 1982 Eranos

In this 1982 photograph on the right, Wolfgang Giegerich is seen delivering his first Eranos lecture. He received his Ph.D. from the University of California at Berkeley, taught at Rutgers University and later trained at the Jung Institute in Stuttgart. Between 1982 and 1988, Giegerich delivered seven Eranos lectures.

Giegerich, 1982 Eranos

Hayao Kawai, 1983 Eranos

The portrait above of Hayao Kawai, the first Jungian analyst in Japan, was taken at the 1983 conference. He lectured at Eranos between 1983 and 1988 on Japanese mythology, spirituality, and fairy tales. Kawai currently holds the distinguished position of Minister of Culture in Japan.

The conference theme for the 1985 Eranos was "The Hidden Course of Events." Hillman is seen in the upper photograph on the opposite page presenting his 1985 lecture, entitled "On Paranoia." Between 1966 and 1987, Hillman delivered a total of 15 Eranos lectures, more lectures than either Jung or Neumann.

In 1978, and again in 1985, Marie Louise von Franz lectured at Eranos. Von Franz earned her doctorate in classical philology before becoming an analyst and working closely with Jung on his alchemical research, especially translating medieval Latin texts. The 1985 conference theme was "In and Out of Time" and von Franz's final Eranos lecture was entitled "Nike and the River Styx."

Hillman, 1985 Eranos

von Franz, 1985 Eranos

Kugler, Hillman, and Giegerich, 1988 Eranos

The picture above was taken at the 1988 conference. Hillman, Giegerich, and myself[23] are looking over photographs taken during previous conferences. The 1988 Eranos conference was the last one based on Froebe's original design. The decision to stop the conferences was made for a variety of reasons, including financial concerns and a shift in focus by Rudolf Ritsema as to the mission of Eranos. Seminars continue to be held at Eranos and conferences conducted at a local hotel, but 1988 was the last conference convened at Casa Eranos in the format originally conceived by Olga Froebe. While the Eranos conferences officially came to an end in 1988, their intellectual, cultural, and psychological legacy continues to live on and grow in historical significance with each passing year.

NOTES

[1] Deirdre Bair, *Jung: A Biography* (New York: Little, Brown and Company, 2003), 411; William McGuire, *Bollingen* (Princeton, NJ: Princeton Univ. Press, 1982), 21. The exact nature of Irwin Froebe's death is unclear. He was either killed in the plane crash or executed shortly after the crash as a spy.

[2] One of her twin daughters was retarded, and was later killed in Germany by the Nazis (Bair, 411).

[3] Olga Froebe-Kapteyn, "A Note on Eranos," in *The Mysteries: Papers from the Eranos Yearbooks, Vol. 2*, ed. J. Campbell (New York: Pantheon Books, 1955), xv. See also, Aniela Jaffé, "Jung and Eranos," *Spring 1977* (Zürich: Spring Publications, 1977), 208.

[4] Bair, 413.

[5] Barbara Hannah, *Jung: His Life and Work* (New York: G. P. Putnam's Sons, 1976), 264.

[6] McGuire, 20.

[7] Hannah, 276; McGuire, 66.

[8] McGuire, 148.

[9] Bair, 484, 538-540.

[10] Debra Knowles, "Along a Path Apart: Conflict and Concordance in Jung and Heidegger," Doctoral dissertation, Pacifica Graduate Institute, 2002, 48.

[11] While Jung did not officially appear on the 1943 program, he did give an impromptu talk on Opicinus de Canistris, a fourteenth-century mystic. His talk was transcribed, but never published (McGuire, 72.)

[12] McGuire, 27.

[13] McGuire, 114.

[14] Gerhard Wehr, *Jung: A Biography* (Boston: Shambhala Publications, 1985), 325; Ronald Hayman, *The Life of Jung* (New York: Norton & Company, 2002), 393.

[15] Wehr, 365-370.

[16] McGuire, 124-125; Hayman, 394.

[17] McGuire, 135.

[18] Jaffé, 202.

[19] McGuire, 109.

[20] McGuire, 156.

[21] Miller tells the following anecdote about his first Eranos experience. "I first attended the Eranos Conferences in 1969 .... The seats for the auditors at Casa Eranos were reserved, and I was assigned a seat in the fourth row. The aisle and Lago Maggiore were on my right and an elderly British woman was on my left. In the intermission of the initial lecture by Scholem, I turned to my seatmate and, in an attempt to make conversation, I asked her whether there would be a question-and-answer time following the lecture. She said to me: 'You must be an American.' I confessed that I was, whereupon she educated me about the spirit of Eranos. 'You see,' she said, 'the presenters are invited to speak at the very edge of their disciplines. If they manage this edge, they are in no better position than the audience to answer questions. It would be premature. On the other hand,' she concluded decisively, 'if they do not manage to speak at the edge, then they are not worth questioning in the first place!'" (Presented to the 16th Congress of the International Association for Analytical Psychology in Barcelona, Spain, on September 1, 2004.)

[22] Steven M. Wasserstrom, *Religion after Religion: Gershom Scholem, Mircea Eliade, and Henry Corbin at Eranos* (Princeton: Princeton University Press, 1999), 8.

[23] I attended the Eranos Conferences between 1972-1988.

ON DEVOTION

JAMES HILLMAN

PART 1

When I began thinking about this theme—piety, devotion, obeisance—the Gods gave me no forewarning in regard to what I might be getting into. I wonder whether my friend David Miller for all his acuity in such matters could have predicted the perils. To utter the word piety, or devotion, implicates the Gods, and invites them nearer. Because we cannot know in which way they may intervene, we need be cautious using their names. Already we can feel the power present in the theme, because devotion affects, if not motivates, the dangers of our present historical moment and the cataclysm that a few men—paragons of devotion—single-handedly impose upon human history, and the nature of the planet.

But let us begin: "devotion"—the word conjures pious images of folded hands in prayer, a mother attending her ill child, a dairy-man milking at four in the morning, a sculptor, sealed away amid the debris of her cold studio. These images show a particular state of being: concentration upon the other whether God, child, cow, or block of marble; a single-minded focus on what is other than myself, a position of deliverance to another.

Even we who are not mothers, milk-men or artists show devotion in more modest and masked styles: simply rising each day, driving to work regardless of mood and weather; cooking dinner, filling out our annual tax-forms with compunction and *gravitas*.

Can we live at all without being devoted to something? Something beyond pleasure and desire, and beyond guilt, drives our days; something urges us to care and to serve and attend regularly, unthinkingly, even obsessively. Does not creaturely existence require devotion to some "other" power—whether it be named a God, a projection, an ideal, or a delusion? Strive as we might to be wholly Nietzschean, beyond good and evil, superbly self-determined, or wholly existential—a mere sequence of unconnected reactive occasions—that very idea of radical freedom by which some fashion, even stake, their lives itself proves the force of devotion. Like the will to believe, the urge to devote provides a well-spring of self-transcendence, a manifestation of Schopenhauer's notion of human being as an "animal metaphysicum." We cannot avoid being devoted; we are devotional beings.

It would seem that devotion is called into play, as if an instinct, in all walks of life and all mundane tasks. And, if an instinct, then the single-minded attention of a turtle burying her eggs on the shore, a bird weaving its nest, a bull elk guarding his herd, are not they too devoted? They too are utterly committed, their very lives at stake. Do they not too demonstrate a "devotion instinct"?

By casting the net so widely to include such a variety of behaviors, I seem to have removed the very heart of devotion, its piety, that religious constraint put upon the word by its conventional usage, where the object of devotion is hardly a milk-cow or a tax-form, but a cult figure to which we bring our *votum*, our vote of assent and vow of faithfulness. To discuss devotion in terms of turtles and tax-forms seems indeed to commit the sin of impious secular humanism, rendering to Caesar as if he were a God.

There must surely be an essential difference between animal behavior and mundane duty on the one hand, and on the other, the noble and pious devotion that the word alone brings to mind. Frankly, I think it mistaken to search for this essential difference. I think another path is more fruitful. The path I would explore leaves behind the familiar divisions between sacred and secular, between God and Caesar, and instead aims to locate devotion in the unreflected instinctual ground of human behavior, tying the highest and holy with our animal selves. And here, I remind you of a statement from Jung:

> ... the animal is a well-behaved citizen in nature, it is pious, it follows the path with great regularity. ... Only man is extravagant. ... So if you assimilate the nature of the animal you become a peculiarly law-abiding citizen; you go very slowly and you become reasonable in your ways ....[1]

By linking the saintly and the beastly, I am moving in hardly a new direction, since religions the world over present animals as objects of devotion. Christian Saints too have their animal counterparts. The value of collapsing the barrier between sacred and secular—the kneeling prayer fingering his rosary and the tax-payer fingering his calculator—takes devotion out of the closet of preciousness. Its beneficent importance can flow into many sorts of acts, a flow of importance that sanctifies, let us say, baptizes, whatever we do with humble respect, regular faithfulness, trepidation, *gravitas* and a ritual-like obsessive attention to the object, thing, or task at hand. If devotion is as basic, as I believe it is, to the character of *homo religiosus*, then whatever we do with full attention upon the other, delivered over to the other as fateful and compelling obligation, implies that we are each religious beings.

If we are each religious beings, then society is potentially already theocratic because we are each devotedly attached to and followers of a vision, an ideal, a task. This means that a theocratic society is already potentially present without a revolution from the right, without a need for Mullahs, Prophets and Priests, or holy writs. Devotion to archetypal powers beyond our invention is given with our animal nature, so that becoming conscious means discovering to which God, at which altar, we are dedicating our lives.

The push to establish literal theocracy, whether Islamic, Christian, Judaic or Hindu is a left-over from the unnecessary separation between

115

sacred and secular, now called Church and State. That distinction became necessary when the Gods were driven from the world, allowed back only on Sunday mornings and the churches were their asylum. But the Gods are waiting around, as Joseph Campbell said, on the very street corners, as Wim Wenders suggests in *Wings of Desire*, still there, even if invisible to our literalist eyes. David Miller exposed the many presences of these powers in his early work *The New Polytheism*. "All things are full of Gods," said Thales[2] at the beginning of Greek science, which means simply that devotion to things is devotion to the Gods, for *here* is where the Gods are. Devotion to the Gods means devotion to the given, to the created, despite orthodoxy's obsessions with a transcendent, non-here Creator.

The emphasis on transcendence with its upward-lifting devotion in all three faiths derived from the Bible has resulted in the lowering, the fallenness of this planet. As long as God is very different from nature and man very different from animal, our devotions will go the wrong way and wrong this world. Spinoza, who equated God with *natura*, the givenness of this world, was excluded at age twenty-four from his synagogue in Holland, a society known for its tolerance! Orthodoxy demands devotion follow dogma, and dogma prefers a sacred that lies beyond, somewhere else, in future time, anywhere but here. And, what is right here includes our symptoms, including the symptoms of devotion such as fanaticism, immolation, murder. Jung added to Thales's "all things are full of Gods" with his own famous epigram—"the Gods have become diseases." To symptoms too we are devoted and by them obsessed.

In conclusion to these first thoughts and there are two more parts to come—I am suggesting that the familiar image of hands folded in prayer does indeed portray devotion in essence. This because there is no object, no cow, no stone. We see effect without cause, obeisance without ideal. The transcendent is not literalized: we remain with the phenomenon, the image only, devotion as such. These hands have yielded to something other; they are as if bound. By what they are bound, to what they are devoted is not, perhaps should not, could not be depicted. Nonetheless, they are invisibly bound by it, attached to it.

I am suggesting that the word "devotion" represents in language the instinct of attachment with all the fervor and zeal of attachment. And this instinct is akin to what Freud called "object libido" which draws the soul into the world and keeps us there; akin as well to what Asian psychologies call *samsara*, to the vortex of ten-thousand things. I am suggesting that this instinct manifesting as devotion is at the root not only of religion but at the root also of service in every field of passionate unswerving fidelity—art-making, science, tending and caring, study and duty. It is the force that makes civilization possible—and also its destruction.

PART 2

The events emanating from and taking place in Afghanistan and Iraq show that devotion includes more than images of folded hands, of the sincere dedication of a monk on Mt. Athos or of van Gogh in Arles. In fact, the painter who infuriated righteous and sentimental patriots by comparing the attacks on September 11th with a great work of art did indeed see into the difficult truth of devotion: its definition also includes fanaticism, asceticism, martyry, masochism, obsessive compulsions, implacable hatred and delusions. The Gods do indeed reveal themselves in diseases.

"Devotion" derives directly from the Latin *devotus, -a, -um,* which has two meanings: "devotedly zealously attached" and "accursed, execrable." *Devoto, -are, -aui, -atum* means "To put a spell on, bewitch." *Devoueo, -ouere* means "to vow as an offering or sacrifice," and it also means in the case of a military commander "To devote himself and his army to the infernal Gods on his country's behalf," extending to mean, in general, devotion "to the infernal Gods, curse; to bewitch, enchant," and finally, "to destine, doom (to a fate)." I warned you! Our topic takes us into perilous territory, and in case you don't know that word "execrable": it means abominable, awful, fearful; bad beyond description.

The fact that devotion calls also upon the infernal Gods or, in modern terms, is a pledge to Hell, is a lesson taught long before September 11th,

2001. Sovanarola and Torquemada, the natives of Mexico and the Caribbean, and the women burned in France and Massachusetts taught us long ago, and also by the thousands, that to be zealously attached as were the Inquisitors is also to be accursed, bewitched by the very zeal which it serves. The most abominable cruelties have been perpetrated by the most devoted. The infernal Gods may enter even if one's attention is single-mindedly focused on the ill child, the milk-cow, the marble block, or a good God in his high heaven. I am simply re-stating a Jungian precept: there is no condition of soul without its shadow.

Moreover, the better and the worse are inseparable because they are one and the same. To be devoted is also to be cursed, caught in destiny, doomed by the very bonds of your vows. Devotion's definition makes this so clear, and that is why an inquiry into our topic is so worthwhile for psychology. We are led to see that the most dedicated devotion does not protect from evil or supplant evil with good, but rather that we are entangled in both because they are entangled with each other. An understanding of devotion makes one quite humble about human possibilities and suspicious about the good intentions of loyal devotees. Fine principles and illumined teachers cannot protect their following from the inherent harm that devotion inflicts. It should therefore not be such a puzzle to hear execrable acts defended with lofty phrases or that service to the best ends can be enacted with horrifying means. Slowly it dawns on us that the glowing aura which the word "devotion" conjures is part of its enchantment, a way in which it suppresses its own psychopathology.

Freud was the first—other than skeptics and cynics in the tradition from Diogenes to Voltaire—to venture into the shadow-lands of religion. In 1907 Freud published on the deviations of devotion in a paper called "Obsessive Acts and Religious Practices"[3] in which rituals, invocations, prayers, and other ceremonies of devotion are reduced to their shadow. At the end of this astounding essay, Freud dares to "regard the obsessional neurosis" as "a private religious system, and religion as a universal obsessional neurosis." [p. 34] He explains their similarity: "The essential resemblance would lie in the fundamental renunciation of the satisfaction of inherent instincts."

Very soon we will come to what is renounced. But first I shall try to make clearer the state of mind of renunciation. Above all, the mind must close itself against all other alternatives which seem to it to be deviations, compromises, temptations, in order to maintain a single-minded focus. The tending mother does not pick up the phone; the sculptor closes the door; the filmmaker does forty-two takes; the assassin checks his weapon, again and again and again. This monotheism of consciousness calls for precisely repetitive formula, compulsive gestures, enigmatic rituals, words and numbers that reinforce and become inherent to devotion. Here we see the two moments of the definition—zeal and enchantment—occurring at the same instant. In both religious practices and obsessive compulsions, behaviors seem externally imposed according to rules that must be obeyed literally to the last letter for fear of doom, yet without thought for their meaning. In fact, Freud says "In all believers ... the motives impelling them to religious practices are unknown" [31] and the devotee "carries out a ceremonial without concerning himself with its significance." [30] So the baseball pitcher touches his cap three times and his crotch once before mounting the mound, and the writer sharpens and arranges his pencils before selecting the one he will begin with. Freud further notes, that not-doing becomes more important than doing. "Prohibitions," he says "replace obsessive acts." [32] "Thou shalt not"s outnumber "Thou shalt"s. More and more monotheistic consciousness requires forbidden areas about touching, eating, clothing, timing, and, of course, imagining. The way is open to repression and those bans notorious in orthodoxies of religion that would exterminate any thought, any person, any feeling, any image that represents alternatives to devotion.

The anthropologist Paul Radin, who wrote along with Jung and Kerényi the famous study of the Trickster figure and who was one of my teachers long ago in Zürich, wrote a basic essay on monotheistic consciousness. That essay is worth noting now since the peril to the world as we enjoy the day is in the hands of avowed monotheists of three persuasions in which religion and terror are coupled; terror as religion, religion as terror.

Radin said that monotheism in religion is not a developmental stage, a unifying improvement over polytheism, as if the many grow, over time, into a unity. Rather, monotheism emerges as a vision and a convincing passion in a certain sort of psyche, a *homo religiosus*, who leads others to follow the same vision and the same renunciation.

What is renounced, says Freud, is the "satisfaction of inherent instincts." For Freud these are sexual and egoistic satisfactions [34], the pleasures of life that satisfy our multitudinous natures. These are renounced and become repressed. But since the repressed always returns in some form or another, devotion can act as a defense against the repressed. Hence, Freud calls ceremonial acts "protective measures." "A ceremonial begins as an act of defence or security," [31] "The patient feels he must do this or that lest misfortune occur." [31] We are back again at the definition of devotion and its link with destiny and doom.

We all know that renunciation of satisfaction cannot be accomplished by will alone; behavior must be ritualized, magical (ceremonial in Freud's sense) to keep the repressed at bay. But even these defenses—performing acts in the right order, repeating them from the beginning, assuming specific body positions, avoiding seductive images and thoughts—these habits of devotion are not enough. The repressed is mighty; desire calls for satisfaction; life is a farce, it will out. So emotions of equal force supply the energy to maintain renunciation.

Primary among these instinctual forces is hatred. Schopenhauer[4] wrote, "Hatred comes from the heart ... we cannot alter our heart." Devotion does not renounce, does not repress hatred, and in fact hatred can feed devotion and maintain its dedication. The savage outbreaks of ethnic cleansing after years and years of neighborly quiescence show how nourishing hatred can be to an idealized obsession with one's own people, race, land. The Freudians as far back as Ernest Jones[5] in 1913 have long paid devoted attention to hatred as a dominant emotion in both paranoia and obsession, as if to say hatred provides the intensity and consistency needed to keep out the other; perhaps it even creates the other as alien and enemy. Hatred secures us in our own hearts, fixed inside our own territory; it is homeland security, and its poison is therefore so difficult to dilute or convert into love.

At the end of this second part it seems we, Freud and I, have together destroyed all the piety of devotion. Why have I dwelt so long with Freud? Why? Because he is the shadow expert; hence necessary for a true devotee of Jung who insisted upon shadow awareness. I read Freud with a Jungian eye, so I do not reduce religious practices to obsessional acts; but rather I read obsessional acts as pointing toward religious practices, as modes of devotion—once we have purified devotion of its overvalued piousness. As we must not lose touch with the religious aspect of obsessions, so we must keep in mind the pathological shadow of devotion. Elsewhere and earlier I tried to show that depression is secularized melancholy, melancholy without the Gods, and paranoia is revelation literalized, and hysteria the return of the God, Dionysos. An archetypal method approaches obsessions and compulsions, including the Hells plumbed in David Miller's theological studies, to be peculiar modes of recognizing the Gods in all things, even such high-minded things as the abstractions of theology. Neurotic practices are ceremonies with religious value and purpose.

The devotion and destruction travel together on one and the same road: If you believe yourself devoted to your God, your cause, your discipline, your art, you will find yourself caught in devotion's shadows— that narrowing, defensive stance of monotheistic consciousness, surprised by your intolerance and hatreds. If you find yourself obsessive about ridiculous things in daily life and compulsive in meaningless ways, you will find yourself drawn into issues of belief: what unnamed, unknown force wants this devotion from me, so ritualistically, so relentlessly?

You see I am trying to make a fundamental therapeutic move. I am trying to relieve the person of obsessive symptoms by placing their source not in the obscure recesses of the personal psyche, but in the obscure mystery of the psyche of the world. For devotion teaches us that not merely do we obsessively devote ourselves to things, but that things, if they are full of Gods, demand obsession from us.

121

PART 3

One of the longer-lasting exemplars of devotion is the Biblical figure of Ruth. The Book of Ruth fortunately is short and easy, and it is not piously moralistic and weighted with the rabbinical sentimentalism that burdens so many marvelous tales in the Bible. It may serve now for discovering another phenomenology of devotion. Moreover, I am turning to this tale also as a personal devotion to my grandfather who was designated its official translator into the English language for the first American Reform Bible.[6]

A widow named Naomi, bereft of husband and sons, is about to return to her homeland in Judah. Her two daughter-in-laws, Orpah and Ruth, also widowed, are Moabites. Naomi beseeches Orpah and Ruth to stay behind in Moab because they are younger and, as Moabites, they have a better chance of finding new husbands and new life in their own land.

Orpah agrees, and stays; but Ruth makes the following famous declaration:

> Entreat me not to leave thee, and to return from following after thee; for whither thou goest, I will go; and where thou lodgest, I will lodge; thy people shall be my people, and thy God my God; where thou diest, will I die, and there will I be buried; the Lord do so to me, and more also, if aught but death part thee and me. [Ruth: I, 16-17]

Let us read the text, phrase by phrase.

A: *"Entreat me not to leave thee"*—Ruth's devotion begins within a personal context. It expresses what Jung calls "kinship libido," similar to Goethe's elective affinity and to what Bradley, the English philosopher, describes as an internal, rather than, external relationship in which the two are co-relative and necessary to each other.

This kinship first presents itself as a refusal, a stand against another possibility (staying behind in Moab.) Ruth refuses to listen to reason, she goes against common sense. Devotion requires obstinacy, ears closed to any other avenue.

B: "*Following after thee*"—Devotion means becoming a follower, a disciple coming "after" (not first), submitting to a discipline. Whether mothering, milking or sculpting, you follow the discipline.

C: "*Wither thou goest, I will go*" —Wither, wherever, anywhere "*Wither thou lodgest, I will lodge*"—whenever the way comes to a halt, wherever it lodges, stops, sticks, is confined, devotion accepts. It accepts the limits of discipline and the rigidity of exclusion. We are not any longer open, nor are all ways open. In fact there may be no way forward at all. Devotion is a lodging place itself, housed within its own walls.

D: "*Thy people shall be my people*"—Kinship implicates a wider circle of family, clan, society, and that wider body of figures, images and memories that people the psyche of both Naomi and Ruth. There is a shared imagination which holds together teacher and pupil, cause and workers for it, theory of art and practitioners. We are devoted not merely to the object of devotion—a leader, a school, a beloved—but to the archetypal images which arouse our kinship libido, enliven its fantasies and magnify the attraction.

The extension of devotion shows clearly in marriage which may begin like Ruth's concentration upon Naomi, but soon implicates the other's people—relatives and friends, and further, the other's fantasies, ideas and values. The widening of devotion follows Plato's theory of love eventually becoming devotion to an invisible ideal, a marriage both by the sacrament and to the sacrament, a marriage to marriage itself, with its restrictive exclusion clause "forsaking all others."

E: "*and thy God my God*"—Not merely your person and your people, but your God. That unformulated dominant which lords over the psyche of the devoted object rules as well the soul of the devotee. They share the same obsession. Here we can resolve the question raised in the first part—is there no real difference between secular devotion of the dairy-man to his cows and the tax-payer to his schedules and the devotion of the artist or the nun? Ruth answers: my devotion is to your God. As long as "God" is the value term all devotion is sacred. There are greater and lesser Gods; as Proclus and Iamblichus laid out, there are many such figures—angels, archons, principles, powers, daimones. There are many visions, missions, ideals, absolutes, but once they are linked with "God," devotion becomes sacred, and perilous.

F: *"ere thou diest, will I die .... aught but death part thee and me."* The Book of Ruth is told in narrative time, a story from beginning to ending. This could lead us to discuss the phenomenology of devotion as it proceeds through stages from person to group to God to death. Do notice that God is not the final term; death is. Not God signifies devotion ultimately; death does. Devotion is secondarily a matter of religion, primarily it is an inevitable, existential, animal necessity.

But a narrative reading through stages is only one way of entering the tale. There is also an imagistic reading, such as we use when entering a painting, a poem, or a dream. Then, we think less of beginning and finishing, but rather of simultaneity, a logic of all-at-once. An image is holistic, completely presented. So devotion can be entered at any of its moments: fidelity to a person, to a group, or the conviction of necessity— that this person, this work, this place where I am lodged calls as if my death were calling.

Death may be conceived not in the usual sense as mortality, the end of the living body on whom the person depends, but rather an existential death outside of mortality, a death of devotion, or in devotion, in which the usual life of the usual body is not the determinant; one has died to it, devotion has already left usual life behind. Thus the utterly devoted one, the ascetics, the fanatics, enter mortal death without fear and trembling because they have already passed it by, are already dead to the claims of life and all that which might have been or could have been otherwise.

When Naomi entreats Ruth not to follow, she is saying, to follow me is a death. Orpah recognizes this, electing to stay in her known territory. Ruth, however, vows unto death. It is her calling, a necessity, that *"notwendigkeit"* which "cannot be otherwise," as Kant defined necessity. In the moment of her declaration Ruth abandons reason and the prospect of a life in a homeland with a husband, and yields to a value that, like a God, claims one's life and invites one's death. This is what I must do; this is where I belong; this is my family, my people, my home country. I am not a migrant worker; I have crossed the border.

124

Therefore, all the obsessional deviations we saw at the beginning. They help to ward off this commitment to death and continue to propitiate, as Freud wrote, the repressed, that part of the psyche—in my idea of it—that is not pledged to Naomi, calling and death. Devotion has renounced the wishes, to "be other-wise," and so one has to obsess in the work in order to stay in the work, else the repressed "old country" and its longings returns as distractions, the roads not taken. Obsession belongs to artists and fanatics. They require a monocularity of negative prohibitions in order to defend against the voice of temptation, who keeps saying "you are killing yourself, slaving away; it all comes to nothing. There's more to living than practicing your tennis serve hour upon hour upon hour."

John Keats perceived something in the Book of Ruth—rare to find a Biblical reference in his poems—that leads to our conclusion. In his great ode, "To a Nightingale," the bird's song, conjuring the longing for the invisible world, finds its way, "Through the sad heart of Ruth, when sick for home, / She stood in tears amid the alien corn." This image of Ruth in tears amid the alien corn has entered the English canon of oft-used poetic images. For our theme we learn that devotion also expresses a longing for home, may even be a mode of managing or compromising or disguising this longing for home.

But then, what place is this "home" for which Ruth longs? The cornfield which she is gleaning in the Bible story and to which Keats refers, is the world itself, the field of the earth Goddess Ceres/Demeter, this mothering world. But Ruth is not "at home" here. And Ruth becomes in Keats' imagination the exemplar of alienated existence, of a longing, so keenly felt all through the Bible and so ponderously fateful in Jewish history, for "home."

Is devotion the other face of alienation? Orpah, who stays where she is, is neither devoted, nor alienated. Ruth is both. Does devotion "take us home"? The suicidal bomber's devotion takes him home to Paradise, and a Christ-devoted President can command "himself and his army to the infernal Gods on his country's behalf" and thereby overcome estrangement. Does devotion provide an exculpatory response to the curse of Biblical history—the primordial homesickness of the Fall out of the Garden, the destruction of the Temple, the exile and the wandering, so that attachment to a new clan, group loyalty to a cause, joining with a principle, a leader, some Naomi, some God offers an earthly answer that assuages the existential thirst of the solitary life, estranged, homeless, where hope itself is exiled because aimed beyond this earth?

Devotion, as I suggested earlier, can attach us to this world, but because of its shadows perilously detaches us too. In other words the darkest shadow—and shadow has colored my thoughts all along—is neither obsession nor fanaticism, but alienation in the field of yellow corn: the loss of the sense of Gods in all things, the glory of this world only gleanings.

NOTES

[1] *Visions Seminar* December 1930. Notes of Mary Foote, p. 282.

[2] John Burnet, *Early Greek Philosophy*, London: Adam & Charles Black, 1948, p. 50n succinctly reviews the sources for the statement attributed to Thales, and refers to parallels in Plato, Aristotle and Herakleitos that "mean only that nothing is more divine than anything else."

[3] Freud, "Obsessive Acts and Religious Practices" (1907), *Collected Papers II*, London: Hogarth Press, 1953.

[4] Arthur Schopenhauer, *Essays from the Parerga and Paralipomena*, London: Allen and Unwin, 1951 ("Studies in Pessimism"), pp. 54-55.

[5] Ernest Jones, "Hate and Anal Eroticism in the Obsessional Neurosis," 1913.

[6] Joseph Krauskopf (transl.), "Ruth," *The Holy Scriptures, according to the Masoretic Text*, Philadelphia: Jewish Publication Society, 1917.

Once More "The Stone Which is Not a Stone": Further Reflections on "Not"

WOLFGANG GIEGERICH

Many years ago, in *Spring 49* (1989), David Miller presented us with his amazing essay entitled "The Stone Which is Not a Stone," full of insights extending far beyond the immediate theme expressed in this alchemical dictum, insights about "C.G. Jung and the Postmodern Meaning of 'Meaning'" at large. Like myths, fairytales, symbols, poetry, and works of art, alchemical notions, too, are so rich that it is worthwhile to return to them again and again. In the following paper in honor of David—for whose learned, thoughtful, stimulating contributions to the field, whose long-standing friendship, intellectual support and always prompt, substantial, inspiring responses in our email exchanges I feel and wish to express deep gratitude—I intend to explore the meaning of the pivotal term in the alchemical phrase, the "not."

The word "not" performs a negation. "Negation," "negativity," and "negative" are tied to their opposites, "position," "positivity," and "positive." These important terms are difficult because they give rise to confusions. "Positive" and "negative" have several meanings, and our first task is to keep them apart.

(1) The most common meaning is that of a valuation, the ego and survival sense: the terms mean something like good vs. bad, advantageous

(prospective, beneficial, desirable) vs. detrimental, malignant. So we speak of a positive or negative development, sometimes even of a "positive" or "negative aspect" of archetypes; to get sick or to lose money is negative, to stay healthy or to get a salary raise is positive. This use of the terms positive and negative, which is clearly guided by the perspective of the ego and its survival interests, is not how they are meant here. We must in this context forget this sense. We need to evoke this sense of positive and negative only for the purpose of consciously and explicitly excluding it, keeping it away. There is always the danger that this so very common meaning will unawares creep in. So we have to be on guard.

(2) "Positive" means, in a strictly *formal sense*, "affirmative," "saying yes," negative then refers to negation, denial, saying "no." E.g., a positive answer, a negative response. In formal logic "positive (or affirmative) judgment." "Negative judgment."

(3) "Positive" is used in the sense of posited, established by human design, in contrast to "given by nature." E.g., positive law in contrast to natural law. Positive law is the actual laws and regulations in a particular state that in our time are put down in writing in the code of law, in statute books. Since the counter-term to this meaning of positive is "natural," "negative" has no place here.

There are also some other meanings that I will not mention here. I will directly go over to that meaning that we need here for our psychological purposes.

(4) "Positive" here means positively existing, having the status of positive fact, empirically real, demonstrable event, etc. This is the meaning that is prevalent in the philosophical movement of *Positivism*. Positive-factual realities can in this sense also be termed *positivities*. Now what is the meaning of the counter-terms to *this* meaning of "positive", i.e., the meaning of "negative" or "negativity"?

A first approximation might be to think here of the already mentioned term positive law. The written laws made by governments are positivities. The idea of justice, by contrast, is something very different. Many actions and many court decisions may be fully in agreement with positive law, but we may nevertheless feel that justice has not been done. Justice is logically negative, which of course does not mean bad or undesirable, but rather the opposite. Justice can*not* easily be spelled out; it is *not* tangible, visible. And in this sense it is "negative." While you can point to the individual laws, justice cannot be pointed at. It is *not* positively there.

A similar distinction can be made between positive religion, the official, institutionalized religion of the established churches, which often is felt not to be all that religious, but very worldly, driven by human power interests or commercial interests, a sterile routine, etc. True religion often is felt not to be found in the positively existing churches, in organized religion. You can point at and document the dogmas of the churches, just as you can demonstrate the positive laws of a state. But true religion cannot be demonstrated in the same sense.

Literalism (Hillman) means something similar, but not exactly the same as positivity. And especially the negation of a literalistic understanding of the image is not the same as alchemy's direct negation of the image itself ("not stone").

When we read in Laotse, *Tao te king*: "The WAY that can be expressed in words is not the eternal WAY," we see the role of negation. "Is not!" A rejection of the positive is obviously needed. You cannot say what you actually want to say. You can only negate the positive, that which is not meant. The moment you would spell out what the eternal WAY, the TAO, is, you would have positivized it again. The negation of the positive equivalent is absolutely necessary.

Moving from China to India we find a similar example for negativity, one of many, in the *Kena Upanishad*: "Not what the eyes can see, but what opens the eyes, that is the Brahma." Again: Not!

I give another example from our Western tradition, the New Testament. In the Gospel of John (ch. 4) we learn that Jesus had to leave Judaea and passed through the neighboring region of Samaria. At a fountain he had a conversation with a woman from Samaria. In the course of this exchange, the woman said:

> (20) Our fathers worshipped in this mountain; and ye say, that in Jerusalem is the place where men ought to worship. (21) Jesus saith

unto her, Woman, believe me, the hour cometh, when ye shall
neither in this mountain, nor yet at Jerusalem, worship the Father.
... (23) But the hour cometh, and now is, when the true worshippers
shall worship the Father in spirit and in truth: for the Father seeketh
such to worship him. (24) God is a Spirit: and they that worship
him must worship him in spirit and in truth.

The question here is what is the right place (the Greek text has *topos*)
for worship. And the passage starts out with two *alternatives* as options,
"this mountain" versus "Jerusalem." Two features deserve our attention.
First, they are obviously both positivities, visible entities in reality. You
can point at them. With these two empirical localities as the true places
of worship, we are in the sphere of positive religion, not of course exactly
in our modern sense of positive religion, but rather as a still ethnic, tribal
form of religion, a local cult, a religion tied to national and often political
interests. The reference to "our fathers" underlines the dependence on an
ethnic tradition. And each ethnic group, tribe, nation with their "fathers"
has its own sacred places, literal places in geographic reality. Thus you
necessarily get otherness, alternatives, a clash of different local traditions:
our true place for worship, *their* or *your* true place for worship.

The second feature of interest is that traditional ethnically bound
religion singles out from all the places within their own local sphere of
empirical or positive reality certain ones as the exclusive (or at least
prioritized) places for worship and calls them sacred in contrast to all the
other ones, which are *profane* places.

What Jesus does, by contrast, is to push off from and altogether
negate both alternatives offered by traditional piety: *neither* on this
mountain, *nor* at Jerusalem. And by extension at *no place* at all: *ou topos*.
In other words, he negates the whole *level* of positivity as such. Instead,
he states that the worship has to take place (!) "in spirit and in truth."
Thus he moves the entire question of the "right place" to a fundamentally
new level. By rejecting all positive places he does not simply give up the
question about the right place. For him, there is indeed a right place. He
insists on an exclusive place: "and they that worship him *must* worship
him in spirit and in truth" and nowhere else. But spirit and truth as the

130

exclusive place are precisely not a place in empirical reality, nothing positive, nothing literal, fixed. They are really the *sublation* of the very *idea* of "place" or of a "where." *Where* is this supposed to be, "in spirit and in truth"? You cannot say. And yet, it is not either a total utopia (*ou topos*), a literal lacuna, a lack, a nihil or naught. Rather, it is indeed a kind of place, but a *logically negative* "place," a *sublated* place, *topos ou topos*, just as *lithos ou lithos*, the stone which is not a stone. The true worship, we could say, has to take place *in* "absolute negativity" ("absolute," because this negativity is "absolved," freed, from the binary opposition of something versus nothing.) So while you cannot say where this place is in external reality, the expression "in spirit and in truth" nevertheless has a specific (determinate) and concrete meaning. And it receives much of its meaning from the very thing that it negates and sublates. Just as the real TAO is not the literal, explicit *tao*, but has a kind of foothold in what is negated, so here too.

We must be wary of not just *acting out* the negation (acting it out in the intellectual realm). Just as in the area of subjective experience and behavior we should not simply live out and let run free any impulses and drives, so that they merely exhaust, spend, waste themselves, but let their dynamic and message come back home to us (*Erinnern*: "remembering," reflection, interiorization into oneself), so the negation should also not just run free. It has to come home to itself, take its own medicine ("self-application"). Then it limits itself, becoming a *determinate* negation. It does not end up in an abstract (empty) nothing, a total uncertainty and not knowing (here I differ from David Miller's 1989 view). It does not become serial, a deferral forever, which would merely show that now the negation itself has become positivized, an end in itself! No, the "not" does land us somewhere. We do arrive. Where? Of course back at the starting point. But at a transformed starting point, because it has absorbed the negation, has become absolute negativity. The "energy" of the negation, rather than horizontally living itself out, came home to, and came to the benefit of, that which was negated and forced *it* (the notion, definition, understanding of it and thus the logical constitution of consciousness at large) vertically to a wholly other level.

The negation ceased to be an (endlessly repeatable) subjective *operation* and instead turned into the goal, the *place* of absolute negativity.

The determinate negation is not the negation of the content, the semantics. It is the negation of the logical form of the content. The acted-out negation negates externally. The alchemical negation negates the thing negated from within itself and reveals it as negativity.

Topos ou topos and *lithos ou lithos* have to be seen as abbreviations. Actually, three statements are collapsed into one. 1. The stone is a stone. 2. The stone is not a stone. 3. Despite being not a stone, it is not anything else nor simply nothing at all, but nevertheless a stone. And only as this *in itself* (innerly) negated stone is it *the philosophers'* stone.

To return to our biblical passage: There is a further point along the same lines. The negation that Jesus expresses does not amount to a wholesale rejection of *worship* as such. He does not say one cannot or should not worship at all any more. No, one should worship, however in a radically new, previously unheard-of way, namely in spirit and in truth.

It is noteworthy that the cultic veneration is here not "psychologized," removed from the external world into the interior of man, as one's inner *mystical* experience or the like. It is not a personal emotion, feeling, attitude. It is something objective, unemotional, sober: *noetic*, something that goes beyond the subjective person: in spirit and in truth. Truth is universal, it is all around us. This is true for scientific truths as much as for the truth that the Gospel of John has in mind. When we speak of the law of gravity or the theorems of geometry, we know that what is meant is not a subjective experience, feeling, or opinion, but something to which everything in the material world is subject. Although in a very different way, the same applies to "in spirit and in truth."

Furthermore, the sublated place "in spirit and in truth" is no longer rooted in an ethnic tradition. It does not belong to any tribe, nation, group. By rejecting this mountain as well as Jerusalem as *the* places to worship God, Jesus (or the writer of this Gospel who puts these words into the mouth of Jesus) of course also negates the ethnic or national rootedness of religion, all local-ness of cult, the tradition of the fathers and thus inherited and in this sense *natural* religion, religion based on kinship, on *blood* relationship. The natural in this sense is what we are born into, like our mother tongue. It precedes our personal existence and as such is, as it were, self-evident. "This is how it has always been." So we can say that what Jesus does with such a statement is to perform an opus *contra naturam.* The negation or sublation disrupts one's innocent, naive containment in and unity with tradition, tradition which is "nature" in a *psychological* sense. The same can be said about the negation of the places of worship. What is negated is the natural places, and what is proposed instead is spiritual places, places that are no longer places, much as alchemy is about a stone that is not a stone, *lithos ou lithos.*

The negative (or: logical negativity in general) does not refer to a "natural," ontological entity or substance, but is the *result of a negation* of the positive, the result of a pushing off from a specific positivity. "Spirit and truth" *exist* only if, to the extent that, and for as long as, you perform this act of negating and pushing of from. Because spirit and truth never have a positive existence, their existence is fundamentally negative. A mountain or temple, a tree or table exist regardless of whether we see them or do anything with them. Not so "spirit and truth." When we stop being in spirit and truth, *they* stop to be.

What Jesus is saying in this passage, amounts to the view that in Christianity there are no sanctuaries, no sacred places at all any more, no temple, no holy mountains, also no holy objects, no holy people; nothing positively real as such is sacred. A church as a building is for this view not a sacred place; it is just an ordinary assembly hall. By contrast, *any* literal place in geographic reality, any building or mountain or valley could become "sacred" in the sense of negativity if there is worship "in spirit and in truth." The sublated place comes out in the other biblical saying (Matt. 18:20), "For where two or three are gathered together in my name, there am I in the midst of them." This "there" is not defined in geographical terms, but by the name—negativity—that brings them together.

It is the *whole difference between sacred and profane* that has (to be sure, not disappeared altogether, but) been sublated, i.e., (a) canceled and (b) preserved on a *new* level. The move that we witness in such a text is that from the *natural* (positive) consciousness to a higher status of consciousness, which is the *result* of a *sublation* of the former. What has been negated by Jesus in what he said is not just two things (this mountain and Jerusalem), but the whole former *form* of religion that distinguishes between the right positive or literal places for worship and those literal places that are not right or at least not as holy. *The whole way of thinking* in terms of sacred versus profane places and objects has been overcome. This difference has been sublated and raised from the *semantic* level of *entities*, things, items, substances, contents that are side by side on the same plane, but have fundamentally different values and dignity (holy vs. profane) to a *syntactical* or *logical* level of truth and spirit, and thereby it has also been interiorized. Now the question is one about where one's soul or heart is, namely whether it is "in spirit and in truth," or not. The question is not whether one is in this building or that one, in this city, holy country, on this holy mountain, or not. It is a movement from positivity to negativity, from nature to spirit.

We can take this thought even a bit more forward. It is not only that this particular difference between sacred and profane is abolished, but also that the "difference as such" or "otherness" is removed. If God is spirit and those who worship him must do so in spirit and in truth—we could also say: they must do so *as* spirit—then we get a uroboric, circular, self-reflective relation. Ultimately it is God himself as spirit who worships himself through man, man having raised himself to the status of spirit and truth. True worship is a self-relation of spirit. All *fundamental* otherness is overcome (in true worship God is no longer "wholly other"). We can think here of Plotinus: like is known through like; one has to oneself become what one wants to see. Or in homeopathy: "Like cures like," *similia similibus curantur.*

I am here of course not interested in propounding Christian religion or giving a lesson in theology, nor in the question of worship in general. I am discussing this text passage only as a striking example for a move into logical negativity and thus also into the alchemical-psychological "not." At the same time, this Christian example of course *deserves* to be mentioned because Christian thinking, its move *contra naturam*, is one of the historical roots of the articulation and development of this logic in the course of Western history and, as a religious idea, a driving force behind it.

With the expression "in spirit and in truth" logical negativity may be a bit vague for us today, because spirit and truth usually do not mean anything to us modern people. They often sound today like empty words, meaningless jingle. Spirit has nothing to do with what "spirituality" means in modernity, in the New Age movement or in esoteric circles. Similarly, but in different ways, the TAO or the Brahma are exotic power words for us, but we do not have our own experience with them *rooted* in and authenticated by our own real tradition. So that we also get an example of logical negativity that is much closer to our own experience, I will briefly discuss the notion of life.

Life does not have a positive existence. It is not an entity, a thing-like substance. For example, while you can cut out from the body of a mammal or a human being their lungs or livers and then you really have these organs in front of you as positive objects, you cannot extract the life of a living being. Certainly, you can kill a plant, an animal or a human being, you can, as we say, "take" their life. If you take somebody's money, he lost it and you have it. But if you "take" his life, you do not have it. Nobody has it. It is simply gone. By "taking" somebody's life, you do not get it and then have it, you cannot even demonstrate it like you can the lungs or livers that you took out of a body. Life is "nothing," no thing. Life is not either like a vapor, a gas, or like heat or light that in many chemical reactions escapes without our being able to see or touch or sense it with our senses, but nevertheless, with certain instruments, can be demonstrated to positively exist and even be measured. This is not possible with life. It is really "nothing." By contrast, what you do get if you take somebody's life, and *all* you get, is a corpse. The corpse has a positive existence.

And yet, life is a powerful *reality*. There *is* life. But its existence is logically negative existence. Hegel would say that life is a *real or concrete Concept* (in contrast to an abstract concept), a Concept that exists, but that, because it is a Concept is not a positive thing or entity, cannot be positivized. Life, we might say with our earlier text, exists "in spirit and in truth." However, *as such*, as concrete or real Concept, *as* being "in spirit and in truth," it also exists—and *only* exists—in living creatures who have a positive existence. So it is this logically negative reality of life that makes the positive entity alive. And death is the moment when the positive and the negative part company.

But if they part company at death, they must have been joined before. How were they joined? Not like, e.g., husband and wife in marriage. Rather, the living organism is alive because, and as long as, it has the strength to negate its own positivity. When it loses its strength to negate its positivity, e.g., because of old age or illness, then this positivity (that before had been reduced to a sublated moment within life's negativity) all of a sudden *gains an independence of its own*; it now makes its presence felt *as something in its own right*, and this is what we call a corpse. The corpse is the positivity of the living being that is no longer subdued by, and integrated into, the negativity of life. It has been released from, fallen out of, life's sphere of jurisdiction. Death is the normal, the natural state. Life is, as it were, an *opus contra naturam*.

The fact that life exists as the negation and subjugation of the positivity of the living being can be seen, although merely in *acted-out* form, from the fact that animals maintain their life by killing and eating other living organisms and integrating them into their own system. This reality was what was celebrated in the myth and cult of Dionysos, who is, according to Kerényi the primordial image of indestructible life.

Like life, soul, too, is logically negative. It is nothing. During earlier times, the ages of mythological thinking, when soul and life were often not really distinguished, one imagined that at death the life or soul of the person left the body through the mouth in the form of breath or a bird, the soul bird. Or later that the devil would lie in wait and try to capture the soul when it leaves the body. This is typical for the mythological imagination: it substantiates and often personifies what in truth is "nothing," namely logically negative or a concrete Concept, a *real* Concept. The soul is of course not literally a bird or a "subtle" substance like a breath of wind. We know this. However, the images or metaphors of the soul bird or a breath leaving the body have a seductive force. They entice us to unconsciously remain in the mode of substantiating thinking despite our conscious insight that we must not take them literally and must not substantiate them. Therefore: beware of metaphors and images. They suggest that one could simply innocently glide into a nonnaturalistic, nonliteralistic understanding without having paid the price: the radical and explicit break with the natural likeness, that break and rejection that is expressed in the hurtful "not" of our alchemical dictum.

In my discussion of the passage from the Gospel of John about the proper place to worhip, I stated, "When we stop being in spirit and truth, *they* stop to be." The same applies to life. When our organism ceases performing the *act* of living, of breathing, digesting, producing hormones, fighting viruses and bacteria, etc., we are dead. Life is an activity and exists only for the duration that this activity is executed. The point is that life is precisely not a substance that we may possess like property and that may get lost or be taken from us. No, we *keep* alive. It is like a fire that lasts only for as long as it burns...

The abstract concept has its referent outside of itself. For Kant the concept of 100 dollars is different from the 100 dollars that you have in your pocket. For Kant—and for our conventional style of thinking—the concept is abstract. But life is a *real*, not an abstract Concept. And it is the *Concept* that makes us alive.

What I said here about life referred to biological life. But it is true also for the higher life of "the soul." From what the alchemist Dorneus exclaimed: "Transmute yourselves from dead stones into living philosophical stones!" we can realize that the stone, too, is in truth a Concept and not a thing or property.

But when Jung after quoting this dictum bemoans that Dorneus "lacked the concept of an unconscious existence which would have enabled him to express the identity of the subjective, psychic centre and the objective, alchemical centre in a satisfactory formula" (*Collected Works* 9ii § 264, punctuation modif.) he shows that he, Jung, has himself not arrived at the stone which is not a stone. Ultimately, his thought remained stuck in positivity; he thought that there were *two* centers and that one would need the auxiliary concept, i.e., the crutch, of "*the* unconscious" as a third to bring the two together. Jung of course did not speak of "the unconscious" here; he said "unconscious existence." But the latter expression only tells us *what* "the unconscious" is thought to be: positive existence. With "unconscious existence" or "the unconscious" Jung introduces the fantasy of a literal, "empirical" place in the stead of the only place where the stone could really exist: the no-place of "in spirit and in truth." And this despite the fact that the very text by Dorneus that is the starting point for Jung's critical comment already explicitly provides us with the notion of *veritas* (truth), as he himself shows in the same paragraph.

Veritas is the direct opposite of the unconscious. Truth means disclosedness, having appeared and being revealed to consciousness, and thus knowing. "Unconscious," by contrast, means hidden, split off from consciousness, ultimately inaccessible to human knowing: unknowable. Even if "unconscious contents" are experienced and thus become empirically and semantically conscious, e.g., through dreams, logically or syntactically (as far as their status is concerned) they stay for Jung, as "archetypes of the unconscious," on the other side, dissociated from consciousness, and do not attain to the status of truth, true knowing. "The concept of the unconscious," Jung states, "*posits nothing*, it designates only my *unknowing*" (*Letters 1*, p. 411, to Frischknecht, 8 Feb. 1946). Jung systematically washes his hands in innocence.

"Un-conscious existence" merely negates the *accessibility* for consciousness of what we could call "the essential place," while nevertheless granting it positive existence. It declares an area of consciousness as off limits for knowing. It thus sets up a spatial difference. "In spirit and in truth," by contrast, negates the notion of place itself as well as of anything supposed to be found at this place (such as "the stone"). One's recourse to "the unconscious" tries to get away with a cheap substitute, external negation as the displacement, deportation of the (in themselves untouched!) contents, in order to avoid having to pay the full price: negation as the internal sublation, distillation, evaporation of the contents in question in their *substance*. In this way it manages to be the secret placeholder for logical positivity, while appearing to be its opposite.

In 18th and early 19th century England, convicts were often physically deported to the colonies, above all to Australia, and for the price of this removal from their legitimate home country could escape capital punishment (their own negation), while at the same time being out of sight for the people in England, removed for the latter from the sphere of knowing and conscious awareness. Because of their "metaphysical" content and general character, certain contents of consciousness, namely the so-called archetypal ideas and images, are modern positivism's psychological convicts. Jung understood this. Having armored his positivism with what he believed was his Kantianism, he was keenly aware of the convict character of the archetypal ideas within the world of the modern scientific mind. And responding to their incompatibility he followed, as it were, the British model and (logically) deported them into the psycho-logical Australia invented by him, "the unconscious,"[1] so that they could likewise escape *their* "capital punishment" (their sublation, their *mortificatio* and *evaporatio*).

Another purpose and result of this move of Jung's was that their home country, human consciousness, could feel relieved of its (in this case: intellectual) responsibility for them (of the duty to take a position as to their truth). Because, having once and for all settled in the position of "unknowing" by having deported the incriminated or condemned contents, consciousness was no longer burdened with and bothered by the question of truth.

A third consequence: in both cases this trick of deportation saved the tender-minded "authorities" from themselves having to go through with the tough "execution" of the "not" and from having to shoulder their concomitant loss of innocence.

Finally, the wholesale removal of those contents from the sphere of knowing and the avoidance of the necessary execution also helped Jung to rescue the status of the contents themselves as (simulated) immediacies, as (alleged) facts of nature, objective events (rather than productions of the thinking mind itself[2]), as well as to retain unscathed their imaginal character as natural likenesses, thereby simulating a naivety of consciousness that, having historically become long obsolete, did only become possible through, and always stayed dependent on, the artificial and not-at-all naive move of logically deporting them.

As far as the "satisfactory formula" for the expression of the identity of the subjective, psychic center and the objective, alchemical center is concerned, "the unconscious" is by definition a *vis-a-vis*, the object for a subject: for the *experiencing* ego. It is historical England's Australia. The concept of the unconscious posits dissociation, fundamental otherness, the distance of a continent at the other end of the world separated by an ocean; it is for Jung "pure nature" and by definition *not* the mind's, *not* thought's, own depth, inner infinity, and inner transcendency.[3] Its contents remain (and are supposed to remain) logically irrevocably alien to the thinking mind. For otherwise, so the idea goes, they would inevitably produce inflation, madness. Thus contrary to Jung's hope the concept of "unconscious existence" cannot express identity.

Our transmutation into living philosophical stones is even made structurally impossible as long as we hold on to "the unconscious." The philosophical stone as something logically negative, as something that is *not* a stone and *not* a thing subsisting independently, thus also *not* "the objective, alchemical centre" opposite to the "subjective, psychic centre," *is*—from the outset and *in itself* and always-already—the desired identity: because it exists only as thought, in spirit and in truth. It is not in need of the fiction of an "unconscious," having, as it does, everything it needs within itself.

But the stone exists only if, only to the extent that, and for as long as *we* exist as *it*, and only *through* our existing as it. And we exist as it only if we *are*, objectively, the living comprehension of it, only if we *in fact* perform (and are capable of performing) the thinking of it, only if we have, in the logical form of our *consciousness* and our *knowing*, risen to the height of the real, existing Concept and thus explicitly *live as* the real, existing Concept: *are* "in spirit and in truth."

140

NOTES

[1] I am of course not suggesting that Jung invented the term and concept "the unconscious." But Jung invented his peculiar concept of it.

[2] The thinking mind of the *homo totus*, the whole man; *not* that of what we call in psychology "the ego," or ego-consciousness.

[3] In this sentence we see the power of the "not." If it is not executed *as execution*, then it inevitably reappears, but now as being executed in the form of denial and logical deportation. In the latter case thought's inner transcendency is positivized as its (intra-psychic) external other, its (intra-psychic) Australia. Freud once expressly called the unconscious the *innere Ausland* (inner foreign country.) The mind's "not" is thus literally acted out instead of being interiorized, instead of self-referentiality coming home to the mind itself. And, inasmuch as psychology is the discipline of interiority and self-relation, psychology becomes unpsychological.

MILLER'S PENTECOST

GREG MOGENSON

D uring the course of a seminar given in 1925, the Swiss psychologist, C.G. Jung drew upon an important image from Christian symbolism to make an equally important point about the analytic experience that his approach to psychology had been conceived to foster. "Analysis," he evocatively declared, "should release an experience that grips us or falls upon us as from above, an experience that has substance and body such as those things [that] occurred to the ancients. If I were going to symbolize it I would choose the Annunciation."[1]

Appearing to the virgin, Mary, prior to her marriage to Joseph, the angel Gabriel announced to her that she was to be made pregnant with the Son of God by the power of the Holy Ghost. Incredulous as to how this could be so, given that she had not had relations with any man, Mary was greatly troubled by what she had been told. But the angel assured her; she had found favour with God and was to have no fear. Faithfully accepting her fate, the virgin replied, "I am the handmaid of the Lord: let it happen to me according to your word" (Luke 1:38).

With his reference to this event, Jung beautifully conveys the revelatory quality of the encounter with the self's alterity which he believed that analysis should facilitate. Patients in analysis, he clearly implies, should be introduced to an attitude that is as receptive to the otherness of the ways in which they happen to themselves as was the Mary of the Annunciation story to the Angel of the Lord.

A question arises. Setting aside Jung's focus upon patients and their experience in analysis, let us ask: *Can Jung's analogy to the Annunciation be applied as well to the "therapy of ideas"?*

The phrase, "therapy of ideas," of course, comes from the honoree of this *festschrift*, David Miller. We find it in the introductions to his books and articles.[2] In these works it is most often Christian ideas, and especially theological ones, that are taken up in this spirit. As Miller explains,

> Both doctrinal and pietistic theologizing tend to deny or defend against the depths of religious meaning, its fundamental mystery and ambiguity, its terror and grace, its autonomous nature that comes and goes as it will, like the Holy Ghost wandering over the face of the deep. Ego theology is a defense mechanism which banalizes religion.[3]

These words of Miller's, taken together with his call for a therapy of ideas, immediately bring G. K. Chesterton and Søren Kierkegaard to mind. In a passage of his book, *Orthodoxy*, Chesterton famously described the modern world as being full of Christian ideas gone mad.[4] And in his iconoclastic book, "Attack Upon Christendom," Kierkegaard compared the state of Christianity in his day to that of a hospital in which patients are dying, not from this germ or that practice, but from the building itself! With this analogy Kierkegaard implies that the whole structure and framework of the Church has gone awry.[5]

Miller's critical remarks with respect to doctrinal and pietistic theology having short-changed the depths of religious meaning are reminiscent of another passage from Jung's writings. In this passage the psychologist also speaks about a resistant theological mentality on the one hand and of the Holy Ghost or Spirit moving upon the face of the deeps on the other.

A theologian who had come to Jung for treatment dreamt that he was looking down from a slope over a low valley. The valley was dense with woods and in the middle of these was a lake. Feeling that he had previously been prevented from going there, the dreamer was now determined to descend into the valley and to approach the lake. As he did so, however, the atmosphere became uncanny. All of a sudden a gust of wind passed across the lake's surface causing it to ripple ominously. Overwhelmed, the dreamer awoke in terror. Commenting upon the dream Jung acknowledges that "at first this dream seems incomprehensible."

> But as a theologian the dreamer should have remembered the "pool" whose waters were stirred by a sudden wind, and in which the sick were bathed—the pool of Bethesda. An angel descended and touched the water, which thereby acquired curative powers. The light wind is the pneuma which bloweth where it listeth. And that terrified the dreamer. An unseen presence is suggested, a numen that lives its own life and in whose presence man shudders. The dreamer was reluctant to accept the association with the pool of Bethesda. He wanted nothing of it, for such things are met with only in the Bible, or at most on Sunday mornings as the subjects of sermons, and have nothing to do with psychology. All very well to speak of the Holy Ghost on occasions—but it is not a phenomenon to be experienced![6]

Miller's therapy of ideas, indeed his entire *oeuvre*, can be understood as the working-through of the religious resistances that figure in this theologian's dream. Working "depth theologically" and "theopoetically" Miller demonstrates the life and autonomy of the spirit by means of a wide-ranging scholarship that takes in the pagan gods that preceded Christianity, on the one hand, and the seemingly (but in fact quite otherwise) secular poetry that now follows, on the other. The upshot of this is that quite apart from the liveliness that Miller brings to his writings (or perhaps interpenetrating with this as a diviner nature through his own), there is something that moves of itself through his many sources. Placed alongside one another the voices he cites become tongues of fire. And just as Pentecost was called a second annunciation because with it the Church was born, so the pentecost of Miller's richly allusive depth theology brings about a third in which what he has referred to as "theology's ego" gives way or becomes transparent to "religion's soul."[7]

Clearly, as Miller's work bears witness, the therapy of ideas *can* come upon us like the Annunciation.[8]

But now we are faced with another question. This question has to do with Miller's having described his work as an attempt to be responsive to Jung's statement, "We must gratefully acknowledge the invaluable support psychology has received from students of ... religion, even if they on their part have not yet learnt how to make use of its insights."[9] Doubtless, this description is very true. Having drawn deeply upon the insights of Freud, Jung, Hillman and Lacan, Miller certainly has made good the lack that Jung points out, offering a compelling and therapeutic analysis of the defensive theologizing of the religion (as he puts it) that religion itself should be against.[10] But—and here is my question—can an approach to the study of religion that has fully integrated the insights of depth psychology bring its therapy of ideas to bear upon the interpretation of psychology? While depth psychology has certainly contributed much to religion in exposing "the religion of false piety, the religion used as human wish- or need-fulfilment, a crutch and opiate, the religion of spiritual pride ..,"[11] must it not apply this same analysis to its own ideas if it is not to be guilty of calling the kettle black? Lacan said that if religion triumphs psychoanalysis is finished.[12] But, by the same token, is not psychoanalysis finished if, like some freed Barabbas, it settles beneath the niveau that religion has long since reached?

The Christian scriptures state that the Holy Ghost will not "leave [it]self without witness" (Acts 14:17).[13] Miller's dialectical reading of depth psychology as postmodern theology allows us to reflect upon psychology in the light of this assurance. Deeply comprehended, and at its most soulful, psychology itself is the form that this witness has taken in our day, as Jung expressly indicates with his comparison of the analytic experience to the Annunciation and with his interpretation of his theologian patient's dream.

Many associations could be cited to support this claim. Reading psychoanalysis through the lens of the Christian motifs that are continued in its theories, we find that a whole host of analogies further to Jung's analogy to the Annunciation can be drawn. I will only give the merest hint of these by reminding the reader of the talking cure's virginal conception in the womb of the hysterically pregnant Anna O., Dora's account in her analysis with Freud of having sat transfixed before the painting of the Sistine Madonna in the Dresden gallery,[14] and Lacan's teaching having been celebrated by his devotees as having "reproduced the annunciation scene with Lacan playing all the parts. Sometimes he was the space that welcomes the word; sometimes, as Christ born of the Virgin, he transmitted it; something, as man-God, he sowed it in others."[15]

Jung, of course, was well aware that psychology is redolent of the motifs of religion and myth, its theories being the expression of archetypes common to all three.[16] The comparative youth of the discipline he even attributed to religion having previously provided a formulation for everything psychic, one that both presaged and forestalled psychology's appearance as such.[17] Given this, it is all the more interesting to read psychology for the witness it provides for what the religion preceding it had called the Holy Ghost or Spirit. The passage from Jung's writings that comes most readily to my mind in this connection is one in which psychology's witness is presented negatively, i.e., in the form of a warning.

> Not for a moment dare we succumb to the illusion that an archetype can be finally explained and disposed of. Even the best attempts at explanation are only more or less successful translations into another metaphorical language .... The most we can do is to *dream the myth onwards* and give it a modern dress. And whatever explanation or interpretation does to it, we do to our own souls as well, with corresponding results for our own well-being. The archetype—let us never forget this—is a psychic organ present in all of us. A bad explanation means a correspondingly bad attitude to this organ, which may thus be injured. But the ultimate sufferer is the bad interpreter himself. Hence the "explanation" should always be such that the functional significance of the archetype remains unimpaired, so that an adequate and meaningful connection between the conscious mind and the archetype is assured. For the archetype is an element of our psychic structure and thus a vital and necessary component in our psychic economy. It represents or personifies

certain instinctive data of the dark, primitive psyche, the real but invisible roots of consciousness. Of what elementary importance the connection with these roots is, we see from the preoccupation of the primitive mentality with certain "magic" factors, which are nothing less than what we would call archetypes. This original form of *religio* ("linking back") is the essence, the working basis of all religious life even today, and always will be, whatever future form this life may take.[18]

Significantly, this warning of Jung's regarding the critical importance of psychology's attitude with respect to the archetype is resonant with Christ's warning with respect to the sin against the Holy Ghost as this is given in the gospels. We could even say, drawing upon the language used by Jung in the last line of the passage from which we have just quoted, that, "as a more or less successful translation into another metaphorical language," it may even be the "future form" that this warning now takes.

> Wherefore I say unto you, all manner of sin and blasphemy shall be forgiven unto men; but the blasphemy against the Holy Ghost shall not be forgiven unto men. ... Whosoever speakest against the Holy Ghost, it shall not be forgiven him, neither in this world, neither in the world to come.[19]

It is an irony, given what we have had to say with respect to its spiritual charter, that psychology is so often guilty of the commission of this sin of which Christ speaks. Indeed, it could even be said that *against itself* psychology everywhere exists as the contemporary form of the unforgivable blasphemy. The most blatant and pernicious example of this comes from the pen of Ernest Jones. In two early papers, "The Madonna's Conception through the Ear"[20] and "A Psycho-Analytic Study of the Holy Ghost Concept,"[21] Jones analyzes the Annunciation to Mary and the Holy Ghost idea in terms of Freudian categories. The result of this is as astonishing as it is perverse. Squeezed into an Oedipal framework that calculates in terms of erogenous zones and childhood sexual theories, the fructifying, pneumatic character of the angel's greeting in the Annunciation scene is interpretively reduced to the intestinal gas which the child's polymorphously perverse mind conceives of as having been emitted from the bowel of its omnipotently deposed father even as the ear of the Virgin that had received the greeting is interpreted to be not an ear at all, but rather the lowly maternal anus into which Everyman's emasculated Joseph farts![22] Hardly a scene for a stained glass window!

Now it is important to understand that Jones's blasphemy against the Holy Ghost does not reside in his having chosen to analyze the Annunciation story and Holy Ghost concept. As we discussed earlier, these can be discussed in psychology in a manner that continues to bear them witness, even if by other, no longer sacred, names. Rather, it is in the absolute reductiveness of his approach that Jones's blasphemy lies. And this would be so regardless of what his subject matter happened to be or what he chose to reduce this to. The mystery of virginal conception and of the life of the spirit that comes and goes of its own accord is just as effaced when the *tertium comparationis* is some other fundamental such as child development, the letter in the unconscious, or transference derivatives of the bi-personal field. For while it is true (as we now say, *contra* Bishop Butler[23]) that nothing is what it is (i.e., identical with itself), no thing can be truly accounted for as being 'really' some other thing, either.

The reference I have just made to the bi-personal field will remind long-time readers of archetypal psychology of the controversial discussion that took place some twenty years ago now in the pages of *Spring Journal*.[24] At issue in that theology-like debate was the status of the psyche as an independent, autonomous reality. James Hillman began this discussion by dialoguing with Paul Kugler about an article that the Jungian analyst William Goodheart had published in the *Journal of Analytical Psychology*.[25] Hillman, as he put it, was "enraged" by this article, which he regarded as "a prolonged attack on basic ideas in Jung's doctoral dissertation."[26] Wishing to understand his reaction better, he discussed Goodheart's article with Kugler and then sought the comments of ten colleagues on their exchange.

It is not necessary here to recapitulate the whole of this fascinating discussion. The main thing to grasp is that in Hillman's view (though he does not put it quite this way himself) the reduction of the soul's life to the bi-personal field (a concept that regards psychic phenomena to be the product of transference\countertransference exchanges of the patient and analyst in the consulting room) is tantamount to the unforgivable blasphemy against that witness to the Holy Spirit that the concept of the autonomous psyche may be taken to be in our time. "What is centrally at stake," Hillman passionately declares, "... is the idea, and my faith in it, of the autonomous psyche, the self-moving, self-forming activity of the soul."[27]

Speaking with a cooler head Kugler summarizes:

> Goodheart asserts that Jung's theoretical concept of the "autonomous psyche" was a reaction-formation derived from the bi-personal field, designed to defend against acknowledging unconscious erotic feelings for Helly [Jung's medium cousin who was the subject of his doctoral dissertation]. This assertion raises important ontological issues. What ontological status is being granted to the "bi-personal field" and to the "autonomous psyche"? For Goodheart, the bi-personal field receives primary ontological status, while the autonomous psyche is viewed as secondary and derivative.[28]

Now it is important to understand that the controversy here is not about the bi-personal field per se. Without a doubt this concept pays tribute to an important phenomenon, as Goodheart clearly demonstrates in his masterful reply.[29] At issue, rather, is the *reduction* of the autonomous psyche to the bi-personal field (or to any more literal reality for that matter) such that it is viewed as "secondary and derivative." As Kugler goes on to explain, by "primary ontological status" he means our "most fundamental fantasy of 'what is real'."[30] To deny this status to the psyche (that animating source of our reality sense[31]) in favor of the dialectical materialism of bi-personal field dynamics is a gesture than can be likened to the one that Jung criticizes as "deny[ing] the great and blam[ing] the petty,"[32] or so Hillman, Kugler, and several of the commentators here insist.

In his comment on the Hillman-Kugler exchange, Wolfgang Giegerich, that most trenchant therapist of ideas, convincingly argues that the autonomous psyche, far from being an idea that psychology can freely adopt or reject, is, rather, "the indispensable prerequisite for doing psychology at all."[33] In making this point, Giegerich draws an analogy to mathematical physics. While we usually attribute the fact that physics has developed into an exact science to its empirical methodology and its application of mathematics to the natural world, these are secondary, Giegerich maintains, to its fundamental gesture which has been its "unconditional surrender to its underlying pre-conception of the world."

> With absolute commitment, physics followed the principle that "nature" has to be explained exclusively from "natural" causes. At no point was science allowed to take recourse in any factor outside of its own vision. It had to fall back on its own resources, and ruthlessly to rid itself of ideas extraneous to its fantasy as Fate, Spirit, God, Ether—not because these are theological or mythical ideas whereas physics' "nature" was not but simply to be true to its own myth. It is as if physics had, with respect to *its* root fantasy, strictly obeyed Jung's advice concerning fantasy images in general, "Above all, don't let anything from outside, that does not belong, get into it, for the fantasy-image has 'everything it needs'."[34]

Read in the light of our previous discussion, Giegerich could here be said to have described the annunciation scene through which physics virginally conceived and gave birth to itself. For the science of physics to be conceived, "nature," like Mary, had to be approached without recourse to any external fathering factor. Its cause had to be found tautologically, parthenogenetically, within itself as its own *archai*. Nothing from outside could be allowed to get in. Nothing more fundamental than its own conception of itself could be appealed to for explanation. For to make such an appeal would have been to have precisely the wrong attitude that Jung warned against above.

Carrying forward into psychology the Annunciation-to-Mary-like action that has been at work in the conception of physics and the other sciences, Giegerich avers that

> In order for psychology to be, it *must* posit an autonomous psyche, because only then is psychological inquiry possible in the first place.

For only if the psyche is granted autonomy and spontaneity does psychology relentlessly bind itself to the unknownness of its own root fantasy, having to explain everything psychic "tautologically" from the psyche herself, and only if psychology strictly refuses to base itself on anything outside the idea of "psyche" (*whatever* "psyche" may be[35]) will it be inescapably forced into the depth of its subject matter and be able to establish its own (psychological) version of exactitude and certainty.[36]

With these reflections in mind, let us now briefly re-examine the passage from Jung that was cited above in which he raises his warning with respect to the attitude to the archetype and then, by way of conclusion, indicate something of Miller's contribution to this issue.

In the Jung passage, immediately prior to the warning that is given, psychological explanations are characterized as "more or less successful translations into another metaphorical language." Reiterating this point, Jung speaks of "dream[ing] the myth onwards" and of "giv[ing] it a modern dress." With these phrases the reflexive, psychology-constituting insight that psychological theory is itself an expression of the autonomous life of the psyche is well conveyed while in the same breath continuing witness is given to Holy Ghost or Spirit, albeit by other names. But what about the unforgivable sin? If we grant that Jung's cautionary remarks concerning the attitude of the interpreter to the archetype is itself archetypally akin to Christ's warning with respect to the blasphemy against the Holy Ghost, the question remains as to whether Jung's statement is up to the level already attained by the religion that it has so frequently looked to as its other, the myth that it dreams onwards.

When considered in the light of the discussion about the autonomous psyche of Hillman, Kugler, Goodheart, Giegerich *et al.*, it is evident that while Jung rightly speaks about the critical importance of the interpreter's attitude, his reifying reference to "*the* archetype," his positivizing reference to this as "an organ in us," and his dissociatively thinking in terms of a subject *here* and objectified archetype *there* contradict the attitude he wishes to recommend. The problem here is very much like the one that Jung discusses with respect to his religious critics. Railing against those theologians who would accuse him of psychologism for speaking of God in psychological terms, Jung writes, "... the theologian is used to giving orders to God, he tells him how he should behave. He has got him in writing, and he says: You are not God any longer if you do not behave as you did two thousand years ago. He has taken God's freedom away from him."[37] Now, it is precisely this taking of freedom away from what he calls the archetype that Jung would see as example of the wrong attitude. But closely examining the way in which Jung has the archetype in writing, we see that his manner of speaking often treats it as an entity or thing. True, Jung does stress what he calls "the indefiniteness of the archetype"[38] even as he is quick to correct "the mistaken notion that an archetype is determined in regard to its content."[39] Ironically, however, with the familiarity of repeated usage the word itself becomes the "nothing but"[40] from which Jung wished to free it. Speaking just as reductively as ever Freud did of sex, Jungian discourse frequently refers to the archetype of *this* and the archetype of *that*. From this we can see that the logic of Jungian thought, while claiming to be against reductive thinking, itself reductively appeals to the archetypes as something behind the phenomena with which reflection is concerned. Following from this, symbols become the signs that Jung contrasted them to when defining what he meant by symbol.[41] While still said to be approximations of the unknown, they are logically reduced to the known.

Keenly appreciative of the tensions between contemporary critical theory, apophatic theology, and Jung's thought, Miller's therapy of ideas has frequently ministered to this problematic. With respect to the archetype concept, for example, Miller could be said to have done for this God-term of Jung's something similar to what negative theology has done for the notion of God.

A passage from the theologian Paul Tillich may serve to make this issue clearer. Releasing religious reflection from the wrong kind of questioning (even as Jung would release psychological reflection from the wrong attitude), Tillich notes that "a God about whose existence or non-existence you can argue is [only] a thing beside others in a universe of existing things."[42] Following upon this Tillich then refers to science. While reading what he has to say about this, let us bear in mind Jung's irritable insistence with respect to his identity as a scientist. "It is regrettable," Tillich continues, "that scientists believe that they have refuted religion when they rightly have shown that there is no evidence whatsoever for the assumption that such a being exists. Actually they have not refuted religion, but they have done it a considerable service. They have forced it to reconsider and to restate the meaning of the tremendous word *God*."[43] The point Tillich is making is that God is not an existing *being* or *thing*, not even the highest being, but the dimension of consciousness, depth, and concern in which all things have their presence. Now, it is true that Jung thought that his science, far from refuting religion, served it. This, certainly, is the prevailing view of his work. But here it must be understood that as a positive scientist Jung's support of religion can be likened to that of those in theology who, in Tillich's view, are "more dangerous for religion than the so-called atheistic scientists" due to their positivistic "assertion that there is a higher being called God."[44]

With a moment's reflection, the distinction that Tillich draws is easily understood. Simply put, it is the very definition of God that He is not an existing being, not a positivity or thing. The complexity of this comes in when we consider the constitution of the consciousness that such a conception involves. Religious consciousness (and here I am talking, not of its animistic precursors, but of its later expressions) is a consciousness that has freed itself from following sense impressions and from thinking in terms of ontic entities and the physics of beings and things. It follows from this that to be up to the level of consciousness of the religion that has preceded it, psychology must recognize its own version of the difference discussed by Tillich. It must reflect, that is to say, in terms of what Miller and Giegerich have called the "psychological difference."[45]

As cited by Miller, a passage of Jung's touches upon this issue. "If you will contemplate [your nothingness], your lack of fantasy, [lack] of inspiration, and [lack] of inner aliveness which you feel as sheer stagnation and a barren wilderness, and impregnate it with the interest born of alarm at your inner death, then something can take shape in you, for your inner emptiness conceals just as great a fullness, if you allow it to

153

penetrate into you."[46] Reading Jung in terms of the apophatic (negative-theology-like) statements that can be found across his many writings, Miller helps analytical psychology to "reconsider and restate" the meaning and non-meaning of its tremendous words—archetype, unconscious, self. We are reminded by Miller, for example, of Jung's views regarding the "impossibility of knowledge of archetypes (*Collected Works* 11 § 460), of 'ego' (*Collected Works* 18 § 10), and the 'unconscious'."[47] And further to this, Miller's citations work against the idolatry that the self concept degenerates into in much of therapeutic parlance. As Jung was careful to point out to his readers, "Nothing is known regarding the self because it is a transcendental hypothesis." Miller adds,

> The implication of Jung's post-Kantian observations about the epistemic status of psychological theory has important implication for therapy or, as Jung called it, "individuation," that is, the becoming of "self." The implication is that to become "self" is to become nothing, that is, no-thing, not some-thing. Where "ego" is, there let "self" be, means (since the notion of "self" does not have a definite empirical referent) let nothing be. The integration of "self" into "ego's" life is the integration of nothingness, just like the people in religions say.[48]

Miller's strategy here, as a therapist of Jungian ideas, is well conveyed in a passage he quotes from Norman O. Brown: "Get the nothing back into words. The aim is words with nothing to them: words that point beyond themselves rather than to themselves, transparencies, empty words. Empty words corresponding to the void in things."[49] Like Brown's empty words, concepts, too, as Miller has so cannily shown, must have nothing in them if they are to point beyond themselves, not to some signified concept or thing, but to the void of things, the airy nothing that imagination bodies forth. "We should never forget," writes Jung expressing a related insight, "that in any psychological discussion we are not saying anything *about* the psyche, but that the psyche is always speaking about *itself.*[50]

*   *   *

We began with an angel's greeting to a virgin and now speak, after having critiqued reductive interpretation, of empty words corresponding to the void in things—the Mary of the Annunciation yet again. This greeting, along with its assurance of a virginal conception, is as much psychology's as it ever was Christianity's. For as the inwardness of whatever its "Mary" may be, psychology must also produce itself without input from some other source. Indeed, it is only in this way, as the "nothing [that] almost sees miracles,"[51] that it can truly be psychology at all. *Ave psychologia.*

Dreaming the myth onwards, it can also be said that just as the Miracle at Pentecost has been called a second Annunciation because with it the Church was born, so psychology rightly understood now constitutes a third. Explicitly making this point himself, Jung writes that

> a further development of myth might well begin with the outpouring of the Holy Spirit upon the apostles, by which they were made into sons of God, and not they only, but all others who through them and after them received the *filiatio*—sonship of God—and thus partook of the certainty that they were more than autochthonous *animalia* sprung from the earth, that as twice-born they had their roots in the divinity itself.[52]

Surely the Jung of this passage could have no better friend and colleague than David Miller. Nor could we who honor David in this volume. Again and again, the gift of his scholarship has shown the self-movement of the spirit by means of felicitous juxtapositions of religion, myth, depth psychology and modern literature. Reading with Miller between these lines, a third expresses itself. Present only as an absence, this third (as Miller has more than once had the therapeutic task of reminding us[53]) is not a thing. A "no-thing," as Miller often says,[54] we give it better witness by saying what it is *like* than what it *is*. And what is it like? Among Jung's many references we have mentioned three: the angel's announcement to Mary that she is to become the mother of God, the jubilant apostles inspired with tongues of fire, and the pool at Bethesda stirred by a sudden wind.[55] Contemporizing this witness with literary references, Miller mentions Wallace Stevens' likening of poetry to "a pheasant disappearing into the brush," Harold Pinter's quip about a "weasel under the cocktail cabinet," D.H. Lawrence's remarks about "this voice of my being I may *never* deny," and Joyce's "sacred pigeon."[56] To this still very partial list we now may add another: Miller's Pentecost.

NOTES

[1] C.G. Jung, *Analytical Psychology: Notes of the Seminar given in 1925*, Wm. McGuire, ed. (Princeton: Princeton University Press, 1989), 80.

[2] David L. Miller, *Hells and Holy Ghosts: A Theopoetics of Christian Belief* (New Orleans: Spring Journal Books, 2004), 7; *Three Faces of God: Traces of the Trinity in Literature and Life* (New Orleans: Spring Journal Books, 2005), 10; "Animadversions," *Spring 54* (1993): 26-29.

[3] Miller, *Three Faces of God*, 5.

[4] The actual reference is to the modern world being "full of the old Christian virtues gone mad." G. K. Chesterton, *Orthodoxy* (London: Fontana Books, 1961), 30.

[5] Søren Kierkegaard, *Attack upon Christendom*, trans. W. Lowrie (Boston: Beacon Press, 1956), 139f. Cited in David L. Miller, "Attack Upon Christendom! The Anti-Christianism of Depth Psychology," in Murray Stein & Robert L. Moore, eds., *Jung's Challenge to Contemporary Religion* (Wilmette, IL: Chiron Publications, 1987), 27-8.

[6] C.G. Jung, *Memories, Dreams, Reflections*, ed. Aniela Jaffé (New York: Vintage Books, 1963), 141f. Cf. *CW* 9, i § 34-38. Discussed by Miller, *Three Faces of God*, 5.

[7] David L. Miller, "Theology's Ego/Religion's Soul," *Spring 1980*, 78-88.

[8] In his analogy to the Annunciation, Jung speaks of analysis as releasing an experience that "falls upon us as from above." Connecting this up with our extension of the Annunciation analogy to the therapy of ideas a few further passages from Jung are apt. Jung writes, "It is true that ... ideas are never the personal property of their so-called author, on the

contrary, the person is the bondservant of ideas.... A person does not make ideas, we could say that a person's ideas make the person" (*CW* 4 § 769; cited by Miller, "Animadversions," 27). See also Jung's discussion of the dove as a "theriomorphic symbol ... capable of 'interpretation from above downwards'" (*CW* 14 § 205).

[9] Miller, *Three Faces of God*, 6-7. Jung citation is to *CW* 18 § 1164.

[10] Miller, "Attack Upon Christendom!," 37.

[11] Miller, "Attack Upon Christendom!," 37.

[12] Cf. Miller, "Attack upon Christendom!," 32.

[13] Cited by Miller, *Hells & Holy Ghosts*, 157.

[14] Sigmund Freud, "Fragment of an Analysis of a Case of Hysteria," *Collected Papers*, vol. III, tr. A. & S. Strachey (London: The Hogarth Press and The Institute of Psycho-Analysis, 1950), 117.

[15] Marcelle Marini, *Jacques Lacan: The French Context*, tr. A. Tomiche (New Brunswick, NJ: Rutgers University Press, 1992), 83.

[16] C.G. Jung, *CW* 9, i § 302.

[17] C.G. Jung, *CW* 9, i § 11.

[18] C.G. Jung, *CW* 9, i § 271.

[19] Matt. 12: 31-32 *KJV*; cf. Mark 3: 28-29 and Luke 12: 10 *KJV*. Cited in Miller, *Hells & Holy Ghosts*, 185.

[20] Ernest Jones, "The Madonna's Conception through the Ear: A Contribution to the Relation between Aesthetics and Religion," in his *Psycho-Myth, Psycho-History (Volume Two)* (New York: The Stonehill Publishing Company, 1974), 266-357.

[21] Ernest Jones, "A Psycho-analytic Study of the Holy Ghost concept," in *ibid.*, 358-373.

[22] With reference to the conception of Christ, which was "effected by the angel's word of greeting and the breath of a dove simultaneously entering the Madonna's ear," Jones writes: "A study of Greek and Hindu physiological philosophy ... shows that breath used to have a much broader connotation, that of the so-called pneuma concept, and that an important constituent of this concept—probably the greater part of at least its sexual aspects—were derived from another gaseous excretion, namely that proceeding from the lower end of the alimentary canal. It is this down-

going breath, as it is termed in Vedic literature, which is the fertilizing element in various beliefs of creation through speech or breath. Similarly, analysis of the idea of the ear as a female receptive organ leads to the conclusion that this is a symbolic replacement, a "displacement from below upwards," of corresponding thoughts relating to the lower orifice of the alimentary canal. Putting these two conclusions together, we can hardly avoid the inference that the mythical legend in question represents a highly refined and disguised elaboration of the "infantile sexual theory"... according to which fecundation is supposed to be effected through the passage of intestinal gas from the Father to the Mother." *ibid.*, 363.

[23] Bishop Joseph Butler is credited the phrasing of the principle of identity, "Everything is what it is and not another thing." Cited in D.D. Raphael, *British Moralists 1650-1800*, vol. 1 (Indianapolis: Hackett Publishing Co. 1991), preface, § 384.

[24] James Hillman & Paul Kugler, "The Autonomous Psyche: A Communication to Goodheart from the Bi-Personal Field of Paul Kugler and James Hillman, *Spring* (1985), 141-185.

[25] William Goodheart, "C.G. Jung's First `Patient': On the Seminal Emergence of Jung's Thought," *Journal of Analytical Psychology*, 1984, vol. 29:1.

[26] James Hillman, "The Autonomous Psyche," 141.

[27] Hillman, "The Autonomous Psyche," 146.

[28] Kugler, "The Autonomous Psyche," 141.

[29] William B. Goodheart, "Comment on 'The Autonomous Psyche'," *Spring 1985*, 161-164.

[30] Kugler, "The Autonomous Psyche," 141.

[31] In a passage in which he discusses the "autonomous activity of the psyche," Jung writes: "The psyche creates reality every day. The only expression that I can use for this is *fantasy*." C.G. Jung, *CW* 6 § 78.

[32] C.G. Jung, *CW* 10 § 367, slightly modified.

[33] Wolfgang Giegerich, "Comment on 'The Autonomous Psyche'," *Spring 1985*, 172.

[34] Giegerich, "Comment on 'The Autonomous Psyche'," 172. Citation of Jung is to *CW* 14 § 749.

35 Cf. "Psychology begins where any phenomenon (whether physical or mental, 'real' or fantasy image) is interiorized absolute-negatively into itself, and I find myself in its internal infinity." Wolfgang Giegerich, "Is the Soul 'Deep'? Entering and Following the Logical Movement of Heraclitus' Fragment 45." *Spring 64* (1998): 31.

36 Giegerich, "Comment on 'Autonomous Psyche'," 173.

37 C.G. Jung, *Dream Analysis: Notes of the Seminar given in 1928-1930*, ed. Wm McGuire (Princeton: Princeton University Press, 1984), 512.

38 C.G. Jung, *CW* 8 § 964; *CW* 12 § 20; *CW* 16 § 497.

39 C.G. Jung, *CW* 9,i § 155.

40 C.G. Jung, *CW* 11 § 379, 777, 800, 843.

41 C.G. Jung, *CW* 6 § 814-829.

42 Paul Tillich, *Theology of Culture* (New York: Oxford University Press, 1959), 5. Tillich adds that if God is conceived of as a being "the question is quite justified whether such a thing does exist, and the answer equally justified that it does not exist."

43 Tillich, *Theology of Culture*, 5.

44 Tillich, *Theology of Culture*, 5.

45 David Miller, "The 'Stone' which is Not a Stone: C.G. Jung and the Postmodern Meaning of 'Meaning'," *Spring 49* (1989), 118; Wolfgang Giegerich, *The Soul's Logical Life* (Frankfurt am Main: Peter Lang GmbH, 1998), 123-124. For Giegerich's discussion of the negativity of God see page 222 of the same volume.

46 C.G. Jung, *CW* 14 § 190. As cited by Miller, "Nothing Almost Sees Miracles! Self & No-Self in Psychology & Religion," *The Journal of the Psychology of Religion*, 4-5 (1995-1996), 1-26.

47 Cited in Miller, "Nothing Almost Sees Miracles," 7.

48 Miller, "Nothing Almost Sees Miracles," 7.

49 David L. Miller, "Why Men are Mad: Nothing-Envy and the Fascration Complex," *Spring 51*, 77.

50 C.G. Jung, *CW* 9, i § 483.

51 William Shakespeare, *King Lear* II.2.165. Cited by Miller in "Nothing Almost Sees Miracles."

[52] Jung, *Memories, Dreams, Reflections*, 333.

[53] Miller, *Three Faces of God*, 80, 137-150, 156.

[54] Miller, "Animadversions," 28.

[55] D.H. Lawrence, *Psychoanalysis and the Unconscious* (New York: Viking Press, 1960), 165. Cited by Miller, *Three Faces of God*, 116.

[56] Miller, *Three Faces of God*, 114, 116, 129, 138-139.

Jesus Hermes and Shifting Worlds: Metanoia as Therapy

Thomas Moore

> The Church Fathers used the mythology of Hermes
> to make a point concerning Christ's function
> for mankind: both of them were "soul guides.[1]

Many times I have sat in therapy with someone feeling stuck in an impasse. The marriage is dead. The mood is dark. The job is not right. Nothing seems to mean or matter. We talk and talk. We look at dreams and remember histories. What are we looking for? What are we waiting for?

We both have the hope that things will change. In my sophistication I may not allow myself to pursue change quickly, knowing that the strong will to change may be the subtlest and most defeating obstacle of all. Still, we want to be on the other side of the impasse.

It's clear that the desired change doesn't come from strategy or experiment or understanding. These multiply as the conversations go on. Change has to come from somewhere else. From some place deep, far away, mysterious, and ethereal.

Over twenty-five years ago, the Jungian analyst Niel Micklem described change being inspired by an intolerable image. "This is no petty discomfort," he wrote, "but an affect that is unendurable. So, too, with psyche the word intolerable means unendurable to the point where some change is compelled."[2]

He referred to Medusa as the mythic image of the intolerable. You can't bear her presence, and so something has to give. She freezes you so you can't move, and yet eventually, in that petrifaction, you find the impetus you need, not a spur to the will but a pressure on the soul.

Patricia Berry says something similar in her essay on Medusa, "Stopping as a Mode of Animation."[3] There is something in the impasse that inspires change, if you can remain close to the source of the immobility. She makes the point that in the tale of Medusa the hero Perseus is protected because he touches, almost caresses the ugly face. Berry suggests that we have to be that close to the impasse and feeling of being stuck. With your hands on the ugly head of a mood, you can sense that there is life in that threatening thing—the snakes that are the monster's hair writhe and squirm.

I have used this theme in my therapeutic work for many years, and often it has been a quiet business, sitting in the stillness with the faith that there is some odd movement waiting for an opening. Many times I have seen bits of life restored through patience and inactivity.

Life stirs. The kundalini wakens. Asklepios's totem animal rises to attention. The serpent of Eden tempts life into action. All from letting it happen. You would like a complete answer to life's dilemmas, but it is enough to awaken and come to life.

But is it enough? Once you wake up to possibilities, you find yourself in a different place, and you may not recognize it. Where are you? What has happened?

THE OLIVE OIL MAN

When I was in my second year of high school, an English teacher came into class with a large print of Salvador Dali's *Crucifixion*. For me, it was *darshan*, a revelation. My life wasn't the same after the first glance at the painting. I didn't become a Dali aficionado, but I did begin a life in art. That brief epiphany changed me permanently. Of course, it really wakened something not yet seen, something innate. Change doesn't always entail novelty *ex nihilo*.

So now we arrive at part two of awakening: the discovery and making of a world. A word, story, or sight, as in my case, pricks the imagination and a tiny chink of light appears in the dense, dark dome of your heaven. Up to then, your "sky" had been meaningless, offering no hope. Suddenly the smallest possibility shows itself. How important that good story or potent image!

I sit in therapy wishing I could find the word or image that would light up, with even a few amperes, my client's closed-in, darkened cosmos. But again, you can't manufacture this kind of change. You can't turn it on and turn it off. There is no obvious switch. Serendipity is your best hope. You wait for an opening.

The Gospels tell of people waiting for an anointed person, a messiah (in its origins the word means "smeared with olive oil"), someone "out of the ordinary," to come and change their condition. It is an archetypal situation. My clients often expect me to be that person, discovering eventually that the messenger is always an angel and never only human. Through luck a therapist may evoke the messiah, and that has to be sufficient. Many people cling to Jesus, almost as a transitional object, a thing to give them comfort, whereas the Gospels say that the new reality is in you. *"The kingdom is within you and it is outside you."* (Gospel of Thomas, 80)

Medusa is one story of waiting, Jesus another. It has been relatively easy in archetypal psychology to see the soul's mysteries in classical myth, more difficult to see them in the Gospels. One brilliant exception is, of course, David Miller, whose many writings model a theology of depth. His spirit whispers to me as I write these words.

Jesus is an eternal mystery, belonging to no particular religion. Sitting in a doctor's office or rushing off to an ashram, everyone waits for the messiah. Rainer Maria Rilke told his young poet friend to celebrate Christmas with devout feeling: "Why don't you think of him as the one who is coming, who has been approaching from all eternity, the one who will someday arrive, the ultimate fruit of a tree whose leaves we are? What keeps you from projecting his birth into the ages that are coming into existence, and living your life as a painful and lovely day in the history of a great pregnancy?"[4]

THE BIRTH OF IMAGINATION

Jesus offers a different strategy for change. It comes in two steps: 1) the awakening of imagination itself, and 2) entry into a particular place of imagination where your soul is alive and neurosis oiled with imagination.

The person in therapy may be looking for a strategy and an explanation, but what makes all the difference and allows life to change is a shift in imagination. You don't get there step by step, building a theory and a practice. You sit and talk and perhaps steep in your dreams, until one day everything looks different. You don't reason your way into new life; you incubate like an Asklepian supplicant until you finally behold a vision of life as a snake: its hidden, squirming, perhaps frightening and alien otherness, but above all, its hidden vitality.

The waking of imagination is not a mental activity. The effect is more that the world has changed, not you yourself. You don't just see differently; you live in a different reality. There is probably no better term for this than the one Henry Corbin suggested that is used often in archetypal psychology: *mundus imaginalis.* You wake to an imaginal world. First, you learn to imagine rather than to drift along in a river of unconsciousness, and then you realize that there are other worlds available to you. You are lifted to a new level of being, not just perception.

Just exiting the stifling realm of compulsion, you breathe easy and find some hope. Your jealousy eases. Your depression lifts. Your decisiveness returns. Not because you have solved your problem, but because you have entered more fully into the imaginal world, where meanings are to be found and where you have some choices. The entry into this *mundus*, this reality and cosmos, is liberating, because the other realm—we call it literalism, heroism, pragmatism, cynicism, narcissism, paranoia—is heavy and opaque. It is like the gorgon in its rock-hardness and density.

Surfaces are important, but meaning is not to be found on the surface. It is woven into the inner fabric, the underlying threads that don't show much on the surface. Only imagination penetrates to those levels, to the narratives, myths, and primal themes that are the stuff of a life. Yet, a shift in imagination is the most difficult challenge of all. It's easier to stew in indecision or get divorced or maintain a boring job than risk living in a different world order, especially if it has that most threatening quality of all—vitality.

JESUS THE IMAGINATION

What appeals in Micklem's essay is change happening without effort or mechanism. When you feel the unendurable, really sense it without any protections of thought or distracting symptom, a tectonic plate shifts. The change may be slight in one way and life-shattering in another. You have an epiphany about your past or about the nature of things, like a hardly perceptible short in the circuitry of your meaning, and you can go forward a step. The opening is like a small tear in a bed sheet: once there, it easily gets bigger.

Still, it isn't easy to create an opening to the unknown without defenses against it. The more you distance yourself from it, the more terrible and foreign it appears. What you don't realize is that the alien you fear is the most intimate part of yourself that has yet to be met and befriended. This is the oiled one that you are expecting. Eventually you may decide to possess an estranged world as your own, be anointed yourself, and recover your native complexity.

People then get up from therapy and wonder what happened. Life is still a problem, but somehow it is essentially different. Sometimes they don't have even that much awareness. They stop smoking, live with their depression, stay agreeably married to the wrong person, or divorce without the expected collapse of the sky. The physical world may not have changed, but the shift in imagination makes it all radically, if microscopically, different. Therapy has little to do with this life we know too well; it is all about another world, the one in which we really live instead of the one that so preoccupies us.

In the *Euthyphro* Plato defines *therapeia* as "service to the gods." You will also find *therapeuo*, the verb form, in the Gospels, where it is used to denote perhaps the key and identifying action that Jesus uses to show the essence of the new world (*mundus*) he is introducing to humanity. *Therapeia* is usually translated as "healing," but the context of the Gospels indicates that it represents *the restoration of the soul to the divine order*. We have to be careful, in reading the Gospels, not to be literal or naïve when we read about the Father, representative of the divine order and Jesus' means of connecting life to its mysterious source.

Above all else, Jesus is a *therapeutes*, a therapist. Followers of John the Baptist came to him and asked (a question many clients wonder about in relation to their therapist) if he was the one they were all waiting for.

> At that very moment he had cured many of their illnesses, diseases, and problematic spirits. So he said to John's envoys, 'Go back and tell John what you've seen and heard. The blind see, the lame walk, those afflicted with sores are healed, the deaf hear, the lifeless are revivified, and the welcome message is given to the poor' (Luke 7: 21-23)

Through his healing of body, soul, and spirit he demonstrates that he is the one they are waiting for. And so it isn't as odd as it may first appear to turn to him for an idea about the change my clients and I are waiting for. He is usually seen as a religious founder, for which I see no evidence in the stories about him, or as an object of adoration, which goes against every rule of religion. These common approaches to the Gospels are so densely part of our thinking that it is difficult to see Jesus with beginner's eyes, as the therapist he was and as the embodiment of the spiritual and psychological figure we always wait for in our distress. We idolize him, so we miss the point of his appearance.

METANOIA: WORM TO BUTTERFLY

In the Gospels Jesus uses a word that parallels Micklem's intolerable image, a word that has been the topic of thousands of sermons surely and many scholarly articles, a word that encapsulates what I have been saying.

It is used twenty-two times in the New Testament including eight times in the canonical Gospels. The word is *metanoia*.

You have probably heard this word translated as "repentance." It is often closely allied to the word "sin," and so it usually has moralistic overtones. But moralism is an unfortunate reduction wherever it occurs, a defense against complexity and against life's tendency to rush riverlike onward. And so our first task is to examine the word closely and see if it can be relieved of its moralistic drag.

Metanoia comes from two strong Greek words. "*Meta*" means before and after, or change. We are familiar with "metamorphosis," a highly significant change in form. We talk about the metamorphosis of a worm into a butterfly. Imagine being a worm and then being a butterfly. Science tells us that this is not a minor change but an essential transformation, with little biologically in common between worm and butterfly. Such is the power of this little word particle "meta."

"*Noia*" is also a strong word. It is a form of *nous,* a term used by religious philosophers like Anaxagoras, Plato, and Plotinus to refer to the aspect of the divine that is order and intelligibility. At the same time it denotes our human capacity for thought and wisdom. *Nous* is in us and out there. In spiritual philosophical writings of the ancient Greeks *nous* is at the origins. Plotinus places *nous* second after the ineffable primary manifestation of divinity and just before the World Soul in the emanations of being. It is the basic and fundamental ordering of existence; it is the fantasy that life has a particular meaning with a corresponding set of values and a hermeneutics.

Jung cites Pseudo-Clement (Homilies XIX, cap. XXII) for the use of the phrase *agnoias hamartema*, the sin of unconsciousness, represented by the Gospel story of the man born blind who was healed by Jesus. *Metanoia* would then mean repentance for being unconscious, or better, a change out of unconsciousness.[5]

So now, look at this word *meta-noia* again. It implies a highly significant shift in the order of things, as they are and as you perceive them. In other words, it is a change of worlds. It is an entry into the *mundus imaginalis*: into imagination as a means and into a particular imaginal world spelled out in the parables and teachings.

KINGDOM AND *MUNDUS*

Some would say that Jesus was announcing a new world as afterlife, some as a church and a belief, some even as a political state. To me it appears that Jesus was intent on offering a *mundus* in which to live and techniques of imagination for achieving that new imaginal cosmos. In that regard Jesus has a shamanic aspect—acting as a go-between of worlds. The miracles, the parables, rituals of baptism and retreat and food, forgiveness and healing, releasing the daimonic—all of these methods, seen as *upaya* or spiritual *techne*, were forms of imaginal passage into the *mundus*, which he described as a kingdom (*basilea*)—not this realm of fact and heroics, but the kingdom of God or the kingdom of heaven, an unearthly or nonliteral alternative *topos,* having its own values and ethos. (Once you stop literalizing heaven, ever so subtly, you understand that it is a real place outside the ordinary and yet within the natural.)

Two words, *metanoia* and *basilea*, change in imagination and kingdom respectively, sum up the Gospel philosophy. *Metanoia* brings you automatically into *basilea tou theou*, the kingdom of God. Once there, as we saw in the case of therapy, life looks much the same, yet it is entirely different. Buddhists say similarly that *samsara* and *nirvana* are the same. You don't place the new world outside of time or outside of secularity; you see it as a dimension of the world you already know. You acquire a sort of Blakean fourfold vision, in which the world of fact is complexified with poetic, spiritual, and mystical reflection.

Another key aspect of the Jesus *mundus* is the resolution of person and other, or individual and community. As Robert Funk says, "Each man [person] was free to enter in upon that reign in accordance with his inmost destiny."[6] It is obviously tempting for some to interpret the kingdom as an organization that directs your life and tells you how to think and live. But the Gospels themselves clearly show that *metanoia* is linked up with baptism, which is not only a concrete ritual but also a passage from one *mundus* to another. In special alchemical and spiritual water, symbolic of many things, including life's tendency to flow on like a river, you are born into your destiny and into the capacity to reflect. Without baptism you are imagination-free, stuck with the unconsciousness of your various environments—family, marriage, profession, culture. Baptism is not essentially a church activity but rather an existential achievement. Surrealists, not thinking of church at all, said that everyone has to be born twice.

According to Robert Funk, "Jesus did not impose the reign of God upon his hearers. He merely let it show itself." What good advice for the therapist and the one seeking counseling. Don't impose anything, but let what has been hidden manifest. The Jesus *mundus* is not new in itself; it is new to us when we have been living one-dimensionally. It is natural, whereas trying to live without it is unnatural, neurotic, and self-defeating.

Human beings are born, at least in their second birth, into magic, poetry, community, and devotion. That these powers are left out of modern secularist values doesn't mean that they are not natural and given. They are inborn and yet they have to be discovered, and you have to have entered the water of second birth to find them. Your imagination has to start flowing, signaling the easing of neurosis.

The man sitting head-down with fingers twitching in front of me in an hour devoted to *therapeia*, in service to the archetypal and spiritual roots of experience, thinks he needs something else, something new and outside, whereas he is really in search of himself and his hidden world. No one would dispute that when you are born, you get your own life, not someone else's. When you are born the second time into imagination, you also get your own life, not something else. You experience it as other and new, but it has been with you from the beginning.

Metanoia as Yeast

The power of this particular imagination of life can be sensed in a Zenlike comic Gospel parable that is often treated too casually and yet conveys the very essence of the Jesus *mundus imaginalis*. *"The kingdom of heaven (basilea tou ouranou) is like yeast that a woman took and hid in three measures of flour until all of it was leavened."* (Luke 13:20) Scholars point out two points in this tiny story that can easily be overlooked. The woman didn't just mix in the yeast; she hid it. The kingdom is hidden in the thick of life. There is even something shady about it. Perhaps you have to transgress the ordinary, respectable world, with its values and interpretations, to discover this kingdom for yourself. Certainly history teaches that the world doesn't always appreciate a philosophy of communal love. I have no doubt that a profound transgression is necessary in therapy. For one thing, you have to break through the wall of sentimentality that keeps many from their imaginal worlds. Every word of the Gospel has been routinely sentimentalized, leaving in its wake a mammoth shadow of control and guilt and violence and conniving. It would be the gravest mistake to redefine *metanoia* in similar sentimental terms.

Furthermore, three measures is a considerable quantity of flour. Some say about half a bushel. This is not a recipe for a teaspoon of yeast in two cups of flour. The woman has hidden some yeast in half a bushel of flour, and the whole thing rises in the oven. It doesn't take much to evoke the kingdom; the smallest shift in imagining, so absurdly insignificant to be comic, makes a new world.

Jesus uses other images for the comedy of *metanoia*. "Jesus said, 'What is the kingdom of God? What's a good comparison? It's like a mustard seed that a man planted in his garden. It grew into a tree, and the birds of the air perched in its branches.'" (Luke 13:18-19)

Again, scholars point out that the tiny mustard seed normally becomes a bush. Never could birds come and perch in it as though it were a tree. In the story scholars also hear echoes of the great Biblical Cedars of Lebanon. Another absurdity. From the dot-like seed comes a Cedar of Lebanon! How much is accomplished by entering the *mundus* or kingdom, by achieving a real *metanoia!*

Funk points out that the kingdom "is not overtly discernible" and that "it arrives as a mystery, as inversion, and as power."[7]

Let's take a moment to consider these three aspects, remembering that we're talking about the *mundus imaginalis* that transforms neurotic life into a life leavened with soul and spirit and with imagination, meaning, and vitality.

MYSTERY

Jesus is neither a preacher nor a counselor. He is interested in neither virtue nor success in life. He concerns himself with healing, miracle, and the daimonic. Shaman-like, he mediates between the most ordinary life and the mysterious. At the beginning of his life work, he stands in a river and, the story says, the sky opens up. At the culmination of his career he announces that bread and wine are his body and blood. Everything he does and says comes out of the aquatic or baptismal imagination, akin to the alchemical *solutio*, that mixes the visible and the invisible, that dissolves the old world and amniotically gives rise to the new. Everything he sees, touches, and discusses turns into the poetic correlative of itself.

Therapeia is mysterious business. It is not life management. It is, as Plato said, service to the gods. The therapist has a shamanic aspect and is called, as Jesus demonstrated, to keep the realm of heaven engaged with the realm of the ordinary. The therapist, in service of heaven, where everything exists in its poetic dimension, helps a life acquire its innate resonance.

POWER

Every malady entails a loss of power. The soul loses its connection to the imagination, and its positive gifts turn into nightmares. Power becomes manipulation and violence. Love becomes slavery. Value becomes money. Shamanic journeys to the many heavens become addictions. The holy becomes the inflated. Every sickness is a condition of the soul, and every sickness reduces the whole of life to symptom.

But the soul can draw immense power from the mysterious source of its life. Jesus refers to this state as one of being attuned to the Father. He tells his students, "Believe me when I say that I am in the Father and the Father is in me." (John 14:11) This union with the fathering principle of

171

life is, Jesus says, responsible for the amazing things he can do. And, he says, anyone can do them, and even more, if they are so attuned.

Such a mystical word of encouragement may seem too much for a sophisticated modern person, but there lies a secret to the change so many crave. The statement doesn't deny the power of the mother image or many other kinds of images that also waken and strengthen the soul; it simply points to the power to be derived from profound identification with the father source.

Jesus is always in dialogue with the father heaven when he speaks and acts. Another sign of the kingdom: a concrete relation to the invisible otherworlds. Imagination is not an interpretation of this world but a mediating power between heaven and earth, between the hidden and the perceived.

Novalis speaks similarly of the soul, which is implicated in everything we are discussing: "The seat of the soul is there, where the inner world and the outer world touch. Where they permeate each other, the seat is in every point of the permeation."[8]

REVERSAL

Funk's third aspect of the kingdom: reversal. I have often noticed the man who complains in therapy about being stepped on at work and having no will of his own does everything in his power to control the therapy. It becomes clear that the very quality he doesn't want—powerlessness—is the one he needs. The woman who can't find love is obsessed with love. There is nothing else in her life or thoughts. Maybe she needs finally to be fully and completely out of love.

In the kingdom, everything is upside down. The first are last. The rich are outcast. The sick get all the attention. The lost and emotionally distraught are at the center. A thief is promised heaven. In many ways, the kingdom is the reverse of the world we know and understand.

> No one has understood this mystery better than Oscar Wilde, who wrote from prison: Christ, through some divine instinct in him, seems to have always loved the sinner as being the nearest possible

172

> approach to the perfection of man. . . To turn an interesting thief
> into a tedious honest man was not his aim. . . But in a manner not
> yet understood of the world he regarded sin and suffering as being
> in themselves beautiful, holy things, and modes of perfection.[9]

So much for moralism. Yet how difficult it is to reverse years of upbringing and torrents of moralistic thinking in contemporary life to sit with someone in search of his soul without judgment. Jesus the therapist always shocks his students and the authorities with the range of his forgiveness and understanding. Clearly, an astounding acceptance of life's difficulties and the human tendencies toward ignorance and blind passion characterized all his work. Out of unlimited forgiveness he constructed a universe, a kingdom.

Metanoia is, then, often a reversal of values and interpretations. John Dominic Crossan, another brilliant Gospel interpreter, says that in the kingdom it is *de rigueur* to be a nobody.[10] You don't assume that the meaning of life is to fulfill your inherent, primary narcissism with self-indulgence and power over others, even your spouse and children. You discover the reverse: power that comes from giving up the illusion of being somebody, from simply doing your work and making your contribution. In other words, you learn that the secret of self-actualization is the emptying of self (*kenosis*) and deepening of the communal self (*agape*).

HERMES THE EVANGELIST

The word "gospel" comes from the Latin *evangelium* or *evangel*, from the Greek *euangelos*, "welcome message." The Greeks used the same word for message, messenger and angel. In this sense, Jesus is the Gospel. He is the angel acting as the go-between connecting the will of the heavens with life on earth. The Gospels and artistic traditions are full of concrete images of angels performing this function.

This role of go-between the Greeks assigned to Hermes and the Romans to Mercury. Jesus, then, has a Hermetic and Mercurial role in the Gospels, a connection David Miller explores in *Christs*, our best model yet for doing archetypal theology.[11] "The Church Fathers," he writes, "were not reticent to link Hermes and Christ by referring to the Logos, Christ being the "Word" (logos) of God and Hermes being the messenger of the gods (their logoi)." Jesus is the message, the messenger, the angel, and the words themselves. Hermes himself is called an evangelist.[12]

Imagination is not secular hermeneutics but Hermes *psychopompos*, guide of the soul and go-between connecting heaven and earth. Jesus in the garden, sweating with anxiety and praying from deep disturbance of soul, the archetypal patient, is Hermes giving his will over to the father. Hermes tireless on his path to and fro, between heaven and earth. Jesus tirelessly connecting the father in heaven to struggles on earth. All of the travel taking place here in our conversations and efforts at change.

Consider this example of Jesus speaking about *metanoia*. Jesus is having dinner with a revenue agent who had recently become convinced of Jesus' philosophy. Like Hermes, Jesus connects parts of worlds that rarely see each other. His friends are complaining about him mixing in such company—tax collectors were despised as agents of the oppressors. Jesus answers them, 'The healthy don't need a doctor; the sick do. I haven't come to address those who live in a just and civil way. I have come to bring a deep change in vision (*metanoian*) to those who are unjust and uncivil (*hamartolous*)."(Luke 5: 27-32)

Here Jesus Hermes connects change of vision with healing. It is sick to live at the level of perception William Blake referred to as Newton's sleep. The sickness is not rooted in the depression or the painful marriage; it is the failure to rise above the lowest level of *nous*, the material perception of facts. In that case you are left, as some therapies are, with the mere engineering of lives. A factual imagination leads to life coaching; *metanoia* has a far greater impact.

Another important word in this Lucan passage is implicated in the *metanoia* complex of ideas. From early in the history of New Testament translation *hamartia* has been rendered as "sin," and *metanoia* accordingly comes out as "repentance." Many people in a church or in a therapy room seem attached to a moralistic view of life: It's simple and manageable, but it doesn't offer the possibility of healing, which requires imagination.

The word in the Lucan passage I translate "those who live in a just and civil way" is *dikainos,* meaning civilized and orderly, just, able to follow laws and customs. To me, this sounds like the capacity to live and participate in community. And so, Jesus seems to be saying, "I'm not here to speak to those capable of civility and justice but to those who have a faulty vision. I offer a deep change in the way they understand human life." The kingdom turns out to be a quality of all human association—marriage, family, friendship, society—people coming together in community.

Metanoia is not just changing your mind and deciding to live a better life. The profound, eternal, reverberant *nous* is always resounding the background of this word. *Metanoia* is a "shaking of the foundations," as Paul Tillich said. A new being. As George Aichele puts it, "Mark's word "repent" (*metanoia*) suggests a hermeneutical crisis, one that is associated with the nearness of the kingdom of God—a disruption of understanding (*noeo*) apart from which belief—or perceiving the kingdom—is impossible."[13]

THERAPY AND THEOLOGY

My client wonders why she can't decide whether to leave her doctor husband and go off with the prison parolee she met at the halfway house where she works. The impasse is driving her crazy. Everything she has tried has failed. But she hasn't stepped outside her known world. She is trying to make sense of things without changing worlds, without *metanoia.* As long as she remains in her world, I don't expect anything significant to happen.

The specifics of the *basilea* are spelled out in Jesus' actions and in the instructions he gives to his students. He tells them *"go out and announce that the kingdom is here. Heal the sick, wake the lifeless, clean those afflicted with disease, and release the demonic."* (Matt: 10:7-8) These actions establish and represent the kingdom.

He doesn't recommend any old new world, but a godly world, one in which you don't keep pursuing your own aggrandizement. You don't weigh your soul with the money you have. You don't feel complete until everyone is complete. Jesus bodhisattva. To be a vital part of community, you have to transcend your narcissism and paranoia, which are signals of a one-dimensional self. Here, psychology and religion are reconciled. Healing is not a matter of resolution but of *a significant shift in imagination,* a decent translation of *metanoia.*

The kingdom is a home for those who can keep poverty and wealth in creative tension, romanticizing neither. It is the condition in which you can only be truly effective when you make miracles. It is the place where everything you say resonates with layer upon layer of significance. It is a place of poetics, hermeneutics, and paradox. It is a place where virtue and passion overlap.

In this realm, everyone is a healer: parent, teacher, businessperson, politician. All work has a therapeutic aspect, and all healing has a miraculous aspect. Miracle need not mean overcoming some natural law and performing some astounding feat. This kind of showmanship magic was apparently not uncommon in Jesus' time, but he practiced miraculous healing that signified *mundus novus,* a new world.

Where Water is Wine

In the kingdom, things are not what they seem. Water is wine. At the wedding of Cana, Jesus didn't actively change water into wine. He simply told the waiters to pour out the water and they tasted it as wine. On another occasions he fed five thousand people lunch with a few pieces of fish and bread. You can do the same once you enter the *mundus imaginalis.* Deeds impossible in the flat realm of fact become readily available.

Water is wine. Imagination not only gives dimension to the flat ordinary; it also complexifies, intensifies, vivifies, and ferments. Where Freud's death principle rules, the Dionysian, which Jesus restored in Cana, is not to be seen, and without the Dionysian there can be no resurrected vitality. We don't need passive reflection as much as fermenting conversation and art. Jesus says that his very blood is wine.

176

In history, tiny communities like those of Epicurus, Marsilio Ficino, and Ralph Waldo Emerson change culture. They raise the intellectual and moral life through conversations in a garden, a villa, and a small town lyceum. Magic is the order of the day. Miracles happen regularly. Life has spice and fermentation.

A woman comes to me with a deep desire to find a new job. I listen closely but I hardly hear her complaint. Her soul is begging for the fresh air of a new imagination. She comes seeking *metanoia*, thinking of it as a change in life. She brings utopian thoughts of an entirely new existence. She is a little disappointed after the first conversation that she hasn't found the messiah, but something hidden moves her to return for more conversation. Within a short time she has reconceived her world, perhaps in a small way. She decides to keep her job. Her expectations, so big and airy, have diminished, but her life has changed essentially. An angel has been invoked between us and has brought some healing. We see traces of olive oil on her head and on mine—some new language, new vitality, and, dare we say it, a new world.

NOTES

[1] David Miller, *Christs* (New York: Seabury Press, 1981), 28-29, (repr. ed. New Orleans: Spring Journal Books, 2005).

[2] Niel Micklem, "The Intolerable Image," *Spring 1979*, 1.

[3] Patricia Berry, "Stopping as a Mode of Animation," in *Echo's Subtle Body* (Dallas: Spring Publications, 1982), 147-161.

[4] Rainer Maria Rilke, *Letters to a Young Poet*, transl. Stephen Mitchell (New York: Random House, 1984), 61.

[5] C. G. Jung, *Aion*, CW 9,ii (Princeton: Princeton University Press, 2nd ed. 1968), § 299. Other views of metanoia are numerous but not precisely relevant, such as Emmanuel Levinas' "from subjectivity to intersubjectivity" and R. D. Laing's "breakdown as breakthrough."

[6] Robert Funk, *Jesus as Precursor* (Philadelphia: Fortress Press, 1975), 92.

[7] *Ibid.*, 64.

[8] Novalis, *Pollen and Fragments*, transl. Arthur Versluis (Grand Rapids: Phanes Press, 1989), 27.

[9] Oscar Wilde, *Complete Works* (New York: Harper & Row, 1966), 933.

[10] John Dominic Crossan, *The Historical Jesus* (San Francisco: HarperSanFrancisco, 1992), 269.

[11] David Miller, *Christs* (New York: Seabury Press, 1981), 30, (repr. ed. New Orleans: Spring Journal Books, 2005).

[12] Henry George Liddell and Robert Scott, *A Greek-English Lexicon* (Oxford: Clarendon Press, Ninth ed. 1940), 905.

[13] George Aichele, "The Poetic Function and the Gospel in/of Mark: A Post-Canonical Reading" 2003, online, 5.

"Intricate Evasions of As": History, Imagination, and Saint Basil's Crab

PATRICIA COX MILLER

Meditating on angels as images of imagination, David Miller observed that "the Angel as poetic image is one of 'the intricate evasions of as' which help us disengage our various idolatries and literalisms. Yet, these as-forms give substance nonsubstantialistically."[1] It seems fitting to entitle an essay in honor of David with a line of poetry, since so much of his work as a scholar has been devoted to images and the poetry of meaning that they provoke.[2] Indeed, he began one of his major books, a true *theologia imaginalis*, with this statement: "It begins—as it will also end—with a poem. This is not only to indicate that things are better said poetically, though that of course is also true, but rather to express the view that some things can be said, if at all, only in image, metaphor, and likeness...."[3] Images as metaphors—those "intricate evasions of as"—can be constitutive of a text's insight, and David's work has consistently conspired with "those forms of thinking that cannot be accomplished without poetry, without image's metaphoric power."[4]

The impact of David's work on the religious texts and traditions that he studies certainly exemplifies a remark that his teacher, Stanley Romaine Hopper, once made: "Metaphors are risky."[5] That is, metaphors have a habit of unsettling tidy interpretive structures and those who, like David,

179

follow (in) their uncanny tracks must occupy, however uncomfortably, a certain liminal space, the space of imagination.[6] Images, however, can only do their iconoclastic work in that liminal space if the interpreter actively engages them. As David has more elegantly phrased this point, "The eye begins to see poetically, metaphorically, inferentially under the conditions of the *descensus ad inferos*, the descent into the interiority of the resonances of the language of its own poetizing."[7] As in the biblical story of Jacob, angels-as-images have to be wrestled, since "idolatries and literalisms" do not loosen their grip so easily.[8] The riskiness of metaphor—as in David's finding a drunken Silenos in the depths of the Christian image of Christ as good shepherd[9]—depends for its transformative power on a certain willingness to allow images to deform one's perception.

This was all news to me when, fresh from the University of Chicago and newly-minted as an assistant professor in the Department of Religion at Syracuse University, I first met David. Even though I had written my dissertation trying to prove that Eusebius of Caesarea's biography of Origen of Alexandria was an artful construct rather than a work of "positivist" history, I had not seen the force or the possibilities of my own approach. More significantly, however, as an historian I had never imagined that the historian's own work might be construed as an imaginal enterprise, that the historian herself might dwell in "a world in which images (simulacra) are honored for themselves, rather than as copies of an original."[10] David's greatest gift to me as a scholar has been his work on the poetic image, and I write this essay in recognition of, and thanks for, that gift.

Following, then, David's articulation of a poetic theology, I have tried to develop a poetic historiography. Having been introduced by David not only to his own work but also to the work of such literary theorists as the French phenomenologist Gaston Bachelard, I now read ancient texts according to the truth of their figures of speech. For an historian, this way of reading is immensely liberating; when one is no longer caught in the grip of historicism, one is free to read ancient texts as literature, not as a trove of facts to be mined for social, political, and institutional data. In a poetic historiography, a text's images are read as performative,

performative in the sense of generative, as in the following formulation by literary critic J. Hillis Miller: there is "no such thing as an innocent image or myth.... No metaphor or myth is a mere 'symbolic convenience,' separable from the thought that it embodies. It is the body of that thought, the secret generator of the concepts it incarnates."[11]

Not only are images complicit with a text's meaning; as David has argued, they also give "thickness or density, thickening the plot of life, leading to make-believe, to imagination, the domain of *mundus imaginalis*."[12] In other words, in a poetic historiography, texts speak otherwise when one is attentive to what might be called the storytelling function of the poetic image, that is, the image that deforms or changes how one apprehends a text's "story" rather than conforming to habituated modes of understanding.[13] Such images, referred to by the poet Ezra Pound as "luminous details," are, as he also observed, "clusters of fused ideas endowed with energy" that "present an intellectual and emotional complex in an instant of time."[14]

Engaging a text's images with these perspectives in mind amounts to what David, following Bachelard, calls "'a systematic education in deformation.'"[15] Indeed, in a remarkable essay on the incandescence of poetic images, David highlighted a central insight of Bachelard's that has been crucial for his own work, and also for mine. "We always think of the imagination as the faculty that *forms* images," Bachelard wrote: "On the contrary," he continued, "it *deforms* what we perceive; it is, above all, the faculty that frees us from immediate images and *changes* them. If there is no change, or unexpected fusion of images, there is no imagination; there is no *imaginative act*. If the image that is *present* does not make us think of one that is *absent*, if an image does not determine an abundance— an explosion—of unusual images, then there is no imagination."[16] Deforming, imagination creates.

With these thoughts in mind concerning what might happen when a text is approached through a striking or discordant image, I offer in what follows a reading of an ancient text as a tribute to David's imaginal scholarly pedagogy. Given that it is a text that concerns animals, my reading is also offered as a tribute to an aspect of David's own writings that perhaps even he has not noticed: they teem with bestial images! There is truly a bestial play at work in David's *mundus imaginalis*. First, there are the felines: ghostly tigers;[17] the Cheshire Cat who disappears, with only his smile remaining;[18] the lion from the zoological garden in the book of Job;[19] and the great cat that "leaps quickly from the fireside and is gone."[20] And then there are the birds: disappearing pheasants and whistling blackbirds,[21] a raven and an ostrich,[22] and that most curious flier, an "unsatiate sparrow" that "animadverts," turning the eye inward toward soulful depths.[23] Finally, along with domestic animals—sheep,[24] bulls,[25] a "mouse in the machine"[26]—there are the aquatic beasts: frogs with a comic, underworldly vision;[27] a giant water bug that eats the frogs,[28] and perhaps best of all, the magnificent Leviathan, created for the sport of angels.[29]

Given this catalogue of some of the poetic animals that romp through David's work, it would seem that he has taken his own advice, not only regarding images as epiphanic vehicles carrying theological and psychological insight but also regarding how a reader might read imaginally, allowing the image to "break the horizontal narrative-movement" of a text such that the reader (and the text) is allowed to dream.[30] Many of the animal images with which David himself has dreamed are from modern poetry, but quite a few of them are from ancient texts. Writing in one article about the iconoclastic function of bestial imagery in relation to the Christian doctrine of Christ's descent into hell, he noted that "ancient theological writers ... depict the *anima*-depths with imagery of animals, as if the descent into hell, into interiority (*ad inferos*), were a descent into a fundamental animality."[31]

It is with this notion of a descent into fundamental animality that I introduce Saint Basil's crab. Basil of Caesarea, Christian theologian and biblical exegete, was one of the so-called Cappadocian Fathers who lived from C.E. 330-379. The crab makes its appearance in one of Saint Basil's most famous texts, the *Hexaemeron*, a series of nine homilies that interpret the six days of creation in the book of Genesis. Complaining, at one point in this text, about what he considered to be the flights of fancy spawned by allegorical interpretation, Saint Basil assures his readers that *he* has certainly not approached the text of Genesis as though it were an imaginal treasure house. Using hearing as a figure for reading and writing, he insists: "As for me, when I hear grass spoken of, I think of grass; and I do the same when I hear plant, fish, wild animal, and domestic animal. I take everything just as it is said."[32] No fancy poetizing for Saint Basil; all he wanted was the letter of the text. As we shall see in a moment, however, despite his profession of literalism, Saint Basil fell prey to the spell of the image. Before inviting the crab more fully into this essay, I want to present the interpretive stance that I am bringing to this text.

The *Hexaemeron* is filled with *ekphrases,* which were exercises in composition for those studying rhetoric. In the rhetorical handbooks in use in the period of the Roman empire, *ekphrasis* was defined as "a descriptive speech bringing the thing shown vividly before the eye," turning listeners into spectators.[33] *Ekphrases* appeal to the ocular imagination and, as one scholar has noted, they are indicative of ancient authors' ability to see more than was (literally) there in the place, building, person, thing, or event being summoned before the eyes in words.[34] The tendency of *ekphrases,* that is, is to undermine mimesis by creating the illusion that images can come to life, that they can "pass from the opacity of words to the luminous scenes behind the words."[35] As described by literary theorist W.J.T. Mitchell, "the basic project of ekphrastic hope" is "the transformation of the dead, passive image into a living creature."[36] Basically, then, ekphrastic hope is founded in *poiesis,* the image honored on its own, rather than in mimesis, the image understood as a copy of an original.

Armed now with this perspective on the imaginal hope of *ekphrases,* let us return to Saint Basil. The overall point of the *Hexaemeron,* stated repeatedly, is that the intricate beauty of the natural world can give human beings an idea of the God who created it.[37] Since the features of the world in the creation story in Genesis—animals, plants, sea creatures, and so on—are called into being only as general groups (that is, Genesis does not mention the names of individual animals, plants, and sea creatures), Saint Basil undertook the task of specifying the diversity of the natural world. Posing, as we have seen, as a plain-sense interpretation of Scripture, what Saint Basil actually presents is a cosmology as he opens out the text of Genesis to embrace the created world in its immense variety. The ekphrastic effects of his text's descriptions of the natural world attempt to overcome the boundary between the book of Genesis and the world of nature. Yet disjunction remains, not only because Saint Basil's own text intervenes between the two, but also because he claims that nature—presumably the "real" nature that exists outside the book—is itself a book whose text conveys the glory of God.[38]

Like any good ekphrasist, Saint Basil leads his reader around in a cosmos that is both itself and something else, a text. His own writing achieves its ekphrastic effect of animating its images not so much by visual description—though we do get word-pictures of such things as camels' necks and elephants' trunks—as by descriptions of the movements and activities of various components of nature. Nonetheless, it is appropriate to call the *Hexaemeron* a collection of *images* because the cosmos as presented by Saint Basil is not only a living text but also a work of art. According to the fourth homily, God is "the great wonder-worker and craftsman" who has invited us humans to witness the display of his works; nature is thus "the grand and intricate workshop of divine creativity."[39]

While cataloguing the aquatic animals that populate part of this divine natural workshop, Saint Basil directs his reader's attention to the crab by means of an extended *ekphrasis*. Here is his account:

> The crab craves the flesh of the oyster, but its prey is hard to get because it is enveloped by a shell. For nature has protected the softness of the oyster's flesh with this unbreakable enclosure—hence the name testacean or hard-shelled. Thus when the two shells, which fit each other exactly, enclose the oyster completely, the crab's claws are necessarily powerless. What is the crab to do? When it sees an oyster in a sheltered spot warming itself voluptuously and opening its shells to the sun's rays, then the crab furtively flicks a pebble into it, making it impossible for the oyster to close its shells. With this trick the crab is able to obtain what it could not by force. Such is the immorality of animals who partake neither of reason nor of speech.

> I myself wish that, while emulating the resourcefulness and
> inventiveness of crabs, you refrain from harming those near you.
> That person is [like a crab] who approaches his brother with cunning,
> is attached to the Mishaps of those near him, and delights in the
> misfortunes of others. Flee any resemblance to these wretches! Be
> satisfied with what you have! For poverty that is truly self-sufficient
> is for the wise more honorable than any other pleasure.[40]

So much for the plain sense of Scripture!

In a stunning leap from the mimetic to the imaginal, Saint Basil's
description of the crab has succumbed to the lure of the story-telling
potential of the image's own craving. As David would (perhaps) say, this
image as a whole is itself a "crab," working its own furtive trick on the
unsuspecting reader. For what Basil has done here is to insert an
anthropology into his catalogue of nature and nature's appetites. When
one "reads" nature along with Saint Basil, one is also reading the self. The
descriptive horizontal movement of the text has suffered a break, such
that the reader is forced to dream about a cosmology that is humanly
inflected. Saint Basil's text is in fact a "translucent overlay of different
planes of perception" of self, world, and divine creativity.[41] Although he
would probably have been surprised and even affronted to hear a modern
interpreter describe him as a poet, Saint Basil seems to me to have provided
an instance of David's view that "[i]n poetizing the world becomes glass,
transparent. Images are for seeing through, not for seeing."[42]

The crab, one might say, was Saint Basil's angel, leading him to *see
through* the image of the crab's behavior toward the oyster, using it as a
lens for viewing human misconduct. The fleshly appetite of the crab
becomes an object lesson in human ethical behavior: emulate the crab's
resourcefulness, but not so as to harm "oysters," those defenseless others
who are prey to the furtive flicks of the cunning selves whom Basil
condemns. The text's abrupt switch from descriptive narrative to direct
address is surely a jolt to the reader, a moment of "deformation" in which
perception is altered by forcing the reader to inhabit this "testacean"
story.

Yet, this is no ordinary crab. It is not, as Hillis Miller would say, an innocent image. Not only does it generate what Bachelard called an "unexpected fusion of images," as the human and the natural worlds slide into each other; and not only does it, as David has remarked, "lead to make-believe," asking the reader to imagine him or herself as a crab; but it also masks—or unmasks—an erotic exuberance that the ethical stance of the text cannot quite suppress.

This animal image is indeed a descent into what David has called a "fundamental animality." The animality in question here is the body and its desires. Saint Basil's text presents the crab's quest for the soft flesh of the voluptuous oyster in unmistakably sexual terms. What the reader sees is a scene of seduction: the canny crab, unable to use force, tricks the oyster into satisfying its desire. Paradoxically, the image petitions the erotic while at the same time condemning it as bestially immoral. On the face of it, Saint Basil's fall into the sensuous allure of this image seems surprising, since he was a leader in the ascetic movement in late-fourth-century Christianity. Founder of monastic brotherhoods and devoted to relief of the poor, Saint Basil spoke the stern language of sexual renunciation and the embrace of celibacy and virginity that swept through late ancient Christianity.[43]

Given his renunciatory stance toward the body and its pleasures, Saint Basil's image of the crab is a telling "luminous detail," that is, it is one of those moments when a text confounds itself in "aporiae, those tears where energies, desires, and repressions flow out into the world."[44] Seduced, perhaps, by his own suppressed eros, the ascetic Saint Basil dreamed, displacing his own sense of the seductive and the voluptuous onto the animal world while giving expression to that sense at the same time. Furthermore, his attempt to convert the story into a moral lesson confounds the very story it petitions; by recommending, at the end of his narrative, the embrace of poverty as the ultimate wisdom of the story, Saint Basil denies the satisfaction of the crab's carnal desire even as he narrates its fulfillment.

Had I not been tutored by David's work concerning the power of images, I might have read Basil's riff on the crab as an example of the naïve credulity and romantic fancy with which late ancient Christians approached the natural world, as other interpreters indeed have. However, as an historian committed to reading the truth of a text's figures of speech, I read Saint Basil's crab as a particularly striking example of the transgressive nature of an apparently "innocent" image. And it does indeed tell a story. In fact, it is part of a larger "story" in late ancient Christianity, recently described by one interpreter as the "eruption of a powerful crosscurrent of asceticized eroticism"[45] in texts like hagiographies—and, I would add, the *Hexaemeron*—where one might least expect to find it. Saint Basil's crab is a sublimely erotic fantasy that disrupts both its naturalist and its ethical contexts. And it is also proof of the power of the image to deform perception, and not only Saint Basil's, but the interpreter's as well.

Images as metaphors—those "intricate evasions of as"—can indeed be constitutive of a text's insight, as David has argued in his work. And so I offer this essay with gratitude for all of David's insights concerning poetic seeing; to paraphrase an aphorism from one of the desert ascetics: "the interpreter ought to be as the cherubim and the seraphim: all eye."[46]

NOTES

[1] David L. Miller, "Theologia Imaginalis," in *The Archaeology of the Imagination*, ed. Charles E. Winquist, *Journal of the American Academy of Religion Thematic Studies* 48/2 (American Academy of Religion, 1981), 2.

[2] The phrase "intricate evasions of as" comes from Wallace Stevens, "An Ordinary Evening in New Haven," in *The Collected Poems of Wallace Stevens* (New York: Alfred A. Knopf, 1957), 486.

[3] David L. Miller, *Christs: Meditations on Archetypal Images in Christian Theology* (New York: The Seabury Press, 1981; repr. ed. Spring Journal Books, 2005), xiii.

[4] *Ibid.*, xviii.

[5] Stanley Romaine Hopper, "The Bucket As It Is," in *Metaphor and Beyond: Conversations with Stanley Romaine Hopper*, ed. Mark D. Lombard (Syracuse, NY: Syracuse University Department of Religion, 1979), 15.

[6] This imaginal interpretive "space" is defined succinctly in David L. Miller, ed., *Jung and the Interpretation of the Bible* (New York: Continuum, 1995), 104: "If assuming a theological and doctrinal significance to texts puts the interpreter in a deductive and rationalistic mode of thinking, and if assuming a historical and experiential significance implies an inductive and empirical strategy, there is yet a third possible way. The historian of religions, Henry Corbin, called this alternative by the name *mundus imaginalis*.... This 'imaginal realm' functions similarly to the celebrated *metaxy* of Plato and Plotinus, for both of whom the 'middle realm,' between mind's intelligibles *(nous)* and experience's sensibles *(aisthetikoi)*, is the domain of soul *(psyche)* and carries the workings of imagination *(phantasia).*"

[7] David L. Miller, *Hells and Holy Ghosts: A Theopoetics of Christian Belief* (Nashville: Abingdon Press, 1989; repr. ed. Spring Journal Books, 2005), 82.

[8] Miller, "Theologia Imaginalis," 4, 11. See also p. 7: "The problem with human ideas is that they tend to stay around, having a marked propensity for fixation, for objectivization and externalization, wanting to be taken for truth itself, leading thinking and feeling unwittingly and witlessly ... toward idolatry and dogma; whereas images, like Angels, tend to turn and transform as they disappear into the brush, like a pheasant" (the latter image is an allusion to one of Wallace Stevens's aphorisms, "Poetry is a pheasant disappearing in the brush," in Wallace Stevens, *Opus Posthumous: Poems, Plays, Prose,* ed. Samuel French Morse [New York: Alfred A. Knopf, 1977], 173).

[9] Miller, *Christs,* chs. 3, 7, 22.

[10] David L. Miller, "Through a Looking Glass—The World as Enigma," *Eranos* 55-1986 (Frankfurt: Insel-Verlag, 1988): 387.

[11] J. Hillis Miller, "Tradition and Difference," *Diacritics* 2 (1972): 10.

[12] David L. Miller, *The New Polytheism,* 2nd ed. (Dallas: Spring Publications, 1981), 20.

[13] See Patricia Cox Miller, *The Poetry of Thought in Late Antiquity: Essays in Imagination and Religion* (Aldershot: Ashgate, 2001), 7.

[14] For Pound's notion of the luminous detail, see Catherine Gallagher and Stephen Greenblatt, *Practicing New Historicism* (Chicago: University of Chicago Press, 2001), 19; for Pound's definition of images, see *Ezra Pound: A Critical Anthology*, ed. J. P. Sullivan (Baltimore: Harmondsworth, 1970), 41, 57.

[15] David L. Miller, *Three Faces of God: Traces of the Trinity in Literature and Life* (Philadelphia: Fortress Press, 1986; repr. ed. Spring Journal Books, 2005), 78, quoting Gaston Bachelard, *The Philosophy of No: A Philosophy of the New Scientific Mind,* trans. G. C. Waterston (New York: Orion, 1968), 110.

[16] David L. Miller, "The Amorist Adjective Aflame in the Works of Gaston Bachelard, Henry Corbin, and Wallace Stevens," unpublished manuscript presented at the Gaston Bachelard Conference, Dallas, Texas, December 4, 1983, sponsored by the Dallas Institute of Humanities and Culture. The quotation from Bachelard is from *Air and Dreams,* tr. Edith R. Farrell and C. Frederick Farrell (Dallas: Dallas Institute Publications, 1988), 1 (emphasis in original).

[17] Miller, *Three Faces of God*, 109-33.

[18] Miller, "Theologia Imaginalis," 1.

[19] David L. Miller, "From Leviathan to Lear: Shades of Play in Language and Literature," *Eranos* 51-1982 (Frankfurt: Insel-Verlag, 1983): 74.

[20] David L. Miller, "Prometheus, St. Peter, and the Rock: Identity and Difference in Modern Literature," *Eranos* 57-1988 (Frankfurt: Insel-Verlag, 1990), 116-17, quoting a line from Wallace Stevens's poem "Montrachet-le-Jardin," *Collected Poems,* 264.

[21] Miller, "Theologia Imaginalis," 2-3.

[22] Miller, "From Leviathan to Lear," 74.

[23] David L. Miller, "Animadversions," *Spring 54* (1993): 21.

[24] Miller, *Christs,* Part I: "Christ, The Good Shepherd," and passim.

[25] *Christs*, 38.

[26] David L. Miller, *Gods and Games: Toward a Theology of Play* (New York and Cleveland: The World Publishing Company, 1970), 3.

[27] David L. Miller, "Hades and Dionysos: The Poetry of Soul," *Journal of the American Academy of Religion* 46/3 (1978), 332-33.

[28] Miller, "From Leviathan to Lear," 59-60.

[29] "Leviathan," 86.

[30] *New Polytheism*, 19-20; see also "Hades and Dionysos," 334: "Images are for seeing through, not for seeing."

[31] David L. Miller, "The Two Sandals of Christ: Descent into History and into Hell," *Eranos* 50-1981 (Frankfurt: Insel-Verlag, 1982): 174.

[32] Basil of Caesarea, *Hexaemeron* 9.1, in *Basile de Césarée: Homélies sur L'Hexaéméron,* ed. Stanislaus Giet (Paris: Les Éditions du Cerf, 1968), 480 (hereafter cited as Hex.)

[33] For discussion, see Liz James and Ruth Webb, "'To Understand Ultimate Things and Enter Secret Places': Ekphrasis and Art in Byzantium," *Art History* 14 (1991): 4.

[34] John Onians, "Abstraction and Imagination in Late Antiquity," *Art History* 3 (1980): 4, 12, 23.

[35] Norman Bryson, "Philostratus and the Imaginary Museum," in *Art and Text in Ancient Greek Culture,* ed. Simon Goldhill and Robin Osborne (Cambridge: Cambridge University Press, 1994), 266.

[36] W.J.T. Mitchell, *Picture Theory: Essays on Verbal and Visual Representation* (Chicago: University of Chicago Press, 1994), 167.

[37] See, for example, *Hex.* 1.11, 3.10, 4.1, 8.7.

[38] *Hex.* 11.4.

[39] *Hex.* 4.1.

[40] *Hex.* 7.3.

[41] Philip Rousseau, *Basil of Caesarea* (Berkeley: University of California Press, 1994), 326.

[42] Miller, "Hades and Dionysos," 334.

[43] See, for example, Peter Brown, *The Body and Society: Men, Women, and Sexual Renunciation in Early Christianity* (New York: Columbia University Press, 1988), 287-91.

[44] Gallagher and Greenblatt, *Practicing New Historicism,* 109.

[45] Virginia Burrus, *The Sex Lives of Saints: An Erotics of Ancient Hagiography* (Philadelphia: University of Pennsylvania Press, 2004), 3.

[46] *Apophthegmata patrum, Bessarion* 11, trans. Benedicta Ward, *The Sayings of the Desert Fathers* (Kalamazoo: Cistercian Press, 1975), 42: "The monk ought to be as the cherubim and the seraphim: all eye."

Narcissus Reflections

CHRISTINE DOWNING

> The way of the soul. . . .leads to the water, to
> the dark mirror that reposes at its bottom.
> —C.G. Jung, *Collected Works* 9.1 § 33

I was led to this quote by David Miller, as I have been led to so much else—themes, images, stories and ideas—in the more than forty-five years we have known one another. Narcissus and narcissism, the story and the idea, reflect one another. Moving back and forth both are illumined, deepened.

The story ends with a flower, the narcissus with its white petals surrounding the yellow center.

But perhaps it *began* there. Not with the boy staring transfixed by his reflection in the still pond but with the flower.

Nor with the other story.

The one about Persephone, captivated by the flower planted by Gaia, that marvelous radiant flower that smelled so sweet that heaven and earth and sea laughed with joy, that awe-inspiring flower from whose root a hundred blooms grew.

NARCISSUS REFLECTIONS

Years ago I wrote of Persephone reaching for that particular flower as a reaching (if only half-consciously) for her own in-her-selfness and for that engagement with death that gives depth to life.

But then I thought the other story, the story of the boy and his image, was already there.

Now I know it came later, much later.

For scholars whom I trust tell me there was no story about the boy until Ovid came to tell it.

So perhaps Ovid moved the flower from one story to another (for it does not appear in his telling of the Persephone story.)

But before there were any stories, there was the flower—and its name. A name derived from association with the word, *narke,* and thus with sleep, unconsciousness, death.

And the flower gets its name because its sweet smell can make the heavens laugh but may overpower us mortals, put us to sleep, remind us of death.

But of course there would come to be stories and of course the stories would be about longing and beauty and being overpowered and death.

And of course eventually there would be ideas, ideas like narcissism and narcolepsy.

But let's begin with the story, the one about the boy and the image. Not as we tend to remember it, as though what it really meant was narcissism all along (even a fine Latinist like William Anderson makes that mistake[1]) but as it was told the first time around in Ovid's *Metamorphoses.*[2]

And let's begin by looking at it *in* the *Metamorphoses,* remembering how important contexts, juxtapositions, repetitions, prefigurings, variations, contrasts, interruptions, flashbacks are to shaping the meanings of any tale that Ovid tells.

Let's begin by remembering how shortly before turning to our tale Ovid writes of Actaeon stumbling upon a pool and being undone by what he sees.

And how just a little later he tells us of another lovely virginal youth, Hermaphroditus, who comes upon another crystal clear pool and there is set upon by a nymph who wraps herself so tightly around the resistant youth that their two bodies become one.

Let's recall that our tale is framed by two about Dionysos.

And that, as Anderson notes, the story about Narcissus is the first account, following so many of divine seductions and rapes, of a human lover.

Though even this one begins with the rape of a struggling nymph, begins with a rivergod imprisoning a waterlily by curving tightly around her.

So the water and the flower are there from the beginning.

A child is born and the mother asks the yet untested prophet Teiresias if her beautiful son will have a long life. "Not if he comes to know himself," she is told.

We've all heard enough stories to recognize this as a warning.

We remember (even though Ovid has not yet come to the story) that Orpheus is told he can have Eurydice back, if he doesn't look back—and we remember that he does.

So we know: this boy will not have a long life. This boy will in some sense come to know himself. And the story will be about how this comes to happen. And if it's a good story, it will look for a while as though it might all turn out differently.

(And of course many read the story as though it *did* turn out differently, as though Narcissus never did come to know himself except in an empty, superficial way.)

But I think we should stay with the story. Narcissus does come to know himself, to know himself as one in love with an image, as still in love with that image even in death. Isn't that more accurate than to say he's in love with himself? Stay with the story.

But we are getting ahead of ourselves.

Let's return to the story.

Narcissus is sixteen, at that age of fugitive bloom that is the equivalent for a youth of Persephone having just reached maidenhood when her story begins.

194

Ovid makes much of Narcissus' soft tender androgynous body, of how he's desired by both youths and young girls. But his heart is hard; he is impervious to their longing, perhaps more unaware than hostilely rejecting. (It is not in Ovid that Narcissus sends a sword to one of the more importunate suitors who uses it to kill himself.) He seems self-enclosed (as Persephone was enclosed in her mother's arms), perhaps imbued with the kind of self-sufficiency Freud (in his essay on narcissism) ascribed to women like Lou Salomé.

One day a nymph, catching sight of him as he is driving frightened deer into his net, is inflamed with love. But this nymph cannot speak her love, she can only reflect the words of others, she can only echo. Ovid has fun with this—but it's also sad. "I'd sooner die than say I'm yours," says he. "I'm yours," echoes Echo. Narcissus flees. (Ovid uses the same word as that describing Actaeon's vain flight.) Spurned she wastes away, becomes only voice.

But, as we've said, many others fall in love with Narcissus, including one rejected male lover who prays, "May Narcissus, too, fall in love and be denied the one he loves." The goddess Nemesis heeds the prayer.

So one day, wearied from a hot day's chase, Narcissus comes upon a sylvan pool, so virginal that its surface has never been disturbed by shepherd or by bird or beast or even fallen branch—not the stream or spring of many translations or pictorial representations. (In Ovid, we might note, the scene of Persephone's abduction is a lakeside grove not a meadow and many water nymphs enter the tale).

Narcissus lies down and while he tries to quench one thirst, he feels another: desire for the image in the pool. He believes that what is but a shade must be a body. He cannot turn away, lies there still as any statue. As Ovid describes his Dionysian locks, his ivory neck, his blushing cheeks, we, too, become viewers—as taken with Ovid's image of Narcissus as he is with the image in the water. (And if what Narcissus sees is but his own reflection, is that not true of us as well? I'm getting ahead of myself again, thinking of how Freud will take this image out of pathology—will help us see that in looking at Narcissus we are looking at ourselves, at an image of ourselves.)

Narcissus knows not what he sees but what he sees invites him; unwittingly he wants himself; he is the seeker and the sought, the longed-for and the one who longs, fixated on the lying shape. "I smile and you smile too. ... bend to kiss and you move to meet me."

Then the narrator's voice intrudes, reminding us that Narcissus himself is an *imago*, a poetic image:

> But why,
> o foolish boy - do you persist? Why try
> to grip an image? He does not exist—
> the one you love and long for. If you turn
> away, he'll fade – the face that you discern
> is but a shadow, your reflected form.
> That shape has nothing of its own: it comes
> with you, with you it stays, it will retreat
> when you have gone—if you can ever leave!

As Narcissus half knows. He knows that though he and the youth in the water are separated only by a thin film, they can never touch. He cries out to the trees that shade the pool as though his situation were the cruelest ever.

> Yes, yes, I'm he. I've seen through that deceit.
> My image cannot trick me anymore.
> I burn with love for my own self; it's I
> who light the flames—the flames that scorch me then.
> What shall I do? Shall I be sought or seek?

As he cries, his tears temporarily erase the image, as his plunging arms will later do so once again. But this is no mirror whose shattering would destroy the image forever. The turbulence settles, the image reappears. Watery reflections, as Bachelard tells us, are like flowers growing in the water; they are not simply replications, they shift, they move, they disappear and reappear.[3]

Narcissus gets it, and doesn't. He turns away, death seems the only way out of the impossible situation. But then he realizes, "With death my pain will end, and yet I'd have my love live past my death. Instead we two will die together in one breath."

Strangely, it is through seeing his own reflection that Narcissus is for the first time made aware of real otherness. He cannot bear that his departure would mean the other's, the image's, death. Reflecting on the reflection takes him out of his self-absorption, not more deeply into it.

Narcissus imagines the other reaching toward him with love, as keen to be embraced. He longs for the other's longing, he dreams of mutuality. As Pygmalion will later dream of mutuality when he gazes upon the statue he has made. Desire, it seems, may always be inspired by an image.

The longing for mutuality enters here as a new theme in Ovid's epic—though not in his poetry, for his early love elegies celebrated the importance of shared pleasure in love as they also revealed how the beloved is always in a sense a fiction, created by the lover's imagination.[4]

Narcissus sees that both moving too eagerly toward and leaving destroy the image.

So he returns, back to the image. And stays, wasting away with love. Almost gone, he cries "Farewell" to the image—and Echo, reappearing, answers back, "Farewell" to him. And when his water nymph sisters come to bury him they find in place of his body, a flower, the white petalled narcissus with which we began.

But Narcissus is still gazing at his image in the pool of Styx, in the underworld. All along Ovid has spoken of the image as *imago* and as *umbra,* words used to describe the soul. Now Narcissus is a soul himself, *imago* and *umbra.* Soul gazing upon soul, image reflected by image.

Hillman is right.[5] Narcissus experiences the image as *real* and is in a sense fulfilled by the image, has come to realize that gazing upon it is enough. It's no longer illusion but *image.* Kristeva says that the object of Narcissus's love is an image,[6] a fantasy, and that if he *knew* that he would be Hölderlin or Freud. But perhaps he does.

* * * * *

So there was the word and the flower and the story about the boy and his image.

And then there was the idea.

And then the story of the idea.

One which we tend to read backwards—as though the idea was always the one purveyed by the *DSM*: that narcissism is a pathology, a personality disorder characterized by arrogance, exploitation, grandiosity and entitlement, by an excessive need for admiration, by a lack of empathy.

But that's not an IDEA in a depth psychological sense, in Giegerich's sense. For that we have to go to Freud. We go to Freud to recover the possibilities opened up by his reflections on the idea, not to read him in the light of what we believe he must have been saying.

When the term narcissism was introduced into psychology by Havelock Ellis, he used it as a synonym for auto-eroticism in its most literal sense: masturbation. (It does seem strange that this first use was about achieving sexual satisfaction through looking and touching one's own body—when in the myth it's such a big issue that Narcissus couldn't touch what he desired and saw only the face.) But then Freud's use of the word brought some of the full richness of Ovid's telling of the myth into psychology, particularly the close association between narcissism and death, though it is important to note that he nowhere explicitly refers to the myth.

As so often LaPlanche and Pontalis's *The Language of Psychoanalysis* helps us trace the story. Freud's first uses the term "narcissism" in 1910 to account for homosexuals taking themselves as their love object: "They look for a young man who resembles themselves and whom they may love as their mother loved them." Without ever directly evoking the myth Freud reminds us of the homoerotic aspect of Narcissus' desiring gaze.

Freud uses the word again in 1911 (in the Schreber case history) for a *stage* in sexual development between auto-eroticism (a stage where there's not yet a sense of having a unified body-ego) and object-love—an intermediate stage where one takes oneself as love-object. Here he also suggests that psychotics may be immured in this stage, may have withdrawn libido from the external world so wholly that they are unable to develop transference in the analytic context.

But in his 1914 paper "On Narcissism"[7] he moves toward a much more complex and richer understanding, one that sees narcissism in structural not just developmental terms and takes it out of a pathological context so that it becomes a descriptive, clearly not a deprecating, term. (Though as always with Freud the more exaggerated manifestations open him to the universal normal ones.)

So he begins by talking about *secondary narcissism,* about the withdrawal of libido from object back to self, a withdrawal of libido from others, even imaginal ones, as a way of introducing us to *primary narcissism*—by which he means that early pre-psychical, pre-verbal stage in which there is no self and no other. This stage exists only in memory, in fantasy, only for the imagination—only afterwards—for consciousness begins with the experience of separation and loss. As self and other are co-created there arise the twin possibilities of self-love and other-love. Originally, Freud says, we humans have two love objects—our mothers and our selves. The Oedipus myth expresses the soul meaning of one, Narcissus of the other.

This primary narcissism represents an earlier, more original stage than Oedipal love; it arises in response to the separation between what is not yet an ego and not yet an object. It arises out of a longing to deny the loss, the dependency, the neediness, out of a longing to claim a self-sufficiency. It represents the fantasy that separation is not the ultimate truth, that to begin with we were whole in ourselves and at one with the world. There is always nostalgia for that imaginal "before." Primary narcissism is poised at that liminal moment between before and after and so for Freud always remains a "border concept." The domain explored by psychoanalysis is psychical experience; anything earlier is outside. Our initial turn to an other expresses our impossible longing for this other to give us back that lost wholeness. It is really an expression of fusion longing, expresses a desire to *be,* not to *have.*

Only after the full acknowledgment of the loss, only after what Freud calls the work of mourning, does there really arise the possibility of turning to other as other, as a genuinely separate other with his or her own desires which are not just for me. Only, we might say, when we acknowledge the existence of a rival, admit that the mother does not exist only in relation to us, only as we enter the Oedipal world, does the possibility of real loving, of Eros, emerge.

For from the outset consciousness entails a departure from primary narcissism, a transfer of some of the love that might be directed toward ourselves to another. Some of the originally undifferentiated libido is directed to the self, some to others. Often we may try somehow to have it both ways, to love someone who reminds us of ourselves, or of our earlier selves, or of our ideal selves. We are also likely to over-estimate the beloved in order to make up for the forfeited self-love—and of course we also demand to be loved back to recover that lost self-love. And when we aren't loved, there is always an enormous temptation to entirely withdraw libido from the outer world and thus fall into "secondary narcissism."

But this, Freud reminds us, is too simple. Secondary narcissism as self-love can't be understood as independent of relationships with others, but rather as an internalization of them. For elsewhere Freud speaks of our becoming selves only gradually, by way of a series of identifications through which we acquire an *image* of ourselves. In his 1917 essay, "Mourning and Melancholia," Freud sees loss as central to the formation of the identifications that form the ego. Lost beloved others are incorporated and imaginally preserved in and as the ego: "The ego is a precipitate of abandoned object-cathexes and contains the history of those object-choices."[8] We are our losses, including the loss of an autonomy we never had. We are but the images of those we've loved—and they? Images, too, of lost beloveds. Image reflecting image. On and on. . .

At first in the essay on narcissism Freud seems to be trying to clarify a distinction between object-libido and ego-libido, between love of the anaclitic/attachment [Oedipal] type and narcissistic love. But by the end of the essay we see it's not so simple: all object-love has a narcissistic aspect. "No matter how it looks even in adults not all ego-libido is turned to others," he says, and a bit further on, "In a real happy love one can't distinguish object libido and ego libido."

By the end of his 1917 essay the initial distinction between mourning and melancholia is deeply problematized. For Freud has come to realize that "melancholia" (unfinished grieving over a never fully nameable loss) is an inescapable part of human life. Since—although in "mourning" the loss is supposedly conscious—the most recent grief always stirs up memories of the never fully grieved losses that precede it, and especially the ungrievable primal loss, of the mother, of one's own wholeness.

Similarly Freud has here in the narcissism essay radically problematized the distinction between object love and narcissism.

Freud's dip into this theme sets in motion ripples that will engage him for the next decade. These early reflections on narcissism lead him to the first hints of what will eventually become the *UeberIch* (superego) in the fully developed structural theory of the 1923 *Ego and the Id*. For he already notes how narcissistic libido is directed toward an "ego ideal," a kind of substitute for the early megalomania when one saw oneself as perfect and whole. Obviously this "ideal'" is an *image:* we love our image of ourselves or of our past or hoped-for selves.

And although Freud has also not yet introduced the notion of the *Es* (id), *the* primary narcissism of this essay is a clear prelude to his later understanding of the primitive psychic stage that precedes the ego's differentiation from the id. He is already writing of a primary undifferentiated energy that "fundamentally persists and is related to the object-cathexes as the body of an amoeba is related to the pseudopodia which it puts out."

Freud's explicit naming of the death drive is also some years away, but he already senses how the self-love of narcissism is death wish. For Freud narcissism is in a sense an illusion; we are in a world with others; we are not self-sufficient, we are not the world. And thus narcissism is death. But it is also true that the narcissistic longings never die. For we all long to return to that earlier fantasized world where self and other were one, all long to believe that separation is not the ultimate truth. Eros is the long way round back to narcissism, to death; Eros is an *aufhebung* of narcissism, its overcoming *and* its continuation by other means. Incest love is already a substitute, but it is life, and then *its* renunciations that lead us toward other substitutes. But they are substitutes. The deeper longing is not erotic but narcissistic—to be free of object love, complete in one.

* * * * *

Freud wrote his paper on narcissism in response to Lou Salomé's urging that he put together reflections that had emerged in their discussions during the year she spent in Vienna. When he sends a copy of it to her she writes him that this essay and its recognition that there is a "good" narcissism has confirmed her commitment to psychoanalysis—and that her own understanding of narcissism, though connected to his, is also significantly different in its emphases.

The journal she kept of her 1912-13 stay in Vienna[9] makes evident that her interest in narcissism, in the role of self-love in love, long antedates her involvement with Freud. Lou came to narcissism independently by way of her reflections on women, love and God—whereas Freud came to it in initially by way of reflections on the difference between neurotics and psychotics. (The year Lou spent in Vienna was the year Freud was working on the Schreber case.)

In her earlier writings Lou says that for women the aim of love is to expand the self, not to reach toward a distant separate other as a romantic man does in his pursuit of the ever-desirable because unattainable woman. Because she begins with a conviction that self and world first exist in a kind of primal union, she is from the outset unwilling to agree to Freud's attempt to clearly distinguish between narcissism and eros, between self love and object love. She believes the separation never fully occurs and understands all object-love as the rediscovery of a lost part of oneself (as Aristophanes had suggested in Plato's *Symposium.*)

Her journal reports on the discussions about narcissism in the 1913 meetings of the Wednesday Evening Group and Lou's reservations even then. She writes that she would want to insist that the narcissist doesn't want to swallow the other; rather, his defect is that "his own love's outburst nearly suffices for him." The other is almost incidental to his enjoying his own loving; he feels gratitude to the other for being the occasion of this experience. She writes of a first narcissism (a universal developmental stage to be transcended) and a second (a later neurotic self-infatuation) and says that finally, a third and beautiful narcissism appears:

No longer just a stage to be transcended; it is rather the persistent accompaniment of all our deeper experience, always present, yet still far beyond any possibility of hewing its way from consciousness into the unconscious. In narcissism the Ucs. still exists only *en bloc*, the primordial form not simply of a foundation but of the all-inclusive.

When (back home in Göttingen) Lou receives Freud's "On Narcissism," she writes him a long four-page letter.[10] She says again that what she most values about this aspect of Freud's thinking—and what she sees makes him, unlike Adler, a *depth* psychologist—is the recognition that the ego is not a given, but emerges from a pre-egoic libido.

Lou's role in persuading Freud to write his piece, her enthusiastic but thoughtful response, his in turn urging her to elaborate that response in a publishable essay, her eventually doing so—help us see how their depth psychological understanding of narcissism emerges out of an ongoing erotic dialogue between them.

In her letter Lou tells Freud that she'd like to call what he calls "primary" narcissism *true* narcissism; she wants to emphasize that this pre-differentiated state (*not* taking oneself as a love-object) is "real" narcissism. She writes of the naïve full-immersion of an artist in his work as a kind of *self-less* creative narcissism. She also understands those (rare) moments—which she believes most often occur in a sexual context—when we feel ourselves to be wholly *at one* with our body, those moments when we *are* body rather than *having* one, as being experiences of this true narcissism.

She insists: narcissism is liminal; one is still affiliated at the roots even when already on the way to self/other discrimination. So Narcissus lingers; he doesn't flee, even when he understands.

In 1921 after a long incubation Lou publishes her own essay, "The Dual Orientation of Narcissism"[11] in which she writes: "We remain embedded in our original narcissism for all our development, as the plants remain in the earth despite their contrary growth toward the light."

She identifies narcissism with a primary undifferentiation; it is too simple to reduce narcissism to self-love. "I want to bring out its other aspect—the persistent feeling of identity with the totality." She speaks of "the primal hurt of all of us—the uncomprehending self-abasement of becoming an individual." Narcissism is the connecting link between the desire for fusion and for individuality. You love another as though he were the world, as you loved yourself—and she relates this love of the whole to the love of God.

Our overvaluation of those we love represents an attempt to make them a substitute for that All. For Lou all love objects are transferences from that original All. She sees our overvaluing of those we love as a blessing, a gift. We enrich the other with our fantasies, if we know that is what we're doing. She speaks of transference when consciously engaged in by lovers or artists as '"festive adornment." There is joyous aspect to this: "We live with ourselves and with the world more fully."

Unlike Freud, Lou Salomé returns directly to the myth and reminds us that Narcissus was not looking into a manmade pool, but into a pool in a natural setting. "The Narcissus of legend gazed not at a manmade mirror but at the mirror of nature." Not just his own face and body but also the trees were reflected in that pool. For her the scene represents a delighted-in experience of total union with the natural world—or, rather, the vision of it. Narcissus "saw himself as if he were all—otherwise he would have fled."

"There is a kind of narcissism that is an experience of being wholly at one with the world, not just absorbed in oneself …. Narcissism is in its creative form no longer just a stage to be transcended; it is rather the persistent accompaniment of all our deeper experience."

"What Narcissus sees is not the trees themselves but their *images,* the world as image."

We've come a long way from that flower, that pool, that boy—but wasn't all of this always already there?

NOTES

[1] William S. Anderson, *Ovid's Metamorphoses: Books 1-5* (Norman: University of Oklahoma Press, 1997), 373-388.

² Most of my quotes and close paraphrases from Ovid are from the translation by Allen Mandelbaum, *The Metamorphoses of Ovid* (New York: Harcourt Brace, 1993). But I have also consulted the Latin text and prose translation in the Loeb Classical Library's edition (Cambridge: Harvard University Press, 1984).

³ Gaston Bachelard, *Water and Dreams* (Dallas: The Dallas Institute, 1983), 24.

⁴ Later in the poem, when Ovid comes to write of Cephalus and Procris, Baucis and Philemon, Ceyx and Alcyone, he will provide images of genuinely passionate sustained reciprocal love, though these loves, too, will mostly end in suffering.

⁵ James Hillman, *The Dream and the Underworld* (New York: HarperCollins, 1979), 119.

⁶ Julia Kristeva, "Freud and Love," in Kelly Oliver, ed., *The Portable Kristeva* (New York: Columbia University Press, 1997), 147.

⁷ Sigmund Freud, "On Narcissism: An Introduction," in James Strachey, ed., *The Standard Edition of the Complete Psychological Works of Sigmund Freud* (London: Hogarth Press, 1953-1974), Vol. XIV, 73-102.

⁸ Sigmund Freud, "Mourning and Melancholia," in James Strachey, ed., *The Standard Edition of the Complete Psychological Works of Sigmund Freud* (London, Hogarth Press, 1953-1974), Vol. XIV, 248-259.

⁹ Lou Andreas-Salomé, *The Freud Journal* (New York: Basic Books, 1964), especially 109, 110.

¹⁰ Ernst Pfeifer, *Sigmund Freud and Lou Andreas-Salomé: Letters* (New York: Harcourt, Brace, Jovanovich, 1972), 22-26.

¹¹ Lou Andreas-Salomé, "The Dual Orientation of Narcissism," (originally in *Imago* 1921), *Psychoanalytic Quarterly XXXI* 1962, 1-30.

"Yes, But Who is Going to Convince the Chicken?": Meditations on the 'Inside' and the 'Outside'

Robert D. Romanyshyn

When this title first came to me, while standing in one of those interminable lines that are one of the hallmarks of bureaucracy, I had no idea about how this title would, or even could, fit the content. But I liked the title and where it came from, a Lacanian joke that I have heard David Miller tell on several public occasions. Anyone who has ever seen and heard David at the podium knows that it is always and unfailingly an unforgettable experience, rich in scholarly content and laced with that kind of easy confidence that inspires an image—at least for me—of a Johnny Carson of the depths, or I would like to say a Johnny Carson who keeps 'soul in mind,' a phrase that once also came to me while 'on line'—see how the phrase has crept into our lives—and of which I am quite fond. So I was caught by the title, trusting that it was a gift of sorts from that complex domain where our insights, intuitions and nightmares are born. And who am I to refuse such a gift? Who is anyone of us to do so? Anyway, there is an energy that collects around this gift and, as it has happened so often before for me, these 'gifts' become a vessel of sorts where ideas, images, intuitions, and feelings stew. I only have to wait, trust and be patient, the last one—patience—being a virtue that serves one well while 'on line.'

"WHO IS GOING TO CONVINCE THE CHICKEN?"

And then, sometime later, the connection between title and content came. My article for this *Festschrift* in honor of David is a meditation on the inside and the outside, for it was in the talk where I most recently heard the joke that David said it was absolutely necessary to rethink the logic of the inside and the outside. I guess in a way this meditation is the best gift I can offer because it is a place where his remark—an invitation—meets one of my enduring passions.

Before I begin, however, I have to tell you the joke, or at least summarize it in order to link title and content. It goes something like this. "A crazy man believed that he was a grain of wheat and so he had a fear of chickens. The psychiatrists convinced him that he was not a grain of wheat. But he came running back to the clinic, having encountered a chicken. The doctors said, 'But didn't we convince you that you were not a grain of wheat'? 'Yes,' he said, 'but who is going to convince the chicken?'"[1]

What is the logic of the inside and the outside for this crazy man? The theory of projection explains it. Its explanation, however, assumes a split between the man who is a grain of wheat and the world where chickens are and can be encountered. It assumes that there is an inside and an outside that are disconnected, a mind space, if you will, that has nothing to do with the material space of the world. The theory of projection reconnects what has been severed. Furthermore, the theory assumes that the inside shapes the outside. The man is a grain of wheat. Of that he is convinced. He believes it. That is his world and in this world a chicken is a danger. And this is how we know he is crazy and would definitely not make a good dinner companion. One man's danger is another man's delicacy!

A phenomenology of embodied perception saves the experience of projection but puts it on a better philosophical base. The man who is a grain of wheat lives a different existence. He lives in a different world. If I go the market with this man and we see a chicken it is clear that the same thing is paradoxically different. His perspective and mine do not agree, but we do agree that we are encountering the 'same' thing—a chicken! How can there be one chicken that is also two? We see the same thing but for the crazy man the chicken mirrors back to him that he is a grain of wheat, while it might mirror back to me the image of the dinner party I am planning for some friends later this evening. His world is one of isolation and anxiety, whereas mine reflects one of friendship and conviviality. His projection is a description of his world and I know this man because I know the world in which he is living. He tells me about himself, which is so much more than knowing he is crazy, by describing his world. My very dear and old friend and mentor J.H. van den Berg would say it this way—he or she who would know the other's experience must know the landscape in which that other dwells.

A phenomenology of embodied experience revisions projection as a matter of mirroring. In this mirroring the world, including others, reflects who we are so that we should say that the other is my 'inside' as much as I am the 'inside' for the other. Through your behavior I see my experience as you see reflected in my behavior an image of your experience. Without this other, without this mutual mirror play we would not know who we are. I count on others to give me back to myself as they also count on me. And when we do a phenomenology of the mirror experience we discover that the mirror reflection is not a duplicate of oneself, as if the mirror was some kind of Xerox machine that makes copies of who I am. On the contrary, a phenomenology of the mirror experience reveals that the mirror, including the mirror of the other, is a deepening of who I am as well as a refiguring of who I am. In the face of the mirror I find myself as a figure in a tale. The anorexic who looks in a mirror sees someone who is too overweight and the whole realm of food reflects back to her a danger not so unlike the man who is a grain of wheat and for whom the chicken is a danger. Both are projecting to be sure, but the projections do not arise from some inside psychological space. The projections arise between each of them and the world that each encounters. The implication here is that the unconscious is a lateral depth. The unconscious is between us. The therapist in this respect is the patient's unconscious.

Note the last sentence and specifically the word 'is.' What does it mean to say that the therapist is the patient's unconscious? Let us take a specific case, which I draw from Jung. In his essay "The Transcendent

Function" Jung notes that the task of an analyst is to mediate the transcendent function by bringing together the conscious and unconscious of the patient. In so doing the analyst takes on the "character of an indispensable figure absolutely necessary for life." In this respect the relation between patient and analyst often seems to repeat the relation between the child and the parent, and Jung notes that there is a tendency to understand this transference relation only in this reductive fashion. He argues, however, that such a reductive reading amounts to taking the fantasy/projection literally. The analyst then is not 'like' the parent; he or she 'is' the parent and this 'is' is an identification. The simile of which the patient could be conscious has become a fact of which the patient is unconscious.

But this way of putting things is still not sufficient because the patient's experience of the analyst is not a simile. The analyst 'is' the parent, just like the crazy man 'is' a grain of wheat in a world of dangerous chickens. He does not say to his psychiatrist, "I am like a grain of wheat." He says he 'is.' So, again, how do we understand this 'is' that also seems to be an 'is not'? Jung is very clear here. The patient's fantasy/projection of the analyst as a parent is a "metaphoric expression of the not consciously realized need for help in a crisis."[2] This metaphoric 'is' is an identity and a difference and in this difference there is a slippage of meaning that leaves the field between them open to other possibilities. Meaning is not fixed and indeed in its metaphoric character meaning is as it were postponed until further notice. The metaphoric 'is' that is also an 'is not' is an allusion to meaning that remains elusive.

A phenomenology of embodiment restores self to other and world in a relation of mirroring in which projection can be understood as an unconscious metaphor. Thus the analyst who mediates the transcendent function facilitates a shift in consciousness from one that is literal to one that is metaphoric, and the symbol, which is the expression of the transcendent function, requires this metaphoric sensibility.

But what does a metaphoric sensibility have to do with the logic of the inside and the outside, which was the starting point of this essay? Over the years I have written about this matter in some detail beginning in 1982 with my first book, *Psychological Life: From Science to Metaphor.* When this book was being prepared for republication in 2001 I asked David Miller to write a new Foreword. I did so because I could think of no one who would be better suited to consider my argument that a metaphoric sensibility is the logic of the soul that dissolves the dualism of an inside and an outside. He had, after all, written that splendid article in 1989 on the stone in alchemy which is not a stone, and if I, as a psychologist who had initially come to this position in 1982 via phenomenology and not Jung's psychology, wanted a Jungian response to it who better than David to do it? Metaphor, I knew from my early studies, refigures the place of meaning and David had written in his article that "If alchemy, in Jung's own view, is the clue to the nature of the logic of his psychological discourse...then a radical transformation of the meaning of so-called 'meaning' is implied in the mature texts of C.G. Jung."[3] On this occasion of his *Festschrift* then it seems quite fitting that we meet at this intersection of the inside and the outside where in addition phenomenology and Jung's psychology meet, and where, I would add, thinking pushes forward toward a phenomenological depth psychology that, like alchemy, is an elemental psychology. This elemental psychology in which matter mirrors soul is alchemy with awareness, a discipline whose metaphoric sensibility makes conscious what is unconscious in alchemy.

I want to return now to the issue of the place of meaning in metaphor in order to show how a metaphoric sensibility does dissolve the dualism of inside/outside.

A metaphor is mirror play. It reflects one thing through something else and in that relation of reflection not only is the meaning of each thing deepened and refigured, but also meaning itself is displaced from either being on the inside as a matter of mind or the outside as a matter of fact. Moreover, as meaning is displaced in this way the logic of identity, which says that something is what it is in itself apart from other things, is dissolved in a logic of difference, which says that something is what it is because it is not what it is. Take for example the statement a purple finch is a sparrow dipped in raspberry juice. Certainly this is not a fact and, if in a fit of empirical frenzy one were to grab in one's garden a purple finch, one's hands would not drip with juice. But neither is it an idea. As Howard Nemerov who uses this example indicates, it was this metaphor from a field guide for birds that convinced him that he was seeing a purple finch in his garden. The metaphor opened his eyes as it were in a way that the purely factual description of the bird did not. Through the metaphor a world was envisioned. Through the metaphor a vision, a way of seeing, was born.

Neither a fact outside in the world to be seen nor an idea inside of mind to be thought, neither a thing nor a thought, the meaning of the metaphor belongs neither to Nemerov nor the bird. It erupts between them in a kind of con-spiracy we might say that allows them to in-spire each other. The metaphor is a perspective and within that perspective the purple finch offers itself as a sparrow dipped in raspberry juice. In doing so both sparrows and purple finches are dissolved as they are reflected through each other. In this dissolution of their separate identities a metaphor, I would suggest, is a piece of alchemy. An interesting consequence of this view is that the poet is kin to the alchemist.

The alchemy of metaphor makes the metaphor of alchemy most suitable to describe the perceptual world of embodied life. The perceptual world is a tissue of metaphors in which things reflect, deepen, refigure and displace each other. It is a tissue of metaphors in which things are displaced from a logic of identity to a logic of difference. Merleau-Ponty makes this quite clear in one of his last essays "Eye and Mind" where he argues that the achievement of painting does not lie in its ability to represent the world as it is for profane vision. Rather, he says, the achievement of painting is that "It gives visible existence to what profane vision believes to be invisible."

To indicate what profane vision forgets Merleau-Ponty offers the following example. Looking at some water in a pool, it is clear, he notes, that it is over there in the pool. That is beyond doubt and if I wish to swim in that water, that is its location. But Merleau-Ponty also says that it is equally clear that the water is not contained there because "if I raise my eyes toward the screen of cypresses where the web of reflections is playing, I cannot gainsay the fact that the water visits it, too, or at least sends into it, upon it, its active and living essence." What profane vision ignores or forgets or discounts are these reflections, which indicate that the water is in the pool because it is also not in the pool, that the water is in the pool because it is also in the trees. It is in Merleau-Ponty's words this "radiation of the visible," this "dehiscence," this bursting or splitting of the ripened visible, this "system of exchanges" that profane vision believes does not matter.[4] It is this relation of reflection, this relation of mirroring in which a thing is that which it is by virtue of the others that surround it, that profane vision dismisses.

Mediating on this same theme of the visible and its radiations Jose Ortega Y Gasset says, "How unimportant a thing would be if it were only what it is in isolation." Contrary to this isolation he adds, "there is in each thing, a certain latent potentiality to be many other things, which is set free and expands when other things come into contact with it." Warming to this insight he continues, "one might say that each thing is fertilized by the others; that they desire each other as male and female; that they love each other and aspire to unite, to collect in communities, in worlds." When we open our eyes it seems, he says, that things "expand, stretch, and break up like a gaseous mass torn by a gust of wind." But gradually the world stabilizes and there is a "settling down and focusing of the outlines that results from our attention." But this moment of looking directly at things, this moment of focused attention, de-animates them. With patience, however, and with a less focused kind of look, a thing slowly becomes "more clearly perceived because we keep finding in it more reflections of and connections with the surrounding things." In this moment Ortega says we know the depth of something, "what there is in it of reflection of other things, allusion to other things." For Ortega something matters because of this depth, because of these allusions to other things. Hence, it is never sufficient, he concludes, "to have the material body of a thing. I need, besides, to know its meaning, that is to say, the mystic shadow which the rest of the universe casts upon it."[5]

Profane vision forgets this alchemy of the natural world, this circuit of reflections that includes us. A phenomenology of embodied experience remembers it and describes it as a tissue of metaphors. In taking us beyond the dualism of inside/outside, a metaphoric sensibility situates us in a field of relations that, like alchemy, is beyond either/or thinking. In this regard I would argue that phenomenology's recovery of the metaphoric character of embodied life is a recovery of alchemy. I would repeat my earlier remark that phenomenology is, or at least can be, alchemy with awareness. In an edited volume of some of Jung's writings on alchemy Nathan Schwarz-Salant leans toward this conjunction of alchemy and phenomenology. He writes, "Alchemy is an old science, but also a new science that is only now beginning to unfold. It reflects upon the mystery of *relations* between things, and upon one's relationship to the cosmos."[6]

The metaphoric sensibility that phenomenology cultivates also makes one ready to appreciate Jung's struggle to reframe alchemy as a way of thinking and being that is beyond projection and its assumption of an inside psychological space and the outside material world. In *Psychology and Alchemy*, for example, he states:

> ...it always remains an obscure point whether the ultimate transformations in the alchemical process ought to be sought more in the material or more in the spiritual realm. Actually, however, the question is wrongly put; there was no 'either-or' for that age, but there did exist an intermediate realm between mind and matter, i.e., a psychic realm of subtle bodies whose characteristic it is to manifest themselves in mental as well as material form. This is the only view that makes sense of alchemical ways of thought, which must otherwise appear non-sensical.[7]

So where has the crazy man in Lacan's joke led us? To his question of who is going to tell the chicken we have replied that Jung will, that the alchemist of old will and that the phenomenologist will. In the space of his question they come together. A metaphoric sensibility takes us beyond the inside/outside dichotomy, and in his reply to my request for a Foreword for the republication of my first book regarding the metaphorical character of psychological life, David Miller supported this view. He spoke of the radicality of metaphoricity and wrote that it "underscores a subversion of interior and exterior binarism." Commenting on the common tendency to think that psychology is interior and subjective, he said, "it is often imagined that the inside and outside of the self are in opposition or are split off from one another, so that when I am 'inside' myself I am not at that moment dealing with what is 'outside.'" With metaphor "there is no 'outside' that is not always and already 'inside,' and vice versa." Metaphor sets up "a space of simultaneity, a reciprocal arc," a circuit of reflections.[8]

I was and I remain grateful for these comments because, as for all of us, a colleague's understanding of one's work assuages the loneliness of thinking. To think that the turn to metaphor is or can be an epistemological revolution has always been for me something of a crazy notion. And, indeed, now at the end of my essay I must confess that I feel somewhat like the crazy man in Lacan's joke. I have my own version of his question about the chicken. In fact it is a series of questions.

In his quote about alchemy Jung speaks about the subtle body world that is beyond either/or ways of thinking. Is a metaphoric sensibility enough for an appreciation of this subtle world, a psycho-physical background world that Jung calls an '*unus mundus*'? Is it enough to have a metaphoric sensibility, which appreciates neither/nor thinking, or is the subtle body world of the '*unus mundus*' an ontological surprise that goes beyond our capacity for metaphor?

In his working notes to his last project, Merleau-Ponty is rethinking the Husserlian project of phenomenology to return to the things themselves. Focusing on language he notes the necessity for a language of which we are not the organizer, a language "where what counts is no longer the manifest meaning of each word and each image, but the lateral relations, the kinships that are implicated in their transfers and their exchanges."[9] Merleau-Ponty is speaking here of metaphorical language and he is suggesting that its powers lie in the capacity to shift meaning away from us toward itself, as if language is not just a means but a being in itself. He is suggesting, I believe, a sense of language in which we are not so much the authors as the agents of meaning.

But if not the author of language and meaning, then the return to the things themselves becomes a bit problematic. How do we know that what we are saying is faithful to what wants to be spoken? The poet Rilke knew this dilemma. At the end of the Ninth Elegy he asks what the Earth wants of us. Is it its dream to one day be invisible? But how? Through us, through language through the alchemy of the spoken word that breathes life into matter! A bit earlier in the elegy he has asked what the wanderer brings back from the mountain slope. It is not a handful of earth. No, what he brings back to his valley is "some word he has won, a pure word, the yellow and blue/gentian." And then in a passage that marks the holy terror of this power, that underscores the awful responsibility of responding to this dream of the earth, Rilke says: "Are we, perhaps, here just for saying: House,/Bridge, Fountain, Gate, Jug, Olive tree, Window—/possibly: pillar, Tower?"[10]

There is, perhaps, no passage in poetry apart from the one word— "Who?"—, which Eurydice softly speaks to Hermes after Orpheus has turned and the God has told her, to match this moment when we are stopped dead in our tracks and forced to turn around to question what seems to be our sacred right and our sole power and possession—to say things, to speak, to proclaim what is. *Perhaps* we are here for saying these things! Already some hesitation has entered, enough to make us pause. And then after the recital of those simple things this other caution— *possibly*: Pillar, Tower? He is not sure. Are the words adequate to what asks to be dreamed into language? Are they faithful? Another poet, Eliot speaks to the same anxiety: "Words strain,/Crack and sometimes break, under the burden,/Under the tension, slip, slide, perish,/Decay with imprecision, will not stay in place,/Will not stay still."[11]

What is this restlessness of language in its struggle with meaning, in its struggle to return to the things themselves? Language seems to have two powers: the power to dream the world into being and the power to betray it. Hence Merleau-Ponty says, "It is by considering language that we would best see how we are to and how we are not to return to the things themselves."[12]

I am asking here if a metaphoric sensibility is adequate to the task of dreaming into being the reality of the subtle world. In his essay "Taboo and Metaphor," Ortega Y Gasset argues that "metaphor is perhaps one of man's most fruitful potentialities. Its efficacy verges on magic," he writes, "and it seems a tool for creation which God forgot inside one of His creatures when he made him." But while Ortega is suggesting here that the capacity for metaphor is the trace of the God left within us, he also draws with approval upon the work of an early twentieth century psychologist, Heinz Werner, who in his search for the origin of metaphor "discovered to his surprise that one of its roots lies in the spirit of the taboo."[13] In this context, a metaphor is a way of avoiding a particular reality. It is the art and means of evasion.

Metaphor as taboo! Metaphor as the art of evasion! Metaphor as the residual spark of the god left within us through which we might participate in the ongoing work of creation! This is a holy tension and might we wonder here if the logos of metaphor is a way of denying metaphor's awesome numinosity. In like manner might we also wonder if the logos of metaphor is a hysterical defense against the ontological shock of the subtle body world that Jung explored in his visions and studies of UFOs, and in his studies of alchemy and synchronicity, and which Veronica Goodchild is extending in her forthcoming book *The Songlines of the Soul,* where she makes a radical case for the ontological difference of the subtle world and raises questions about the path of metaphor. Do we, even with an awareness of our metaphors, which is an absolute necessity, still imprison the subtle world of alchemy that Jung is speaking about in epistemological strategies that ward off the ontological demands that the subtle body world makes? Maybe a metaphoric sensibility gets us ready for this surprise, but in the face of the epiphanies of the subtle world is this sensibility sufficient?

Perhaps in getting us to the threshold of the subtle world a metaphoric sensibility is about the dis-solution of the meanings that language makes and not about the meanings as a solution, and in this there lies perhaps the true alchemy of metaphor. Perhaps its true alchemy lies not in the visible 'is' of metaphor but in its invisible 'is not.' In this regard maybe what most matters about metaphor is not the meaning to which it alludes but to the open space that remains elusive, making the evasion of metaphor an act of liberation. Perhaps the most important thing about a metaphoric sensibility is that it allows us to embrace our ignorance with awareness and allows us never to confuse what we know with the fullness of what is. And in this regard perhaps in the end a metaphoric sensibility is the negative capability that John Keats described as the art "of being in uncertainties, Mysteries, doubts, without any irritable reaching after fact and reason."[14]

But where do these questions and speculations leave us? Maybe, to borrow the title of one of David's essays, we are left in that place where we have "Nothing to Teach! No Way to Teach It! Together with the Obligation to Teach!"[15] That lecture is a critique of the imposition of the language of assessment and accountability onto those realms of human experience that cannot be counted but which nevertheless do count. And in defense of that realm we are called to speak however much we might fail. Or maybe, to borrow the title of one of my own articles, we are left in that place where "Psychology is Useless; Or, It Should Be." That essay is a sustained meditation on Jung's long struggle with the poet and an apology for the language of psychology to be "as useless as a dream, as practical as a fantasy, as helpful as a moment of reverie."[16] Or maybe we are left in that place that the poet Rilke describes in his *Duino Elegies*, which begin so beautifully with the question, "Who, if I cried, would hear me among the Angelic/ orders?" A few lines later Rilke has already taken the measure of that distance between the Angel whose Beauty is "but beginning of Terror we're still just able to bear" and this home of ours where "already the knowing brutes are aware/that we don't feel very securely at home/within our interpreted world."[17]

To these questions I have no answers. They simply upend a journey that I have been on and return me to its starting point. I can think of no other way to truly honor my colleague David Miller on this occasion of his *Festschrift* than to offer him these questions and speculations because in the end what makes him an exemplary colleague is this challenge to let go of your thought for the sake of thinking, even when you know that thinking at its best must end in the silence where it began.

NOTES

[1] David L. Miller, "Holy and Not So Holy Ghosts," Lecture Notes, IAAP/IAJS Conference, Texas A&M University, July 8, 2005.

[2] C.G. Jung, "The Transcendent Function," *The Structure and Dynamics of the Psyche, The Collected Works of C.G. Jung, Vol. 8*, trans. R.F.C. Hull (Princeton University Press, 1960), § 146.

[3] David L. Miller, "The 'Stone' Which Is Not A Stone: C.G. Jung and the Postmodern Meaning of 'Meaning,'" *Spring 49: A Journal of Archetype and Culture,*" (1989): 115.

[4] Maurice Merleau-Ponty, *The Primacy of Perception* (Evanston: Northwestern University Press, 1964), 166, 182, 164.

[5] Jose Ortega y Gasset, *Meditations on Quixote* (New York: W.W. Norton & Company, 1961), 88-89.

[6] Nathan Schwartz-Salant, *Encountering Jung on Alchemy* (Princeton: Princeton University Press, 1995), 19.

[7] C.G. Jung, *Psychology and Alchemy, The Collected Works of C.G. Jung, Vol. 12*, trans. R.F.C. Hull (Princeton University Press, 1953), par. 394.

[8] David L. Miller, "Foreword" to Robert D. Romanyshyn's *Mirror and Metaphor: Images and Stories of Psychological Life* (Pittsburgh: Trivium Publications, 2001), xiv-xv.

[9] Maurice Merleau-Ponty, *The Visible and the Invisible*, trans. Alphonso Lingis (Evanston: Northwestern University Press, 1968), 125.

[10] Rainer Maria Rilke, *Duino Elegies*, trans. J.B. Leishman and Stephen Spender (New York: W.W. Norton & Company, 1939), 75.

[11] T.S. Eliot, *Four Quartets* (New York: Harcourt, Brace and Company, 1943), 7-8.

[12] Merleau-Ponty, *ibid.*

[13] Jose Ortega Y Gasset, *The Dehumanization of Art* (Princeton: Princeton University Press, 1948), 33-34.

[14] John Keats, *The Complete Poems*, ed. John Barnard (New York: Penguin, 1973), 539.

[15] David L. Miller, "Nothing to Teach! No Way to Teach It! Together with the Obligation to Teach!" http://web.utk.edu/~unistudy/values/ethics98/miller.htm.

[16] Robert D. Romanyshyn, "Psychology is Useless; Or It Should Be," *Ways of the Heart: Essays Toward an Imaginal Psychology* (Pittsburgh: Trivium Publications, 2002), 131.

[17] Rainer Maria Rilke, *ibid.*, 21.

DISTURBING THE SECULAR

J. HEATH ATCHLEY

W hat do we expect from a disturbance? The paradox of such a question should be obvious: Disturbances are typically things we don't expect—interruptions of the ordinary, the routine, the established. A disturbance becomes an issue only when there is a desired consistency of condition that is vulnerable to change. Hence, disturbance can be rendered as motion, and the condition it changes can be rendered as rest, stability, or stillness. Disturbances move.

Nevertheless, are there not things we expect from disturbances?— Shock, anger, awe? For many reasons this moment within the first decade of the second millennium is a rich time for such a question. Most obvious, of course, is the place religious and political terrorism now occupies in the minds of many. We board trains, planes, and buses (sometimes defiantly with sentiments of stoicism or patriotism) possessed by irrepressible apprehensions about the next violent strike, the next subterranean group, the next political reality that will create monsters. Less obvious, however, is how we have come to see disturbance as a catalyst of culture. We expect new creations when status quos are disrupted: new technologies, new products, new works of art. Thus, according to this pattern, disturbance can produce both terror and delight. Such a thought can be upsetting because it acknowledges structural similarities between the terrorist, the entrepreneur, the scientist, and the artist. Novelist Don DeLillo has one of his characters say: "For some time now I've had the feeling that novelists and terrorists are playing a zero-sum game....What terrorists gain, novelists lose."[1]

I begin with these reflections because I want to think about the possibilities for disturbing the secular. Of course, any disturbance of this kind is likely to be rendered as parallel to terror. After all, isn't one of the primary motivations of contemporary terrorism to protest and disrupt a civilization that has chosen to separate religion from political government and public life? So we have often been told by our leaders and media readers. Hence, secular modernity, as we typically understand it, is most disturbed by the extreme demand that, instead of our own finite capacities, God should be demonstrably running things. We are right, of course, to be disturbed by such a demand. But the force of this demand and the simplicity of our current responses to it keep us from seeing how what we take as secular can be upset by something other than bombs, airplanes, and holy war.

* * *

One reason for bringing up this topic in this context (America? the West?) is that many of us assume the secular, take it for granted, even if we don't know it, acknowledge it, or articulate it. Even if we are traditionally religious. The secular is our status quo, not only because we separate religion from government, but even more because we consider religion to be something special, something set apart (the meaning of *religare*, one of the two possible etymologies of "religion"). For those gripped by a traditional religion, it is special because it is sacred (that is, *really* important). For those not gripped by a traditional religion, it is set apart because it is retrograde (something we should allow others to do, but it shouldn't get in our way). Also, there is the pervasive, Protestant-driven notion that religion is something deeply personal, a matter of fundamental belief and commitment—its most natural and appropriate place is in the heart, not the public. Meanwhile, doesn't the fact that we do with the world what we will, that the world is a collection of objects we exchange to satisfy our needs and desires, indicate that religion (if not also the object of religion—the sacred, the divine, the gods) is situated in some innocuous, even invisible, place in culture?

I do not mean to sound like a holy-roller preaching that we should all get a little more religion in our lives. In fact, it is the idea that religion is something to go and get, that it is something separate from world and culture, that I want to criticize. This idea presupposes the secular. We typically understand the secular as what is not religion, and the secular is what greets us at our doors, whether we welcome it or not. Hence, it is a prevailing condition vulnerable to disturbance—call this also critique. Such a critique, however, need not be made only with bombs, bullets, or even sermons, and its result need not be a return to religion (in whatever form that can be imagined to take). Indeed, the secular as we find it (a state in which religion is thought to transcend culture and aims itself at a transcendent deity) can fall under a critique (think philosophical attention) that shows its status to be ambiguous. One conclusion worth drawing from this ambiguity is that religion can be anywhere, or even more, that the things sought by religion appear in unlikely places.

* * *

I have been brought to such thoughts, not by current headlines, but by a poem. Listen to A.R. Ammons' "Ars Poetica":

> The gods (for
> whom I work) are
> refreshing realists:
>
> they let you into
> paradise (which is
> the best pay—
>
> and pay they
> know's the best
> equalizer,
>
> disobliging
> all concerned)
> and say, sing:

that's all: they
have their own
business: and

you can't begin
by saying, I've
been in

Hudson, Partisan,
and *Poetry*: the
gods are

jealous of their
own judgment: and
you can't say, I

feel sort of
stove-up today, just
got rejected

by *Epoch*: the
gods, as with other
species, don't give

a damn about
you, only the song,
and song is all

protects you there:
tough: but the
pay is good enough.[2]

The problem with this poem that warrants thought is its straightforward and nonchalant talk of the gods, as if it were a kind of pagan theology. Far from an effort of nostalgia or imitation of the ancients, the poem's modernity is assured by its mention of literary journals (publication in which only a self-unassured modern poet would be concerned) and its contemporary idiom (giving a damn and being stove-up). One might, then, expect some kind of irony to be at work, Ammons engaging in an archaic vocabulary to mock his contemporaries. Though mockery is certainly present, it does not appear to be the principal point of the poem, and furthermore, there is not the aloof, distanced tone so common to irony. In other words, Ammons means what he says: he works for the gods. What could it mean for a poet with no expressed religious adherence to say that he works for the gods? And what gods does he mean? He doesn't call any by name. Like that of nearly all other contemporary poets, Ammons' work is not religious in that it does not illustrate the ideas, images, or practices of a recognizable religion. In other words, he is a secular poet. So what are the gods doing in his lines, among his words? Perhaps it would be melodramatic to consider such a strange encounter a disturbance. After all, how seriously do any of us take poetry? Nevertheless, I am inclined to describe this appearance of the gods in an otherwise ostensibly nonreligious poetry as a disturbance of the secular we normally assume, if for no other reason than it beckons the question: What is a god?

* * *

In an essay entitled "Of Divine Places," Jean-Luc Nancy explains that the questions "What is God?," and "What is a god?," emerge only after the death of God. I take this to mean that the philosophical examination of the concept 'god' becomes possible, or prominent, primarily within the secular. One can imagine questioning the will or even the existence of (the) god(s) from within a religious milieu, but to question what *a* god is seems likely to occur only in a context that has drawn some distance—critical or otherwise—from religion. What makes such a question philosophical, and not simply theological, is its typological quality—What type of thing is a god? Nancy answers that God is a strange half-proper, half-common name. It is a common noun that becomes proper when it designates a god lacking a name. Because we no longer call god by a name, *god* becomes a name. Hence, the term can designate a divine being, one who can be real or unreal, present or absent, malevolent, benevolent or benign. This could be a root of monotheism. But Nancy gives a different take on divine names. According to him, the divine manifests itself through names, but ones which offer no knowledge, ones that are not simply designations. Instead, a divine name is a gesture of

224

invitation or seduction, a call. A god signifies nothing, it only gestures like an infant before the arrival of language. This sounds like Nancy's way of saying that a god is not us, not a being with a will that guides its words. The lack of proper divine names (a condition that could be called monotheism, or the secular, or both) does not indicate an incapacity of signification; it precisely designates the absence of the seductive divine gesture. The god present in this gesture, the god that is this gesture, expels one outside of the self into a state of destitution and exhaustion:

> The god expels man outside of himself....It is always in extreme destitution, in abandonment without shelter or protection, that man appears, waxes, or wanes before the face of god.[3]

Destitution, however, is not necessarily misery. The unprotectedness described above is also, in Nancy's eyes, a joy.

Nancy adds further that a god or goddess offers us art.[4] All art is sacred, and there is no sacred save through art, but this can only be the case if art is no more, if art has reached its limit.[5] In other words, Nancy implies, when art becomes a question rather than a method or milieu (i.e. "the artworld"), it names a god, it becomes the sign of a god, it is a gesture, a call. The implication is that art doesn't, or shouldn't, designate gods, either old ones (Zeus, Apollo, Marduk, Yahweh) or new ones that have yet to be properly named. Rather, without the mention of such proper names, art names gods; it is the place of the divine. Due to the lack of such proper names, I would add, this place is also secular. Art offers us the gods in the secular. Nancy reinforces this point when he says that naming a god really requires more than a single name:

> Naming or calling the gods perhaps always necessarily resides not in a name, even one equipped with sublime epithets, but in whole phrases, with their rhythms and their tones.[6]

Rhythms and tones suggest song. Naming a god is something like singing, something like poetry, not a language which uses specific names to denote an already-existing metaphysical entity, but one which seduces the self into its own exhaustion, destitution, and joy.

* * *

But what happens when the gods show up literally in poetry, not as properly named entities, but as common, even abstract, nouns? This is, of course, the challenge, or disturbance, of Ammons' work. It is as if he takes Nancy's point about art offering us the divine and playfully puts it in our faces, refusing to be coy or ironic, but also refusing to be doctrinaire, which is a way of saying that Ammons doesn't *believe* in the gods. He has little faith in belief:

> what we believe in requires no
> believing: if the axe falls on the toe, severances will
>
> follow promptly: put the burner on Hi the coffee will boil:
> push down the fence it will no longer be standing: walk off
> the cliff, air greets you: so much we do not need to
>
> be urged to believe, we're true, true believers with no
> expenditure of will: to believe what runs against the
> evidence requires belief—concentration, imagination, stubbornness,
>
> art and some magic: the need to disbelieve belief so disbelief
> can be believed: there are infidels only of fictions....[7]

The urge to believe in disbelief suggests that we savor our states of disbelief—terror and awe, joy and rapture. But these states are ordinary, not grandiose, to Ammons' eyes, like boiling coffee and knocking down a fence.

* * *

Ammons' poetry complicates the thoughts of another philosopher who thinks of the gods. In a role resembling a prophet, Martin Heidegger claims that the contemporary era is a time of default, a between-time when the old gods have departed and the new god has yet to be named. This is strange because prophecy is traditionally ecstatic speech, the nonsense ravings of those sensitive souls evicted from themselves by the divine. It is nearly miraculous when such speech manages to be predictive of the future (as we typically take prophecy to be), and it certainly differs significantly from the carefully methodical reflections of philosophy. For what could Heidegger's claim mean, or even better, what might it imply? It seems to parallel Nietzsche's dictum that God is dead. Heidegger's notion seems less modern than Nietzsche's, however, because it suggests a transition from polytheism to monotheism, a transition that has apparently already happened. Consider also that Heidegger's declaration sounds suspiciously theological, and he insists that philosophy—his philosophy especially—has nothing to do with theology.[8] So in this instance Heidegger resembles a theologian—which he is not supposed to do—and he resembles a prophet—which doesn't seem possible.

Such confusion could be the result of Heidegger's source of inspiration: the German poet Hölderlin. For him, Hölderlin is the poet's poet, the poet who sings of the essence of poetry. It is he who gives the clue to this time of default: "It is that Hölderlin, in the act of establishing the essence of poetry, first determines a new time. It is the time of the gods that have fled *and* of the god that is coming. It is the time of *need*, because it lies under a double lack, a double Not."[9] One might note that Heidegger's source is unreliable, because poets are liars, as Nietzsche says, and because the source of their words (like art and prophecy) is ecstasy. In other words, there is no controlling poetry.

Ammons makes Heidegger's diagnosis of the contemporary era more complicated and more interesting, because he thinks the gods are still around:

if the gods have gone away, only the foolish think them gone

for good: only certain temporal guises have been shaken
away from their confinements among us: they will return, quick
appearances in the material, and shine our eyes blind with adoration

and astonish us with fear: the mechanics of this have to do with the way
our minds work, the concrete, the overinvested concrete,
the symbol, the seedless radiance, the giving up into meaninglessness

and the return of meaning...[10]

DISTURBANCES IN THE FIELD

* * *

The gods are not gone, and they are not to be believed. That is, they are not objects or beings that demand belief in order to dispense their radiance. Though it is often associated with things thought mysterious, ultimate, and supernatural, belief is, after all, really about certainty. One may say "I believe...," with enough hesitation to indicate an epistemological lack of confidence. But when one speaks of "my beliefs," it refers to the ideas and principles that structure one's life, the formulations that give the most important guidance for life. Hence, belief behaves, for all practical purposes, like knowledge. So if one were to make the common theoretical distinction between belief and knowledge—the former requiring a faith, an assent of will, and the latter being the result of inquiry and resulting in some level of certainty—this distinction is essentially meaningless if one acts on beliefs ("lives them") as if they were knowledge—which is almost always the case. This is one of the principal points of Jacques Derrida's essay, "Faith and Knowledge: The Two Sources of 'Religion' at the Limits of Reason Alone": that within the realm of 'religion' (a singular abstraction that occurs only in the West and is implicated with how the West dominates the world) faith and knowledge (rendered also as the sacred and technoscience, belief and calculability) appear and often proclaim themselves to be antithetical to each other, when in fact they rely on each other, or put another way, they are versions of each other. In Derrida's words, the point sounds like this: "We are constantly trying to think the interconnectedness, albeit otherwise, of knowledge *and* faith, technoscience *and* religious belief, calculation *and* the sacrosanct."[11] Ammons' poems suggest that *both* belief and knowledge are things we can do without, or at least, we would be better off with a little less of them, especially when it concerns the gods. He insists that gods do not have to do with clear states of apprehending and experiencing. They are not the objects of subjects:

...the gods near

their elemental or invisible selves turn or sweep or
stand still and fill us with the terror of apprehending[12]

228

Also, the gods are absent and unavailable for easy grasping:

> but the real gods, why talk
> about them, unavailable: they appear in our sight when they
> choose when we think we see them whole, they stall
> and vanish or widen out of scope...[13]

And in a move resembling aphairetic negative theology,[14] Ammons cautions against an anthropomorphic divinizing that make deities objects of knowledge:

> take my advice: the forces are there all right
>
> and mostly beyond us but if we must be swayed by the forces
> then at least let's be the only personalities around, the
> sort of greatness a raft in a rapids is and at the top
>
> let's put nothingness, good old.[15]

* * *

As an aside, but also as further thought on the issue of belief, one could look at Nietzsche's complex attitude toward Christianity. The philosopher who declares the death of god more forthrightly and boldly than any other thinker of the nineteenth century, of course, despises Christianity. Attempts to reconcile Nietzsche with the religion, for example by psychoanalyzing his relationship with his Pietist mother, aunts, and sister or by claiming that his thought opens the way for a new revitalized Christian thinking, these ignore the palpable pathos present in Nietzsche's criticisms of the religion, a pathos that is as much the content as the style of his thinking. Thus, when Nietzsche claims that Christian metaphysics places the value of life outside of life, causing life to lose its value, and that Christian morals breed passivity, resentment, and a hatred of the body (not to mention a hidden lust for power), we should believe that he means what he says. Nevertheless, how can we ignore the fact that Nietzsche sees something valuable in Christianity? As a set of metaphysical ideas and moral dictums—both of which are things that are to be believed—Christianity is repugnant to this philosopher. But as a way of life modeled on that of Jesus of Nazareth (the portrait portrayed in the Gospels, not the theology of Paul's letters), Christianity inspires Nietzsche. According to him, the life of Jesus is the perfect example of the refusal of resentment, and his message that the kingdom of god is here (that god's presence is immanent, not imminent) stands in stark contrast to the emphasis on god's transcendence that develops out of Paul's theology.[16] In other words, Nietzsche thinks that when Christianity loses its preoccupation with believing and places its attention on living, then it affirms the value of life itself. He says it most clearly in these paragraphs:

> Christianity is still possible at any time. It is not tied to any of the impudent dogmas that have adorned themselves with its name: it requires neither the doctrine of a personal God, nor that of sin, nor that of immortality, nor that of redemption, nor that of faith; it has absolutely no need of metaphysics, and even less of asceticism, even less of Christian "natural science." Christianity is a *way of life*, not a system of beliefs. It tells us how to act, not what we ought to believe.
>
> Whoever says today: "I will not be a soldier," "I care nothing for the courts," "I shall not claim the services of the police," "I will do nothing that may disturb the peace within me: and if I must suffer on that account, nothing will serve better to maintain my peace than suffering"—he would be a Christian.[17]

Again, Nietzsche's pathos is important, because here it indicates that giving up on belief does not lead to nihilism. (I would also add that it does not lead to capitalism. One often hears that when belief in transcendent values is abandoned, what remains is unchecked capitalism, rampant materialism. But perhaps the reason it appears as such is because capitalism itself is filled with transcendent values. In other words, it is based on faith and belief, specifically the belief in a predictable, prosperous future.[18] As an example one could contrast, in a slightly simplistic way, the current politics of the United States and Europe. In the US where Christianity, often in its fundamentalist form, exercises much influence on government, the social righteousness of capitalism itself is never questioned, not even by "liberals." Europe, where traditional religion's influence on government is considerably less apparent, seems to be the last remaining place in the "First World" where capitalism is curbed. Not even communist China is willing to put the brakes on the unfettered flow of money.) The emotional intensity of this nearly aphoristic writing reveals Nietzsche's thought that values and commitments do not lie solely within the sphere of belief. In truth, belief, being a form of knowledge (hence, caculability), preserves and protects the self and cannot deliver on the transcendence it offers.

* * *

Also worth considering here is Nietzsche's answer to the question, What is a god? Psychologically speaking, according to this philosopher who refers to himself as the first psychologist, a divinity is an abnormal feeling of power, experienced as terror, joy, or even both, whose cause cannot be attributed to one's own will. But the religious person, says Nietzsche, is compelled to find some kind of will as the cause of such exalted feeling. Hence, a god is determined to be its source. In his own words:

> When a man is suddenly and overwhelmingly suffused with the *feeling of power*—and this is what happens with all great affects—it raises in him a doubt about his own person: he does not dare to think himself the cause of this astonishing feeling—and so he posits a stronger person, a divinity, to account for it....Religion is a cause of *"altération de la personalité."* A sort of feeling of fear and terror at oneself—But also feeling of extraordinary happiness and exaltation.[19]

Also:

> ...when man experiences the conditions of power, the imputation is that he is not their cause, that he is not responsible for them: they come without being willed, consequently we are not their author: the will that is not free (i.e. the consciousness that we have been changed without having willed it) needs an external will.[20]

At first glance, these thoughts appear to define divinity as a subjective, emotional state. Consider this the romantic reading of these words. A closer inspection, however, reveals something different. Because the feeling

231

of power cannot be attributed to the will as cause, it cannot be said to be part of the will. It is something else, something fully different. Hence, a "great affect" is a sort of presence pushing the will off its own center, an intruder in the house of consciousness. By explaining this phenomenon, Nietzsche does not criticize the reality of a god, just its agency, its willfulness. In other words, he implies that in the shock of its own mysterious displacement, the human will needs another will for the comfort of explanation. The occurrence of a god is real. The anthropomorphism of a god is questionable. It is as if the human will pictures its own disruption with a familiar image so as to suffer or enjoy the disruption more easily. Another way of saying all of this is to describe a god as a disturbance.

* * *

Disturbances move. To be disturbed is to be shaken out of place, something that happens even to inanimate objects. This is a thought I expressed earlier. What it can mean in this current context is that a god is a movement. It could be called a movement within the soul (to use a romantic, probably misleading, term), but one where the soul (considered here synonymously with Nietzsche's will) does not charitably go for a ride but is invaded by something different—the movement itself. As if the self present only to itself (or to the images it produces) staves off motion, seeks the solid and stable. The self present to something else (anything else, as Derrida might imply[21]) cannot sit still. According to Ammons:

> all movements are religious: inside
> where motions making up and rising turn about and proceed,
> node and come to pass, prayer is the working in the currents....[22]

(Ammons words above suggest that one should not get too personal with this talk of soul. If all movements are religious, then perhaps becoming part of a movement of any sort exposes one to a god as much as waiting to be moved does.)

232

DISTURBING THE SECULAR

* * *

Noticing the gods (in Ammons' poetry or anywhere else) need not result in a new piety or new cultus.[23] Seeing the gods in the secular (especially in abstract form, as common nouns) raises the questions: What is a god? What can the secular be if it admits gods? Questions such as these mark a philosophical practice that seeks a movement that is a disturbance of the divine.

* * *

No doubt you have noticed how this essay has been jagged with asterisks. Not the effect of an effort to be aphoristic or even fragmentary, this condition is the result of an inability to hold together completely the concerns of this writing: the prevalence of the secular; the gods in Ammons' poems; the question of what is a god; the criticism of belief; and the description of a god as disturbance and motion. This reminds me of David L. Miller's essay, "Spirit," written for the *Festschrift* for his teacher Stanley Romaine Hopper.[24] That piece, too, is composed of brief sections, each of which contains a gathering of quotations and citations, a myriad of other voices that somehow resist chaos and engage in thought. Though his work as a whole is most known for tracking the traces of the divine in myth, literature, and the human psyche, it has always been for me this composed, yet jarring, jaggedness in his writing and speech that testifies to a movement and event within language and experience that is worth calling a god.

NOTES

[1] Don DeLillo, *Mao II* (New York: Penguin, 1991), 156-7.

[2] A.R. Ammons, *Diversifications* (New York: Norton, 1975), 63-4.

[3] Jean-Luc Nancy, "Of Divine Places," in *The Inoperative Community*, trans. Peter Conner, Lisa Garbus, Michael Holland, and Simona Sawhney (Minneapolis: University of Minnesota Press, 1991), 147.

[4] Of this point, Nancy says, "...that is something we still have to think about," *ibid.*, 127. In its own way, this essay of mine could be

characterized as an attempt to think about how it is that the divine offers us art. All too often in criticism, drawing a connection between art and the divine becomes a place to stop rather than a place to start thought.

[5] *Ibid.,* 127.

[6] *Ibid.,* 146.

[7] Ammons, *Sphere: The Form of a Motion* (New York: Norton, 1974), 35.

[8] Martin Heidegger, "Phenomenology and Theology," in *The Piety of Thinking: Essays,* trans. James G. Hart & John C. Maraldo (Bloomington: Indiana University Press, 1976), 6. For an elaboration of the significance of Heidegger's distinction between philosophy and theology, see Jeffrey W. Robbins, *Between Faith and Thought: An Essay on the Ontotheological Condition* (Charlottesville: University of Virginia Press, 2003), 30.

[9] Heidegger, " Hölderlin and the Essence of Poetry," in *Existence and Being,* trans. Douglas Scott (Washington, DC: Gateway, 1988), 289.

[10] Ammons, *Sphere,* 48-9.

[11] Jacques Derrida, "Faith and Knowledge: The Two Sources of 'Religion' at the Limits of Reason Alone," in *Religion,* eds. Derrida & Gianni Vattimo, trans. Samuel Weber (Stanford, CA: Stanford University Press, 1998), 54. Derrida elaborates the point this way: "Religion today allies itself with tele-technoscience, to which it reacts with all its forces. It is, *on the one hand,* globalization; it produces, weds, exploits the capital and knowledge of tele-mediatization: neither the trips and global spectacularizing of the Pope, nor the interstate dimensions of the 'Rushdie affair', nor planetary terrorism would otherwise be possible....But, *on the other hand,* it reacts immediately, *simultaneously,* declaring war against that which gives it this new power...," 46.

[12] *Ibid.,* 16.

[13] *Ibid.,* 17.

[14] See Raoul Mortley, *From Word To Silence, Vol. I* (Bonn: Hanstein, 1986), 126-58.

[15] *Ibid.,* 32.

[16] Being a good philologist, Nietzsche knows that, textually speaking, there is no Jesus without Paul. But despite Paul's theological influence

on the Gospel writers, the *images* of Jesus' action in the Gospels make these texts substantially different from the theological advice given in Paul's letters. Hence, a distinction, even opposition, between Paul and Jesus can be made, especially by a philosopher concerned more with immanent value in life than theological belief. Indeed, Nietzsche portrays Jesus *as a kind philosopher* akin to the Stoics, Epicureans, and Cynics— philosophical schools that place a practice of life at the center of their thought. Contrast this view with that of Alain Badiou who sees Paul as a religious and political thinker who articulates a universal faith and creates a universal community partly in opposition to the cool rationalisms of Greco-Roman philosophies. For Nietzsche, however, the comforts of faith and community are far cooler than the affirmative life of philosophy. See Alain Badiou, *Saint Paul: The Foundation of Universalism*, trans. Ray Brassier (Stanford, CA: Stanford University Press, 2003).

[17] Nietzsche, *The Will to Power*, ed. Walter Kaufmann, trans. & eds. Kaufmann and R. J. Hollingdale (New York: Vintage, 1967), 124-5.

[18] Cf. Goodchild, *Capitalism and Religion*, and Mark C. Taylor, *Confidence Games: Money and Markets in a World Without Redemption* (Chicago: University of Chicago Press, 2004); especially pertinent is the second chapter, "Marketing Providence," 55-89.

[19] *Ibid.*, 86.

[20] *Ibid.*

[21] Derrida, *The Gift of Death*, trans. David Wills (Chicago: University of Chicago Press, 1995), 68: "*Every other(one) is every (bit) other [tout autre est tout autre]*, every one else is completely or wholly other."

[22] Ammons, *Sphere*, 33.

[23] Compare these lines from Philip Goodchild: "For the essence of the contemporary predicament [capitalism's threat to human experience] lies in misdirected attention, a mismanagement of piety," in *Capitalism and Religion: The Price of Piety* (New York: Routledge, 2002), 248; also these from Emerson's "Divinity School Address": "I confess, all attempts to project and establish a Cultus with new rites and forms, seem to me vain," in *Selected Essays, Lectures, and Poems*, ed. Robert Richardson (New York: Bantam, 1990), 122.

[24] David L. Miller, "Spirit," in *Echoes of the Wordless 'Word'*, ed. Daniel C. Noel (Missoula, Montana: American Academy of Religion, 1973), 93-110.

Magic, Irrationality, and the Shifting Tectonics of Beauty

(Inspired by the mentorship and scholarship of David L. Miller,
especially *Gods and Games* and *The New Polytheism*)

SUSAN L. SCHWARTZ

The history of magic owes not a little to deliberate obfuscation on the part of practitioners, who prefer to keep their secrets shrouded. The multi-layered veils of time and geography have added to the mystery, as have the prejudices of academic and theological analysis. Whenever we try to define what we mean by "magic," whether as a type of performance or as a lens for understanding a type of experience, words become slippery, categories become elusive and unstable. And when we try to distinguish between magic and religion, particularly across cultures, the obstacles to clarity become truly formidable. If religion is a worldview that provides meaning and value to life experience, and this very broad definition is a useful one beyond the theological monotheisms of the West, then particular practices designed to influence the flow of power in the world in keeping with that lens are omnipresent, as much in the West as they are elsewhere. If magic is the artful performance of impossible events, religious specialists everywhere are members of the guild. Moreover, both current magicians in the West and the history of magic are linked irrevocably to both religion and the multiple, magical beliefs and practices of South, East and West Asia, whence the magi of biblical reference, and so many of the images and forms of magic, originated. The Indian lens, in particular, may offer a unique view of those tremorous, shifting plates upon which the magical arts transform and transfix us.

Asian magics are multiform and extremely ancient, and lie at the root of those cultures to this day in many locations. It is controversial but essential to observe that the worldviews that provide context for these practices are different in kind, as well as in quality, from those that have been predominant in the West. That is the meaning of "exotic," and the term does not imply judgment. But this difference has been misappropriated and manipulated by colonialist and missionary interests; it has formed the basis of negative judgments and dismissive attitudes, and it has obscured the meaning and value that reside in those cultures. This essay cannot pretend to address the enormous range of beliefs and practices associated with magic in Asia. But by highlighting a few examples, it may be possible to explore some of the parameters of difference in worldview that empower magic there.

While Eastern concepts from Persia, Egypt and India were acknowledged as influential by the significant Greek thinkers such as Pythagoras, Plato, Pausanias and Solon, by the Christian era, what had been admiration tempered by some suspicion of manipulation and probably the presence of envy, gave way to distaste and rejection. Egypt's technological wonders, particularly in hydraulics, impressed and amazed. Technological achievement always appears magical when first it appears. When one cannot explain how it works, one can conclude either that it has mysterious qualities or that one is not clever enough to understand it. The former is usually the choice of preference. Relegating the explanation to mystery is much safer, and associating mystery with irrationality was the standard move historically. "The West's longstanding image of the East as a home of irrationality may be accounted for partly by the transmission of ancient magics westward."[1] By the colonial period, the use of magic by non-Western societies was an essential justification applied to support the colonialist enterprise. "This was based on the claim that the mentalities of "savages" (that is, colonizable peoples) and the "civilized" (that is, their colonizers) were as different from one another as magic is from reason ...."[2]

MAGIC, IRRATIONALITY, AND BEAUTY

The British Empire enabled exposure to foreign practices, which were then imported, along with their practitioners, as curiosities. By the early nineteenth century Indian conjurers and jugglers as well as Chinese performers were amazing European audiences with their skill.

> The success of Indian and Chinese jugglers/conjurers in Europe around 1800 enabled magic to demonstrate its transcultural appealand openness to outsiders. That is to say the importation by European and American entrepreneurs of Asian illusionists, jugglers, and sleight-of-hand artists in the romantic epoch is an early example of how a fascination with magic would consistently occupy the foreground of cultural globalization.[3]

The French magician Phillippe (Jacques Talon: 1802-1878) was hugely successful costumed as an "Eastern Magus" (mistransliterating the Persian source of the word "magic"). It became preferable for Western performers to imitate their Eastern counterparts, thus making possible a measure of mystery, a dose of legitimacy, and an increased comfort level. Costumed as a stereotypical Eastern conjurer, a magician could prove his superiority by mastering Asian techniques as well as Western ones and, in so doing, "he secured a safe distance between white and Asian magics."[4] Here is the origin of the generic turbaned magician ubiquitous in Western magic; much like white performers in blackface, this practice served to neutralize, marginalize and disempower the actual artists, implying superiority where actually there was insecurity. Various scholarly and theological techniques were utilized to bolster Western confidence, including the labeling of those other cultures as "primitive." These "served through much of the past century as an important ideological tool in the aid of European and American imperialism and colonialism."[5] "Particularly in anthropological and ethnographic literature, this juxtaposition of cultures could produce a heightened sense of cultural difference, rendering non-Western societies an 'oppositional other.'"[6] Increasingly, magic served as a marker of difference and inferiority, serving as a foil for both religion and modernity,[7] and attributing the effeminate "weaker" descriptor to the other. Attributing irrationality, physical and moral weakness to societies that were engaged in magical thought and practices enabled colonizers and other adventurers

239

to conclude that just as women needed (and wanted) structure and control, cultures that practiced magic not only required, but actually desired, their European masters.

John Nevil Meskelyne, British entrepenuer and performer, produced "the levitation illusion of Daniel Dunglas Home (1833-1886) that was probably borrowed from Robert-Houdin, who had himself taken it—perhaps indirectly—from accounts of Indian magic."[8] "Indian magic ... had the most lasting impact on Western performers."[9] Jean-Eugène Robert-Houdin (1805-1871) appropriated Asian magics freely and, presenting them alongside his mechanical wonders, succeeded most famously in the effort to co-opt Asian traditions into effective Western performance art. The caricature of the Asian magician survives to this day, as is apparent in so many magic acts.

This essay will concentrate on one non-Western culture whose influence on European cultures has been considerable, and that embodies the characteristics of great antiquity, namely India. It will be apparent that Western theological and scholarly categories that seek to distinguish between magic and religion are inappropriate in Hindu South Asia. Clearly, religious and cultural systems that have embraced the role of ritual in the private and public spheres of activity have a very different approach to the use of magic from those that do not. Western theological traditions have cast a long shadow on ritual in the West, and the Protestant Reformation intensified a suspicion that the use of images, the incorporation of the body, and the availability of supernatural power for human needs were insidious to the theological agenda. This sensibility was not present elsewhere; on the contrary, all of these elements retain a high-profile existence in most of the world's cultures to this day as part of the larger worldview.

INDIA: A PROPENSITY TO MAGIC

It would be difficult to overstate the significance of performance in Bharat, that ancient civilization now known as India. Performance infuses the culture still, as is apparent from its innumerable forms of music and dance, its active celebration of festivals, and its

240

engagement with images and icons, both on the altars and in the streets.[10]

India's rich and varied philosophical and religious traditions provide a rich context for understanding the role of magic in a non-Western milieu. Its textual traditions are ancient, from the *Vedas* in the second and first millennia before the common era, through the *Upanishads* and the *Puranas*, and onward. The Sanskrit word *māyā* lies at the heart of Indian concepts of magic, and its etymology implies both to measure and to display, but also may have a close connection to the creative and efficacious power of thought. Hence, in the *Vedas*, "the gods were described as *māyin*, that is, as 'possessed of the power of *māyā*.'"[11] They acted "as powerful magicians or artists."[12] The Sanskrit word *Rta* (the *R* in this word is vocalic, a vowel, in Sanskrit) is the etymological ancestor of "rite" and "ritual" as well as of "harmony" and "art." The term means "that which has moved in a fitting manner,"[13] and implies an alliance between the spheres of divine, macrocosmic creativity and proper human microcosmic ritual performance. The human ritual enactment emulates divine creative design, and together they sustain and forward the artistic impulse that imagines the cosmos into existence. It is through the divine imagination that the world is given form in these early texts; ultimately, the imaginative act becomes both art and artifice. By the time of the *Yogavāsiṣṭha*, probably composed in Kashmir between the sixth and twelfth centuries of the common era,[14] the transformative qualities of *māyā* have taken on a paradoxical and mercurial dimension. "The world is a magic trick, and man is the dupe, and God is the magician."[15] Magic, in Ancient India, was quite a powerful reality, but ultimately an ambivalent one. When used by human specialists, it could be a very dangerous tool.[16]

The oral, iconographic and ritual traditions of South Asia are equally powerful, sometimes in accordance with the texts, but often parallel and occasionally divergent from them. India's worldview is rich in ritual practices, from the vast and public to the domestic and intimate, allowing for extraordinary variety. Localized practice and belief draw on varied influences that shift over time. There is no one source, no one text, image or practice that is authoritative or definitive, providing a fluid and layered theological landscape. Over time, this approach has enabled India to explore and define a worldview perhaps best described as a multivalent universe, or a polyvalent multiverse. The dominant (but by no means exclusive) religious sensibility, Hinduism, operates on three theological levels: it is monotheistic, in that it recognizes one ultimate reality, *Brahman;* it is polytheistic, in that it recognizes an infinite number of manifestations of that reality; and it is henotheistic, in that it offers the ability to choose one of those manifestations as the prevailing or dominant theistic presence at any given time. The dominant deities are usually related to Vishnu, Shiva and/or one of the many forms of the Divine Goddess, often in relation to one another. In whatever form, however,

> the divine is inherently "playful," and the term here includes not only a mysterious form of ludic activity but also its inherently dramatic nature. Divine playfulness is not only, or even primarily, a diversionary activity. Rather, it is the means by which the gods create, sustain and destroy the world. Gods' play is instrumental, it is the origin of all there is. To aspire to participate in lila is to seek to participate in that process. ... The concept is known as *maya* in Indian philosophy, and the term is often defined as "illusion." The world as we know it, according to Hindu philosophy, is a dream, a play, an artful construction devised by the divine realm. It is both comedy and tragedy, often simultaneously, and it is ultimately unreal. [17]

To imagine the divine as playful, and the world as illusion, is to engage a magical sensibility as an essential, defining element of both the macrocosm, the divine realm, and the microcosm, the human realm, and to suggest that the interaction between them is magical as well. That dynamic is ultimately transformative: "A human being might achieve an identification with the god, not communion with the deity, but an actual incorporation of the divinity's essential energy."[18] The power flows both ways in Indian traditions and therefore illusion, reality, transformation, trickery and gaming are human and divine activities with cosmic implications. It is not surprising that many of the games in the global repertoire are derived from India: chess, Snakes and Ladders, Parcheesi. Both playing and Tarot cards may have their origin here as well. All of the major deities and many of the minor ones participate in these activities; the mythology is rich with narratives about the powers available to both the divine and human spheres as a result of yogic practice, and ritual performance. In fact, the work of play is a prerequisite to the existence of the world.

The rich mythological heritage of South Asia offers many cosmogonies, and since time is cyclical in this tradition, the universe may be created in the diverse ways the texts describe over and over into infinity. These creation narratives themselves are quite magical and include such phenomena as a golden egg, the *Hiranyagarba*, magical churns that produce the stuff of existence itself, divine cows whose milk is the genesis of the cosmos. The deity Indra is often the grand master of the conjuring arts in these traditional cosmologies, and thus is often the patron of the magical arts. "The magician recreates images of what the Magician creates."[19]

THE DIE IS CAST

Don Handelman and David Shulman, in *God Inside Out, Śiva's Game of Dice*, investigate one of the most compelling narrative clusters relevant to our topic. Shiva and his wife, the Goddess Parvati, play a game most often linked to Parcheesi, but also possibly related to "the game of karma," known in the west as Snakes and Ladders. The game "is closely linked to divination, the dice disclosing, in external clarity, the karmic-existential state of the player in his every move."[20] In this game, Shiva loses, generating both a theological crisis and an ontological transformation of existence: his defeat makes the world possible through Parvati's inherent creative power. In order for the world to exist, Parvati must win. She "embodies and accentuates otherness, disguise, illusion,"[21] that is, all that comes to be associated in Indian traditions with *māyā*. The substance of the world, and its illusory nature, are manifestations of *Shakti*, the primordial feminine. *Shakti-Māyā* provides the stage upon which the game of existence is played, a game whose own existence is made possible, in this case, by the game played by Shiva and Parvati. The paradox inherent in this outcome is the theme of Handelman and Shulman's work; for our purposes, we may concentrate on the qualities and central location of a magical sensibility in this case.

One of the more compelling qualities of gaming and play is that "the ludic impulse is pervaded with uncertainty."[22] How can the divine realm be uncertain? The tradition implies that, in fact, it is not, that the suggestion of loss of control is part of the illusion, at the level of the macrocosm. And indeed, ritual gaming, for example as part of the *Rājasūya* initiation for kings in ancient India, was completely under control, for the outcome was the support of the cosmos and could not be left to chance.[23] In the microcosm, however, as in the famous dice game of the *Mahābhārata*, ontological destabilization was entirely possible, and in fact, essential.[24] Here, in one of the world's greatest living epics, the dice game is played between two factions of an embattled family to determine the future of the kingdom. Just as different forms of dice have been used in Asian cultures for divinatory purposes for millennia, this "game of chance" does in fact determine the future, albeit not in ways immediately discernable within the narrative itself. For the game is fixed by the Kuru clan to disadvantage their cousins, the Pandavas. From the macrocosmic perspective, the Pandavas must ultimately triumph and the kingdom must be theirs. But it is first necessary for them to be sent into exile, and the dice game is the means by which that microcosmic goal will be achieved. This is one of the notorious scenes in this great epic tale; the disgrace of the Pandavas is played out with high dramatic effect, as the eldest and normally most controlled and wise Yuddhistira is again and again lured into wagering his kingdom, his wealth, his brothers and finally his wife, Draupadi. She is protected from ultimate shame by the intercession of the lord Krishna, who famously extends her sari so that she may not be stripped before the court. The God will not, however, alter the outcome of the game, for this microcosmic disaster to the Pandava clan is required for the divine agenda ultimately to be fulfilled. Draupadi's curse against her enemy in this scene is to be fulfilled on the battlefield of their future. Uncertainty, divination, prophecy and the trope of larger purpose have been players in games of dice in India since ancient times, indeed, "ontological destabilization" may be described as a defining quality of life lived in the realm of *māyā*.

In the "ritual model of the dice game, the rules are fixed and predictable. ... Or, the game may be a module of uncertainty that opens the cosmos toward new shapings."[25] The crux of the matter is that there is a "homology of game and cosmos."[26] As is often the case, there is a myth parallel to that of Shiva and Parvati about a game of dice between the God Vishnu and his female counterpart, Lakshmi. The tenor of this version is different and includes trickery and cheating. Since both are closely linked with *māyā*, "the issue assumes an ironic ontic cast, the overt question being which of the two *māyās*—his illusion or hers, the male or female—is "real."[27]

"The processual qualities of the ludic—fluidity and malleability, movement and change—are deeply and centrally embedded, under a variety of rubrics, in Indic cosmologies and cultural ideologies."[28] Magical play and its prerequisite, magical thought, flow in India from the top down, from the divine to the human. In western monotheisms, on the other hand, where complete difference, segmentation and "hardened boundaries" exist between the divine and the human, the ludic sensibility resides only on the bottom layers.[29] Paradox, radical transformation, and the infinite possibilities that accompany them, are endowed with divine acknowledgement and existence in India.

THE MAGICAL SELF

At ground level, India's many ethnic and religious communities are infused with beliefs and practices that reflect and echo the magical nature of divine reality. Healing, conjuring, illusion, transubstantiation, charms, spells, mantras used as incantations, divination, astrology, exorcisms, possessions, channeling, transformations of space with mandalas and yantras: there are more forms of magical practice in India than we probably can name.

Ariel Glucklich's fieldwork for *The End of Magic* focused on Banaras, India, arguably the oldest continuously and consistently utilized sacred city in the world. He was witness to the application of magical techniques

245

in temples, ashrams, homes and on the streets. In this location, he was forced to reject western distinctions such as natural/supernatural, the latter of which has no cognate in the Hindi of his informants,[30] since what is understood as "natural" is largely culturally determined. "Magical consciousness" or "magical experience," is "the awareness of the interrelatedness of all things in the world by means of a simple but refined sense perception." A practitioner "creates the context" in which that relatedness is performed, perceived and experienced by the use of empathy.[31] The role of the senses is essential and contextualizes magic as a performative act.[32] According to Glucklich, both ego strength and the mind/body split, notable characteristics of the western worldview, work against the transformative nature of the magical experience,[33] and their influence accounts for the decline of magic in western, European cultures more than any other factor. He rejects the use of the noun, in fact, insisting that "there is no such thing as magic, only a magical attitude."[34] He notes that the propensity to magic transcends even the most highly-charged distinctions in Indian cultures, notably caste, economic class, and even religious affiliation.[35]

Anthropologist McKim Marriott's expression "open person" is used by Glucklich to attempt to describe the specifically Indian experience of personhood, that is not bounded by physical or psychological distinctions, that is transactional, interrelated, fluid, and that does not define the "inner" versus the "outer" self.[36] This fluidity, the porous qualities of boundaries among people, environments, and objects, the elusive nature of competing realities, are examples of the ways in which the religious philosophy of the subcontinent as described by Handelman and Shulman both influences and is influenced by life experience in India.

Taking It to the Streets

The characteristics of magical transformation permeate Hindu polytheism and its correlate, psychological polytheism, making for a propensity to magic. Psychological polytheism, as opposed to its monotheistic counterpart, invites and celebrates multiplicity on many levels. Far from the monolithic focus on one path of thought, one form of practice, one truth, one reality, this perspective values and prefers the multifaceted and multi-layered universe. It transcends by its nature parochialisms, tribalisms, and fundamentalisms. It is ironic that in India today, where caste hierarchy and religious and sectarian rigidity have become political tools of manipulation, the underlying ethos remains magical, fluid, paradoxical. Evidence of the surviving perspective may still be found in the street, as Lee Siegel so engagingly documented in his *Net of Magic: Wonders and Deceptions in India.*

Paradox: the street magicians interviewed by Siegel in Delhi and other northern Indian cities and towns are members of a Muslim subcaste, Maslets, but their performances are certainly infused by India's ancient Hindu worldview.[37] They inhabit a liminal vocational category, drawing on the ancient images and practices of the magician-yogis whose ascetic practices, present in revered texts and living mythologies, empowered them with sacred skills. Confused both within and without India with magician-entertainers, such street practitioners have probably always had a symbiotic relationship with them. The *siddhi* religious specialists associated with Hindu deity Shiva are particularly well known for their powers of transformation and materialization. The Buddha, born of Queen Mahamaya (grand illusion), is described in a variety of contexts as able to perform many of the feats street magicians utilize to this day, including levitation, dismemberment and restoration, the manipulation of fire and water.[38] Siegel's hypothesis is that that the Maslets were late converts to Islam, probably in the nineteenth century.[39] A combination of economic, political and sociological forces would have made the decision to convert sensible at that point in the British Raj.

In public performance, these street magicians, the *Jādūgars*, will cater to whatever theological predisposition their audience displays, crossing the apparent boundaries between them with a facility that is spiritually dexterous and visibly manipulative, like many of their tricks. Indian Street Magic is graphic and explicit, often featuring the apparent mutilation and/or sacrifice of a child, images replete with blood, death and dismemberment, culminating in a miraculous re-memberment and restoration of the apprentice. The legendary Rope Trick embodies this deeply evocative trope. These performances effectively integrate magic with religious narrative and imagery, and they succeed because magic's connection with religion is part of India's cultures, whereas in the west, the historically required distancing from religious traditions eviscerated from magic that traditional link. There is still beheading and dismemberment aplenty in western stage performance, but it is sterilized, with barely a hint of blood and gore, and the restoration of the victim's body veils its religious derivation by necessity. It is "only" illusion for us, whereas it evokes *Mahāmāyā*, "great" and divine illusion in India.

By appealing to the more mystical aspects of religious sensibility, the distinction between Hindu and Muslim has been negotiated in the performing arts of India for centuries.[40] In private, Siegel's street magicians reject the possibility of real magic in incendiary terms:

> "Are there people with real power" I asked. "Is there real magic?" and both Shankar and Naseeb were eager to answer. Naseeb said no: "No, but I shouldn't ever say it. I earn a living only if people believe these things, only if they believe at least in the possibility of miracles. But there are no real miracles, and all the holy men and god-men, Sai Baba and Jesus and other men like them, are just doing tricks, tricks that I can do, that I can teach you to do, tricks that all the street magicians can do. Those miracles described in the Qur'an, the *Ramayana*, and the Bible—those were all just tricks." [41]

Their legendary abilities in performance, and their ability to glean enough money to survive, depends on their ability to convince their audiences that the possibility of real magic is inherent in the nature of the universe, thus their sale of magical objects and talismans is both sensible and profitable. Their understanding of the history of religions and its generic relationship to the history of magic East and West is striking:

> I was surprised when he disagreed with my conjecture that it was Houdini who first popularized the typically Indian Buried Alive Trick in the West. No, no, he shook his head, "It was another Western magician, another Jew in fact, a street magician, who made the illusion popular in the West. It was your very own Jesus Christ. He brought so many tricks back with him from his tour of India. But of all of

them, that resurrection trick was the greatest, the one that has fooled the most people."[42]

India's ability to generate illusion may be infamous, but its opposite, the ability to cast doubt, is equally formidable. The legend of Jesus' apprenticeship in the subcontinent is omnipresent there. India confounds assumptions at the most fundamental level, one of any magician's most ancient tropes. Both gullibility and the propensity to magic are countered by skepticism and ambivalence at every turn.

The magician was a fixture in the royal courts of India from ancient times until the dissolution of the princely states during the withdrawal of the British in the 1940's. He was probably often indistinguishable from members of the official priesthood. "Magic could be practical accomplishment, effective ritual or courtly entertainment; the three functions were linked."[43] During the Mogul domination of northern India, the court magician would have taken on a different cast, since the dominant Islamic perspective was less welcoming to the ancient, indigenous ambivalence regarding the performer's role and religious identity. Typically, the magicians adapted by emphasizing the entertainment model. It is probably to this milieu that we owe the image of the richly turbaned and costumed performer that has saturated Western magic shows.

Closely allied to the image of the magician in India is the inveterate snake charmer. The infamous Indian Rope Trick, in which a child is dismembered and then resurrected, is the major theme of Lee Siegel's *Net of Magic* and is closely related to the powers associated with the mysterious regenerative abilities of the serpent. To understand the magical nature of this particular genre of performance, it is necessary first to place the serpent in its proper theological and mythological context. For the snake charmers of South Asia are not the same as the snake handlers of the United States, whose theology, derived from the biblical text, teaches them that snakes are evil and that control over them is a way to display and perform power over Satan. On the contrary, in India as in Ancient Egypt, the serpent is worshipped as a progenitor of creativity, fertility and healing. In Hindu iconography, many major deities, both Gods and Goddesses, are adorned with snakes. Snakes of all kinds are closely associated with the monsoon, for it is during the rainy months that snakes emerge, washed out of their holes. The monsoon, like the serpent, brings both life and death, and is therefore a natural arbiter of ultimate meaning. The cobra in particular is a powerful image of ambivalent power: its venom is deadly, but milked from the glands and processed, it is a curative antivenin. He who causes the serpent to dance plays a game of life and death, echoing the snake-adorned Shiva, who, as Nataraja, is the cause and the very image of creation and destruction. Manasha, the Goddess of Snakes, worshipped in many forms in villages during the monsoon season in rural India to this day, is the daughter of Shiva, whose seed fell to the earth and was swallowed by a cobra. Ritual worship of this deity includes harvesting wild cobras from the flooded fields and "playing" with them in long processions through the towns, mesmerizing them with the movement of the bean, a gourd wind instrument, for the snakes, of course, are deaf.[44] Dancing in the streets, the cobras perform the magical essence of all that is, its illusory, ephemeral nature and its prodigious creativity.

LOCATION, THE EXOTIC, AND THE TECTONIC PLATES OF ILLUSION

> The power of magic, a trick itself, is always brought here and now
> from another time and space, a mysterious then and there, the greater
> the distance, the more magnificent the power.[45]

There is something about magic that wants to be foreign, even in its home setting. It thrives on differences both perceived and historical. Its exotic otherness is part of its charm, even as it taunts the familiar with resemblance. As resistant as magic may be to the commonplace, it loses its edge if it is too far removed from experience. The flow of techniques, costumes and imagery from East to West is well documented, but there has also been a feedback loop, from West to East. Whichever way it flows, however, it must find its psychological and spiritual location by incorporating that which is perceived as other, and that which is perceived as indigenous. To make the familiar strange, and the strange, familiar, may be one of the magic performance's most enjoyable tropes. But to conflate

250

the two completely, and to empower one over the other, has been the conqueror's approach, and it has caused untold damage.

Even in India, it is always the case that "real" magic is "on its way out," in a decline, not what it used to be. To be sure, magic is always in metamorphosis; that is one of its essential features everywhere. It was Shakespeare, after all, who wrote Prospero's speech:

> Now my charms are all o'erthrown,
> And what strength I have's mine own
> Which is most faint ....
> —Prospero, in the Epilogue to Shakespeare's *The Tempest*

A new age was dawning as he wrote; it seemed that the end of magic was near, and so it was, at least as magic had been known. But magic is notoriously mercurial and resilient; reports of its demise are always greatly exaggerated.

Western influences, economic, philosophical and theological, have been particularly destructive in India. In the face of the insidious penetration of technology and linear thinking, both for good and for ill, the time and interest required to support the magical arts in traditional modalities may not survive. But then from traditional India's perspective, all of this is *māyā*. The illusion of rationality, along with the illusion of control, may be the predominant metaphors of Western colonialisms. Through another lens, magic both generates and infuses the universe and it is difficult, if not impossible, to discern its layers within layers. Only the magicians know where the current illusion leaves off and the next begins. Older societies may be better positioned to appreciate this irony. In South Asia, there are many forms of tectonic plates: geological, religious, political and, embracing them all, imaginal. They are all in perpetual motion.

NOTES

[1] Simon During, *Modern Enchantments: The Cultural Power of Secular Magic* Cambridge: Harvard University Press, 2002, 5.

[2] *Ibid.,* 16.

[3] *Ibid.,* 106.

[4] *Ibid.,* 112.

[5] Randall Styers, *Making Magic* (New York: American Academy of Religion/Oxford University Press, 2004), 14.

[6] *Ibid.,* 16, (quoting Marc Manganaro and Joseph Gruber).

[7] Compare *Ibid.,* 6, 13, 88.

[8] During, *Modern Enchantments,* 161.

[9] *Ibid.,* 109.

[10] Susan L. Schwartz, *Rasa: Performing The Divine in India* (New York: Columbia University Press, 2004), 1.

[11] William K. Mahoney, *The Artful Universe: An Introduction to the Vedic Religious Imagination* (Albany: State University of New York Press, 1998), 32-33.

[12] *Ibid.,* 6.

[13] *Ibid.,* 3.

[14] Wendy Doniger O'Flaherty, *Dreams, Illusions and Other Realities* (Chicago: University of Chicago Press, 1986), 5.

[15] *Ibid.,* 290.

[16] *Ibid.,* 292.

[17] Schwartz, *Rasa,* 10-11.

[18] Lee Siegel, *The Net of Magic: Wonders and Deceptions in India* (Chicago: University of Chicago Press, 1991), 151.

[19] *Ibid.,* 162.

[20] Don Handelman and David Shulman, *God Inside Out, Śiva's Game of Dice* (New York: Oxford University Press, 1997), 33.

[21] *Ibid.,* 53.

[22] *Ibid.,* 52.

[23] *Ibid.,* 67-68.

[24] *Ibid.,* 68-71.

[25] *Ibid.,* 74.

[26] *Ibid.,* 89.

[27] *Ibid.,* 95.

[28] *Ibid.,* 44.

[29] *Ibid.,* 45, 47.

[30] Ariel Glucklich, *The End of Magic* (New York: Oxford University Press, 1997), 11, 169.

[31] *Ibid.*, 12-13.

[32] *Ibid.*, 97-98.

[33] *Ibid.*, 113, 165.

[34] *Ibid.*, 22-23.

[35] *Ibid.*, 85.

[36] *Ibid.*, 176-177.

[37] Siegel, *Net of Magic*, 3.

[38] *Ibid.*, 150.

[39] *Ibid.*, 3.

[40] Schwartz, *Rasa*, 82, 98.

[41] Siegel, *Net of Magic*, 43.

[42] *Ibid.*, 171.

[43] *Ibid.*, 384-385.

[44] Allen Moore and Akos Ostor, *Serpent Mother* (videotape), The Film Study Center, Harvard University (Irwindale, CA: Centre Productions, 1985).

[45] Siegel, *Net of Magic*, 381.

GENIUS LOCI: A GHOST STORY

JEAN GRAYBEAL

These old places are jealous as God.
For they hold us in their thralldom
and they will never let us go.[1]
—*C. Warren Sherwood*

In the woods to the east of Lily Lake in New York's Hudson Valley stand a few ruined stone foundations, the outlines of tiny one-room houses, their walls now only a few feet high, surrounded by deep undergrowth and covered by vines and fallen branches. Buried by vegetation in summer, just shadowy snowy suggestions in winter, they sit in shallow hollows in the undulating terrain. They are said by the neighbors to be the homes of the Pang Yang people, a group who traveled here from Connecticut around 1799 and stopped, although they had been on their way further north and west. No one knows for certain exactly who they were, why they chose this place and stayed, or why the place is called Pang Yang. The local story has it that they had been on their way to Penn Yan, near the Finger Lakes in upstate New York, to join a frontier settlement established by the charismatic American-born

254

preacher Jemima Wilkinson, who called herself the "Publick Universal Friend."[2]

Later, as the Penn Yan connection faded into the past, and perhaps because the group seemed to live differently from the surrounding community, the name of the place evolved to the Chinese-sounding, and probably derogatory, Pang Yang. The Pang Yangers worshiped in a tiny chapel or their homes in a spirit-filled way, in what they called experience meetings; they worked on neighboring farms, and kept to themselves. They buried their dead in groves in the woods, and marked the graves with uncarved stones, in the Quaker style that made up part of Wilkinson's heritage.

If the story is to be believed, what made the Pang Yangers stop here? Having pulled up their New England roots and begun the arduous journey away from home and friends, why would they settle here, so far short of their original destination, so far from the presence and leadership of the woman they had decided to follow? The rocky tract they chose was mostly uninhabited and hard to cultivate; its ownership was ambiguous, since it was on a "gore" or narrow triangle of land formed by oddities and overlaps in the original patents of the territory.[3] There must have been something that made them stop, not even halfway in their journey. It's possible that bad weather or winter overtook them and they intended at first just to rest and wait for spring. It's also possible that the news had somehow reached them from Penn Yan in the winter of 1799 that Wilkinson was involved in legal troubles, including a grand jury hearing on the charge of blasphemy, since some of her enemies claimed she represented herself as the returned Christ.[4] Maybe Wilkinson herself or one of her associates warned them off for the moment, and by the time the situation had cleared up, the little group no longer had the resources for the journey. There is no evidence of any correspondence between the groups in the several boxes of letters left by the Penn Yan settlement,[5] and in fact I have been able to find no documentary evidence of any kind, aside from local folklore, that the families who settled here actually had any historical connection with the Penn Yan group.

DISTURBANCES IN THE FIELD

If the Pang Yangers were indeed Wilkinson followers, Jemimakins. as they were sometimes called in those days, and they were just passing through, did something else reach out and hold them here? Was it some aspect of this place itself, or something about their experience of it? Was it the same attraction that later entangled a man named Warren Sherwood here, and that now has me wound into its aura? Maybe the Pang Yangers sensed in this place some element of the experience they had originally enjoyed in Wilkinson's presence, a sense of spirit and power. Or maybe the Publick Universal Friend appeared to them, as she still does to some of us here, without need of letter or courier, and told them that this was a fine place to worship in the way she called them to.

* * * * *

I arrived here two hundred years after the Pang Yangers did, though I didn't yet know at all where I was. I sat on the rocks behind a little house and listened to the wind in the branches above me. I seemed to hear something more, but what it was I couldn't say. At twilight I was drawn to the woods, to a tiny hilltop burying ground with unmarked stones, to the paths and creeks and boggy ponds, to the old foxes' den and turkey runs; I seemed to sense someone there in the forest, a presence speaking to me in wordless murmurs. I saw ruined stone walls, tangled in vines and berry bushes, and wondered how whole families lived through long winters in those one-room cabins deep in the woods. I wandered, following the trails, until I lost myself, and didn't know how I came to the spots where I woke up. At times I thought I saw someone, or heard a soft voice.

Finally I asked my neighbors about the place. I began to hear about Pang Yang, and Jemima Wilkinson, and about someone called the Woman in Gray. Someone handed me a history book by a man named Warren Sherwood, and a little posthumous volume of his poems about the place.[6] Warren had gotten caught here, some said. Some said he should have moved on, found a wider world, but wasn't able to. He was hooked by the stories of the place, and kept getting down into the grave to find the answers he wanted. I began to want to know more about him, at first because he was my only link to the Pang Yangers, the only one who might have learned what I wanted to know, and then because of what I began to learn about him . . . and to imagine . . . and to dream.

* * * * *

In 1901, about a century after the arrival of the Pang Yang people, Warren Sherwood was born in his parents' home on the opposite side of Lily Lake. He grew up on the farm, a spot a bit more fertile and hospitable than those of the Pang Yangers across the lake, but still requiring hours of stone picking and wall building. Warren was not a Pang Yanger himself, but he knew a few of their descendants, who still lived nearby. He wandered freely through the acres of woods where they lived, between his house and the one-room schoolhouse a few miles away, and he drank up the intoxicating sounds and sights of the woods, the subtle changes of season and weather, the mysterious but learnable ways of woodpeckers, beavers, snakes, and foxes. Lily Lake itself was home to geese, frogs, fish, and dangerous snapping turtles. Swimming in the creeks was safer than in the lake, though it often meant yet more stone-shifting to create spots deep enough to really get wet in.

The Pang Yangers and other people of the neighborhood talked about a figure they sometimes saw, the Woman in Gray. Some said she was the ghost of Jemima Wilkinson, visiting the descendants of her group of followers. People mostly didn't want to see her, since they believed that if you did, someone you knew was about to die. Still, Warren felt it might be worth the risk, and when he thought of it, he kept his senses tuned when rounding a turn in the path, in case she might be walking in the woods near the Pang Yang settlement. The little Pang Yang burying ground at the top of a knoll held a few dozen nameless crooked stones, and this seemed a likely place to run into the Woman in Gray.

Warren felt he wouldn't be afraid of anything he could see, even a ghost. It was the things he couldn't see that concerned him, things in the night, or under the dark water of the pond, or taking place without his knowledge in town, or even riding on the wordless undercurrents of meaning that sometimes seemed to flow between adults. When such things troubled him, the best remedy seemed to be to strike out into the woods again, where all he encountered seemed visible, audible, or touchable. Even a ghost spied in the woods would have belonged in that category, since it was in that place of clarity. Many creatures lived there who only rarely appeared, but their traces were as apparent to him as the words in books, and just as he could read more subtle books as he grew, he could also read with increasing understanding the stories of what the animals were doing. So many of them were night creatures: beavers, possums, and foxes all roamed and hunted in the dark, but their signs showed where they had been and how they lived.

The woods were more to Warren than the plants and animals there, and more even than the possibility of seeing a lady's ghost, for most of the time he spent there became a slipping away from the things he saw and out from any sort of thinking or understanding, a drifting away into a state of openness. Nearly every time he went there he shifted gradually into that mode that seemed to be no longer an awareness of any thing, of any object of thinking or sensing, but instead a formless, thoughtless, directionless emptiness. There were paths he followed and spots where he stopped and sat—the ledge overlooking a swamp, a rock beside the beaver pond—but he often found that he had arrived in those spots without knowing how he had come. Instead of him stopping there, the place stopped him. Or there was just no more walking. He had no memory of the walk, no awareness of thinking of anything, no sense of himself at all. He was taken up into the things of the woods, into the breathing of the woods themselves, and if he came to himself or somehow woke up, oddly, from his already awake state, he was surprised to find himself there at all. Yet once he was back, he felt really less present than he had been just before, when he hadn't known he was there, hadn't known it in any way that meant being outside of being there. At least, that is what I think happened to him.

I imagine that Warren never spoke of such experience to anyone. He must already have been in some trouble for his dreaminess, as his teacher called it, and he realized that this habit of losing himself would be seen as part of that. His father tolerated his long walks in the woods, but preferred that he spend his time helping in the gardens. His older brothers were practical and hard workers, and they sometimes made fun of him for being such a layabout. Only his mother and his sister seemed to understand his need to wander. His mother's tenderness was a balm for him, and a few times, when she sat on the edge of his bed at night, he nearly told her about what happened to him in the woods, and how he seemed to disappear even from himself out there. He decided, though, that it was something he should keep to himself, aware that even the most sympathetic mother might mistrust it and find reason to limit his time alone. He felt that would be the worst thing that could happen to him, and so never took the risk of telling anyone about it.

When Warren was fourteen years old, his father died. Warren had returned from school one Friday afternoon, and heard his sick father make a rattling noise. He turned to see him "seized and rigid, his head thrown back, his eyes staring."[7] While his mother tried in vain to revive his father, Warren ran for the doctor. By the time he returned his father was gone. After a time of struggling on the farm without their father, the family moved away from Lily Lake and Pang Yang, closer to the center of the little hamlet of Highland, part of the town of Lloyd, and Warren was sent to high school in the neighboring college town of New Paltz. The long days of aimless wandering in the woods were over, for now, but Warren began to find new ways of accessing the solace he had first discovered there.

Warren found his new school challenging. It was run by the state teachers' college, and the young student teachers, though inexperienced, were enthusiastic. They introduced him to history and literature in ways that stimulated his curiosity and made him want to write. His essays and stories were rambling and imaginative and earned the admiration of his teachers, though not high grades. He didn't conform to the expectations set for his work, and didn't understand why he should try, when the writers he most admired clearly found them useless. Still, several teachers saw a kind of talent in him, and let him write and talk about the things he loved. He now dreamed away as many days in books as he had in the woods as a child, and the college library became a new kind of home for him, a place where traces and hints drew him as the tracks of animals and birds had in the forest.

During the years when Warren went to school in New Paltz, he was sometimes able to ride the trolley between the towns, or to catch a ride on the road with a farmer making the trip, but often he boarded during the week at the home of a friend, in exchange for helping at the store after school. As often as he could, and always on the weekends, he traveled the six miles home to Highland. The long walk on Friday afternoon, the first half of it uphill, was not a burden for a boy who had grown up wandering in the woods. A two-hour walk was a gift for him, especially when he didn't have many books to carry, and the weather was fine; he found paths and trails that took him through the woods, skirting swamps and jumping creeks, moving back into Pang Yang.

Walking and thinking, rehearsing the stories and poems he had read during the week, matching the phrases to the rhythm of his steps, Warren must have entered the state of open awareness he had cultivated as a child. After a time words fell away, and trees and clouds took their place. He often couldn't start out for home until after four o'clock, and in winter dark was not far off. Even in fall and spring daylight began to fade as he came closer to home. The woods of the ridge had a different character from those of New Paltz. A little upland, closer to the Hudson River, and less densely inhabited, these woods of Pang Yang smelled different, and were full of rocks and rivulets, vines and dens. In the growing twilight, sounds and smells became more vivid, while colors faded and the shapes of things softened. The world became a palette of grays, in infinite variety, nothing black or white, but dark stony grays, light weblike shimmering grays, opaque marbled grays. A few times Warren thought he saw a figure in the shadows, but when he looked directly at it, it was gone. He began again to look for her, the woman he had heard about, the Woman in Gray, but she shimmered at the edge of his vision only when he wasn't thinking of her, or of anything. Warren sometimes awoke from his reverie to find he had been nearly sleepwalking. He never stumbled, or veered far from his direction home, but where had he been?

During his senior year of high school, Warren's English teacher recommended him for a state tuition scholarship at Cornell. She told him he must continue his education, and convinced him to talk to his mother about it. They knew that the money for room and board would be hard to come by, but his mother saw it was important, and found a way to send him. It seems clear that Warren's first year at Cornell, 1919-20, would have been miserable. He certainly lived in a cheap boarding house with other poor students; the food would have been tasteless and meager and the room cold and bare. Winter started early, and climbing the steep icy hills to class was exhausting and rarely seemed worth the trouble. When he did make it to campus, Warren felt surrounded by students with more money and greater opportunities than he had, and his self-consciousness grew to the point where it was a torture to go to class at all. The social changes and upheaval of that year were also reflected in the atmosphere of the university. Prohibition had the most impact on Warren's life, because it turned him, with many others, into a drinking man.

Wine had always been a part of life in Warren's home town. Many Italians were among his family's neighbors and friends, and they grew grapes and made their own wine. They drank it with dinner and sometimes on weekends with friends and family. At birthdays and weddings and holidays people got tipsy; they acted giddy, flirted with the wrong people, shot off fireworks and even guns, and generally showed the sides of themselves that daily life had little room for. There were few consequences, aside from a common recognition that everybody could be a fool sometimes. But drunkenness was rare, and the kind of drinking that Warren began to see at Cornell was completely new to him. Since alcohol couldn't be served in public, it drew those who couldn't afford the speakeasies into the isolation of their rooms, and created a culture of private drinking. Warren fell into the temptation. Every night the first glass or two provided respite from the loneliness he experienced, but too often he woke the next morning, or afternoon, to a pounding head and dry mouth. His work suffered, and his grades the first semester were dismal.

Home for Christmas, Warren slept and ate well for the first time in months. He went to church with his mother, and was comforted by a warmth and sense of community that he hadn't felt for months. He resolved to find a church when he returned to Cornell, and he did. The campus had a lovely, soaring wood-paneled chapel, and the minister, the Rev. Hugh Moran, was a charismatic, engaging man, who attracted many students to its activities. One Sunday morning, late in the spring semester, Moran mentioned the Cornell-in-China Club, and on behalf of its student president, Wang Yang, invited those interested in friendship with China to attend.

Warren sat immobilized; he had grown up in Pang Yang, but had never questioned its name or why it might be called that. Suddenly Pang Yang sounded Chinese to him, as it never had before. Why did a neighborhood in the Hudson Valley have a Chinese name? What did it mean? Had Chinese people lived there, or named it? Who were the Chinese? Indeed what *was* China? The whole globe seemed to open out before him as he sat unhearing and unseeing in the chapel pew; the service was going on around him, but he was seeing across oceans and centuries, as images of things and people "Chinese" flashed across his awareness. He was suddenly deeply conscious of how little he knew of anything that mattered. His images and ideas of what was Chinese were so unformed and indistinct that they impressed upon him his own ignorance and illiteracy.

Warren had never wondered about why his neighborhood was called Pang Yang, any more than he had thought about his own name. He could probably have recalled something about the legendary connection with Penn Yan if he had tried, but now he was off on a different quest. Had there been Chinese in his area? Was there something Chinese about it? One night he dreamed of digging a hole to China, as he had once tried to do when he was a boy. He discovered, to his surprise, that there were more than a few Chinese students at Cornell, and he tried to get to know them, but his shyness and social awkwardness made it difficult. He went to the Cornell-in-China Club once or twice, but found only Americans interested in fund-raising for Nanking University. He looked for a course on China, but found little in the curriculum. I think he must have found a newly established collection of East Asian materials in the library, and he would have pored over art books and religious texts, including early translations of Chinese classics, like the *Tao Te Ching*. In his search he did discover the history department, and determined to take courses in whatever they did offer. The way things came to be as they are now was suddenly a burning question for him. But the first-year courses in which he was already enrolled seemed more dull and unimportant than ever. His grades slipped further and further, and at the end of the year, he was told that when he came back he would be on probation.

At home for the summer, Warren did odd jobs to raise money, but any time he could get away, he was off to the old Pang Yang settlement in the woods. He paced off the ruins of the stone and log houses, dug up potsherds, bottles, and buttons, and got people to talk to him. He started sitting the old folks down to talk and collecting stories of Pang Yangers, and of others in the neighborhood. Soon he was retelling the stories too, passing on what he had heard up the road. No matter who he asked, there was never anything about China or the Chinese, but plenty of stories about characters and remarkable feats, about Bess Lane, the witch, who got the best of the devil, and Blind Tom Palmiteer, who had laid the straight stone walls through the woods. He was told that Pang Yang came from Penn Yan, not from anything Chinese. The old Pang Yangers and their descendants were independent, nonconforming types and not a few of them were reputed to have powers. He heard again about the Woman in Gray, and again he looked for her when he wandered the woods, reciting chants of his own composition and urging her to appear and tell him what she knew. Twilight seemed the best time for this, when gray shapes and shadows were everywhere, but still not yet the Woman he sought. Liquor was not such a temptation now; he drank a glass of homemade wine here and there with the story tellers, and that seemed to be enough.

Back at Cornell Warren became deeply engaged with his studies. Determined to learn the stories of his corner of the world, he began to focus on English and American history, with a few courses in philosophy mixed in. He even took courses in the summers, having found enough work in a rooming house to cover his room and board. In his final year at

Cornell, Warren took no fewer than fifteen courses in the History Department, on topics ranging from American foreign relations to Assyrian history. Warren was a tireless reader, and could lose himself in the stacks of the library as easily as in the woods of Pang Yang. Both were infused for him with human stories, and these came to seem to him the thing that his life was for, learning and telling those stories, trying to make sense or at least a kind of rhythm out of them. For they didn't make much sense in the ordinary meaning of the word; there was too much madness, conflict, perversity and blindness in them to allow him to find much order or any kind of progress. There were deeply frustrating gaps, places where he couldn't make out the motive or intention guiding people's actions, and many spots where history seemed to remain completely silent. But he found he could enhance the stories' meaning by telling them in certain ways; he played with poetry to give form to apparently shapeless sequences of happenings, and he wrote late into the night. He was consumed with learning, remembering and retelling his stories; they gave him a place where he could live with the intensity he sought. Before they had captured him, he had found it only in the woods and drink.

Warren didn't make close friends at Cornell. He fell in love once, but the girl's father refused to give him a second glass of wine at dinner at their home, having noticed that he had drunk the first too fast. Warren felt he had been marked as a tippler, and his shyness and sense of difference made it difficult for him ever to attempt another courtship. And it seems he was on the trail of another elusive feminine figure, one whom real girls resembled not at all.

When Warren graduated from Cornell in 1923, he returned to Highland. He again took up his pursuit of local history, but he suffered both from the murkiness of the stories he wanted to pin down, and from the isolation of trying to learn what few others found important. He wrote, and talked, and tried to pull his old friends into his world, but they found him odd. At last he found work teaching at the tiny one-room schoolhouse four miles from his home, and then the Rev. Moran helped him find a scholarship to return to Cornell to study history.

GENIUS LOCI: A GHOST STORY

Warren was virtually on his own in the graduate program. Moran was away from campus on a research project, and though Warren's professors were available if he asked to see them, they let him alone. He took no courses, and wrote to Moran, "I may do what I please, when, where, and how I please. No definite statements have been made to me, and so I am going ahead, largely on my own book."[8] He began working on an assigned thesis topic within English church history, but felt it was necessary first to master all of English history, "architecture, and painting, and music and poetry, and Science and Philosophy and customs and manners as well as politics and economics and institutions of a more technical sort."[9] He was aware that this was not the way his professors would prefer that he proceed, but he was unwilling to make the "complete intellectual surrender"[10] he felt they demanded when they told him to focus.

Early in the spring semester of 1926, Warren found a more definite way to distract himself from the requirement to get to work. He took it on himself to re-classify and index all the books in the chapel's large library, since it had been "universally (in the widest sense of the word) agreed that the present system . . . is in need of immediate revision."[11] This large, apparently urgent project was just what he needed to pull him away from his thesis. Warren wrote that the librarian "doesn't seem yet to have decided whether I am a lunatic or a jumping jack. Sometimes in the midst of an animated conversation he looks positively scared."[12] It is easy to imagine why. Warren careened between periods of intense activity and engagement, when he talked, read, and began unfinishable projects, and days of lethargy and darkness, when he retreated into his room. He could not find a way to make any kind of steady progress toward the goal that he was presumably pursuing.

And his work at Cornell lacked the grounding that the woods at Pang Yang had given his original interest in history. When he was able to wander the paths that the Pang Yangers had made, and to dig in the earth between the low stone walls of their old houses, and to talk to descendants of the people he wanted to know, the spirit of the place kept him tied to earth and helped him feel that he was part of a connected web of meaning, tenuous and elusive though it was. At Ithaca, though, the history he was trying to master was both large and remote; he was trying to understand English ecclesiastical history with no connection to the people who had made it, or the land where it had happened. And I must think that Pang Yang kept calling him back, with no way for him to respond. He walked in the famous Botanical Garden of Cornell at times, but it bore little resemblance to the twisting, vine-wrapped hills of Pang Yang; Ithaca's misty gorges and waterfalls tempted him but were not the place he needed to be. He had lost his muse and without even a trace of her presence did not know who he was, or what he was doing.

Near the end of the school year, Warren's professors asked for a progress report. He gave them a few pages about his plans for mastering all of English history and culture, along with a long list of books that he was planning to read, and a promise that his research would lead to the first truly worthy examination of the Bishops Exclusion Bill of the Westminster Assembly. The faculty let him know that his work was insufficient, given the time he had spent on it, and told him that his scholarship would not be renewed. After a few days of futile attempts to explain himself, Warren packed his things and left Ithaca for the last time.

Back in Highland at last, Warren again found work teaching at another one-room schoolhouse, and in the spring bought a tiny three-acre farm. Though he didn't have the money for it, it was a place he felt he had to have, a spot that called to him and had the sense of presence and power that was his most reliable source of comfort. About to lose the farm for non-payment in January of 1928, he wired Rev. Moran for a loan and started washing dishes at a holiday camp in addition to teaching. A month later, he wrote to Moran that he still had ambitions in history:

> I'd like to write the rest of the Colonial History of the State of New York. I'd like to write a history of the Westminster Assembly of Divines. I'd like to trace historically the development of the canon law of the Presbyterian Church. I'd like to write the History of the Evolutionary Controversy insofar as it applied to the history of the Christian Church. I'd like to write a nice little illustrated monograph of some nine hundred odd pages on Avernacular Furniture of the Early National Period and I'd like to wind up my days teaching

Ecclesiastical History. And by midsummer I definitely shall have
the "Patroons" ready for rejection by all the publishers.[13]

But soon he again found distraction from his ambitious plans by
allowing himself to be elected a trustee of the tiny independent
neighborhood chapel, in the midst of the old Pang Yang territory, and
getting involved in extensive renovations and squabbles over money and
control. He wrote, "I get a lot of private laughter out of it, and I may
have a chance to show them what a chapel can really be made to look
like."[14]

Finally, Warren got a job teaching history at Highland High School.
Though this seemed better suited to his ambitions than the one-room
elementary school, he wasn't a success. He knew and loved the material,
but he wanted to teach just as he wanted to do everything else: thoroughly
and in exhaustive detail. The students didn't respond; he later said himself
that he had "bombarded" them with material until they were stultified."[15]
Eventually he was fired for losing his patience in class and slapping a
female student.

This episode opened a period of intense disturbance for Warren. Out
of work, he was unable to make payments on his mortgage and many
loans, and he lost his little farm. He had to move back to his mother's
home, and was apparently closed out from future work as a teacher, and
without the hope of further graduate study. He began to drink heavily
and sometimes seemed to rave. Everything looked dark; the woods provided
no solace, no inspiration came, and he felt that his pursuit of history
only wound him deeper and deeper into insoluble puzzles. Who were
the people who settled Pang Yang? Why did he need to know? Why did
no one else seem to care as he did? Where were the answers to the questions
that trapped him and kept him circling helplessly back to the place where
he had been born?

At last his mother became frightened for him, and a friend took him
across the Hudson to the state psychiatric hospital in Poughkeepsie.[16]
Although the doctor didn't find that he required hospitalization, Warren
felt he had had his first enjoyable conversation in months. He voluntarily
committed himself, and spent several months at the institution. It was a

humane place, and Warren took to the orderly way of life and the leisurely pace of the days, walking in the expansive, Olmsted-designed grounds overlooking the Hudson, drawing and painting in the therapeutic studios, and reveling in the long water therapy baths. He ate well, slept well, and generally took a vacation from the pressures of life. He benefited from talk therapy as well, and eventually came to believe that most of his problems stemmed from trying to fit into a pattern of expectations that was not right for him.

Maybe while browsing in the extensive library of the hospital, Warren came across a copy of the *Tao Te Ching*, a book he had read and re-read in his undergraduate years at Cornell, when he was imagining that there was some sort of Chinese history in Pang Yang. The *Tao Te Ching* proposed a view of life radically different from the Protestant emphasis on work and achievement. It seemed to say that life itself was a miracle, that balance and harmony with nature were the most rewarding goals a person could pursue, and that simplicity and even poverty allowed people to see what is truly important. Warren found a refreshing sense of comfort and release in the poems of the book, which reminded him of the homely attitudes of Pang Yang, and its perspectives began to infuse his drawings and his writing. At last he felt ready to go back to Highland, and to find a way to ground himself in the land he loved and to pursue its history while making some kind of simple living for himself.

Warren was well liked in the little town, and he found many kinds of work, moving from job to job, picking apples and pruning trees, tending chickens, digging graves, and mowing the cemetery lawns. He stayed in many places, sometimes at home, but mainly in rooms provided by his employers, in barns, outbuildings, and sometimes the farmhouses themselves. He continued to research local history, and to write stories and poetry about the people and places that he had come to know so well; he searched the woods for Indian artifacts and Pang Yang evidence, even traveling to libraries in New York and Washington to track down documents that he thought would help in his history of the area. He wrote a long manuscript, but was reluctant to show it to anyone who was really interested for fear that it would be copied or stolen. He sometimes gave it to friends, though, as collateral for small loans to get him through lean periods, and finally had it typed up and burned the original handwritten copy, so that no one would get hold of it.[17] He drew maps of the locale with all the old place names and keys to explain their origins. He wrote dozens of rambling and colorful letters to Louis C. Jones, the New York folklorist and historian, and told him, "There is more in any one square mile than can be compassed in lifetime."[18]

He walked everywhere, and stopped in at people's houses to say hello. He was usually invited to stay on for supper and he always accepted. He repaid the hospitality of the neighbors with stories and bits of history, talking late into the night with whoever could stay up as late as he did. He also published short pieces in the local newspaper, but always refused compensation, saying he never again wanted to be paid for doing what he loved to do.

Near the end of his life, Warren worked mainly in the Lloyd Cemetery, a bigger, more orderly place than the tiny Pang Yang burying ground, and his friends built him a tiny wooden shack across the road from the cemetery—they called it "Sherwood's Rest"—where he passed his last years. He deeply enjoyed the cemetery work, for he felt he was at last among the people who really seemed most alive to him. The rhythmic clacking of the blades of the push mower started him off, and he sang and composed poems about the residents of the graves as he went along. As evening came on he wrote letters in his shack by candlelight, and then sat in the back, holding a glass, facing the trees of the forest, watching the shadows deepen and the gray shades arrive, the shades he loved more than the brilliant colors of the day. He communed until night fell with the ever-shifting interplay of light and dark that the *Tao* spoke of, and felt that he had at last gained the vision of the Woman in Gray that he had sought all his life. Warren died in 1947, doubtless of the effects of alcohol.

* * * * *

I have spent many years looking first for the people of Pang Yang, and then for Warren. I still live here by the little graveyard with unmarked stones. Long ago I traveled to Penn Yan to read Jemima Wilkinson's documents, and to the Cornell library to read Warren's letters to the Rev. Moran. I went to Connecticut to look for records of the people who had followed Jemima to Penn Yan, but I never found the names of the Pang Yang families mentioned in any of these places. I read Warren's letters to the folklorist Louis C. Jones, who wanted him to publish his stories, and I spent years looking for a publisher for the letters. I have tried over and over to write the parts of the story that I know and think I understand, but the gaps are too big and I have had to invent and imagine so much. At last I have begun to lose track of the difference between what I know and what I have had to imagine.

And then of course there is the other problem, the bigger one I finally had to admit, that I really do need to master the whole of American history, religion and culture, folklore and poetry, before the story can be properly told. I'm just getting started on that, and it seems it may take me a few years yet. And then just what was it exactly that Warren really read? Did he actually have the *Tao Te Ching*? Where is his old set of the *Encyclopedia Britannica*, the one that I have been told he moved on a child's wagon to his little farmhouse?[19] And the other books that I am so sure must have been in his library? I feel sure they are hiding in used book stores all up and down this valley, with Warren's distinctive handwriting filling the margins. I put on my warm gray wrap and open every dusty history book in the chilly basements, just in case.

I've spent hours with Warren's niece and with younger brothers and sisters of people who were his students in the old one-room schoolhouse. But I still have to talk to all the remaining living people who ever knew Warren—they grow fewer every year, so there is some urgency—and track down the remaining Pang Yang descendants. Lately I've been walking from house to house in Pang Yang, asking to take a peek in the attic. Do they have any old letters in boxes somewhere? Maybe there are other little graves behind their houses—are there names on the stones? I don't seem to find people at home much any more, so I just go around back and see for myself.

GENIUS LOCI: A GHOST STORY

And I must find that handwritten manuscript, with all the illustrated maps, though it may lie at the bottom of Lily Lake; I know that Warren wouldn't have burned his life's work. I believe he sealed it in a crock and sank it in the lake. I've found a little old boat hidden on the shore near the house where he was born; when it isn't raining too hard, I pole around, feeling for unusual things among the roots of reeds and lilies. The best time is twilight, when the glare of the surface is dimmer, and I can see a bit below the surface. And I follow the trails through the woods. Sometimes at dusk, I linger by the graves. I occasionally see a child near there, but I hide before he can see me clearly. I just whisper a little, to start him thinking; maybe he'll carry on when I am gone.

There is so much to do, and yet I still have to make a little living, just enough to get by on. I pick apples, and tend the graves in the little burying ground, and trim the grass, listening to the voices on the wind. At last I have grown gray with history, as Warren said he wanted to do, and my gray hair matches my dress.

NOTES

[1] Warren G. Sherwood, letter to Louis C. Jones, from Highland, N.Y., July 25, 1943 (Haviland-Heidgerd Historical Collection, Elting Memorial Library, New Paltz, N.Y.)

[2] Herbert A. Wisbey, Jr., *Pioneer Prophetess: Jemima Wilkinson, The Publick Universal Friend* (Ithaca: Cornell University Press, 1964). Wisbey notes, "The name Jemima Wilkinson is an established part of the folklore of a neighborhood that she never visited and probably never heard of. A distinctive group of people known as Pang Yangers lived for several generations in isolation in a section of Lloyd Township in Ulster County, New York." (Note to Chapter X, page 215.)

[3] Warren G. Sherwood, *History of the Town of Lloyd* (Poughkeepsie, NY: Artcraft Press, 1953), 91.

[4] Wisbey, *Pioneer Prophetess*, 151.

[5] Jemima Wilkinson papers, 1771-1849. (Yates County Genealogical and Historical Society, 200 Main Street, Penn Yan, New York.)

[6] Sherwood, *op.cit.,* and *Poems from the Platt Binnewater* (compiled by Mabel E. Lent, privately printed, 1967).

[7] Warren Sherwood, "When Pa Died," in *History of the Town of Lloyd,* 176.

[8] Warren Sherwood, letter to the Rev. Hugh Moran, from Ithaca, presumed fall 1925 (Rare and Manuscript Collections, Carl A. Kroch Library, Cornell University, Ithaca, New York. Item 39/2/972, Box 1).

[9] *Ibid.*

[10] *Ibid.*

[11] Sherwood, letter to the Rev. Hugh Moran, January 18, 1926. (Cornell collection.)

[12] *Ibid.*

[13] Sherwood, letter to the Rev. Moran from Highland, February 19, 1928. (Cornell collection.)

[14] *Ibid.*

[15] Sherwood, letter to Louis C. Jones, from Highland, N.Y., March 7, 1941. (Haviland-Heidgerd Historical Collection, Elting Memorial Library, New Paltz, N.Y.)

[16] Personal conversation with Eleanor Quick, niece of Warren Sherwood, June 2003.

[17] Sherwood, letter to Louis C. Jones, from New Paltz, N.Y., Sept. 13, 1940. (Haviland-Heidgerd Historical Collection, Elting Memorial Library, New Paltz, N.Y.)

[18] Sherwood, letter to Louis C. Jones, from Highland, N.Y., May 14, 1941.

[19] Personal conversation with Eleanor Quick, niece of Warren Sherwood, May 2003.

KARL KERÉNYI: HUMANISM AT THE MARGIN

VICTOR FAESSEL

> To lead a discordant, indeed, split human race, lying there
> dismembered, to humanity is more than an educational problem
> for grammar school teachers, more than a task in the style of the old
> humanists. — *Karl Kerényi*

To honor David Miller on the celebratory occasion of this *Festschrift*, I have decided to submit a few reflections on the humanism of Karl Kerényi: classical philologist, historian of religion, and fellow member, with David—though slightly before David's time there—of the esteemed Eranos circle.

Honoring David this way is, in effect, to acknowledge his humanism by association, a juxtaposition that I hope sufficiently to qualify in my initial and closing remarks. But first I want to suggest explicitly that David has a place within a strand of the humanist tradition that has learned the lessons of the 1930s and '40s with which Kerényi and others grappled, and sublated them into scholarly careers "marginal," in a very particular sense, to their fields. To mention the names of two such others, whose inspiration had come from Vico—Erich Auerbach and, somewhat later, Edward Said—is to evoke the diverse personal, intellectual, and

273

ethical styles of a humanism transformed by the twentieth-century's *ricorso* to a "barbarism of reflection." I refer to that late symptom of a cyclically recurring decay at the moorings of civil society which drives oversophisticated minds, as Vico says, to acts of savagery.[1]

What Kerényi, Auerbach, and Said also have in common, of course, is the peculiar destiny of having been not just emigrants, but, to varying degrees, self-imposed exiles from their homelands. In different ways they lived as strangers among others and—turning Kristeva's[2] fecund idea a notch—as 'strangers to ourselves.' They took up in their personal as well as their scholarly lives a kind of itinerant "position" on the "margins" which is not manifestly nostalgic, and which entails more than shoring up or asserting cultural coherence in an incoherent age, as Kerényi and Auerbach clearly also did. This marginal stance presupposes an estranged[3] way of looking at boundaries, is attuned to "gaps" and lacunae in the surfaces of carefully delineated domains: whether of conventional wisdom in its complacency, of the culture's root metaphors and images in their reified glory, or of the ego in its citadel. It was to these lacunae that David, with penetration, brilliance, and wit, directed us to attend.

Great teachers direct attention and exert influence. Central to the educator's art, this requires no apology. David's influence—I am not alone in testifying that he ranks as an educator *par excellence*—points to what it can mean *still* to be a humanist in the skeptical, "scare quote"-obsessed climate of the late 20th and early 21st centuries. Beyond all irony, I want to insist that David embodies that humanist ideal, cornerstone of the entire tradition, which situates pedagogy at the center of the care of souls. A perennially difficult burden, such caring, because it aims for the coherence of a mutable sociality undergoing constant change; how much more difficult, then, in times of lengthening, and dangerously under-scrutinized shadows.

As a concrete, if eccentric, example of this pedagogical caring, I would like to share a personal anecdote. David, like other Pacifica faculty in this esteemed gathering, had frequently to deal with a tenacious habit of intellectual abstraction that pervaded my thinking and writing as their student. In an email exchange soon after research for my doctoral thesis began, David, my advisor, had the following to say in one of several attempts to wean me of this habit; the context is a discussion clarifying David's assessment of paragraphs I had sent for his review:

> There is one mis-reading of my e-mail. In your first paragraph you quote me as saying "big bloody." I actually wrote "big blobby." "Bloody" is a good word for me, and if I had written it, I would have been not against it; blobby is, on the other hand, problematic in my view, because it is big, abstract, undifferentiated, imprecise, not concrete and not down-to-earth. Aristophanes called it "cloudcuckooland" and accused Socrates of it!

About Aristophanes David has taught us much, but at the time my distinguished role as analogue of the comedian's Socrates was somehow lost on me. Yet, I *have* learned from David. For what did occur to me upon reading his playful corrective—though perhaps typically, more in the tragic than in the comic register—was a passage of Kerényi's from a letter written not long after the end of the Second World War. The text is saved in his collected works under the title "Lob des Konkreten," or, "In Praise of the Concrete." It reads, in my own translation, as follows:

> With 'man', [who is] simply the result of an abstraction, one can do anything. One can turn him into the wheel of a machine and send the machine hurtling against a wall. Five machines, a hundred machines—as many as it takes to break through the wall. Fewer is better. Abstract thinking thinks in terms of numbers. Fewer wheels, fewer "men," is an advantageous solution to this problem, the wall. For now the wall is no longer even a wall: it is a problem. The result of an abstraction.[4]

This passage is representative of a side of Kerényi little evident in the English-language bibliography of his writings. It reveals an engagement with the crisis of his day that shall serve to introduce my remaining reflections on this ardent European humanist and his "turn" to depth psychology. For it is as a response to humanism's seemingly helpless encounter with a grim face of Western humanity—one that had turned souls to stone and stone to rubble in the middle years of the last century—that Kerényi's turn sustains its abiding significance.

I.

In a March 1945 open letter "to young humanists," Kerényi responds to having been addressed as a classical philologist from the standpoint of humanism's traditional relationship with philological education. He writes of the challenge to humanism posed by the atrocities of the not yet concluded war, reflecting on humanity's "typhonic" nature and its "Gorgon's face." He was, of course, referring primarily to its European manifestation in the collective swoon of fascism during the 1930s and '40s.[5] The letter from Christmas 1946 quoted above ("In Praise of the Concrete") meditates on the paradoxical nature of intellectual abstraction in Europe's cultural heritage, and specifically, its consequences for the humanist tradition. That letter, too, ends with an evocation of this "Gorgon's face."[6]

Writing in 1945-46, the paradoxes and dangers of abstraction could perhaps only be rendered in such stark images, forged in the searing awareness of what had just transpired on the world stage. The idea of *humanity* (Latin: *humanitas*), on which modern Western political and legal institutions are built, enables precisely through its abstraction the possibility of transcending individual, racial, and cultural differences that too frequently occlude recognition of human 'others' as people. Yet it was from within an abstract manner of thinking that many Europeans of the 1930s and '40s were seduced by the ideology of fascism: *the Communist, the Jew, the Aryan, racial purity, national self-realization*—all are abstractions. Noteworthy here is the extent to which this ideology of exclusion was bolstered by "scientific" theories of folklore and mythology, of philosophy, even biology, and how it was sold to the public through deft manipulation of traditional images. The implications were not lost on Kerényi, nor on other contemporaries who also saw Nietzsche's hyperbolic (and highly ironic) notion of the "higher man" co-opted and turned to blatantly murderous ends by the Nazis.[7]

KARL KERÉNYI: HUMANISM AT THE MARGIN

The striking image from the Christmas 1946 letter underscores a lingering timeliness in Kerényi's words, now almost sixty years after he wrote them. The instrumental abstraction that can set the machine against a problem, man the machine with human beings and "send the machine hurtling against a wall"—such technical perfection and rational expediency imagine it as a quite simple thing to "erase cities from the map."[8] In a late essay bearing the title "Wesen und Gegenwärtigkeit des Mythos" ("Essence and Actuality of Myth," 1965/'67), Kerényi bemoans how technical objectives in the service of an abstract notion of human progress seem too often incapable of heeding the fragile particularity of human lives and local places. Technology, he says, "is *techné* ['craft'] on its way to autonomy, to being for itself."[9] Such examples indicate the range of concerns that animate Kerényi's humanism. It can be said that he tried to come to grips with these challenges by, perforce, reinvigorating humanism both from within and from outside the study of Greek and Roman antiquity—the traditions of philology and pedagogy at humanism's center. But this involved a progression along an increasingly eccentric path, responding to challenges at different moments in time beginning early in his career.

A novel conception of ancient religion and mythology already emerges in Kerényi's intellectual struggle with the prevailing dogmatism in classical philology during his formative years as a scholar. In the German academic sphere at that time (1910s and 20s), the field was dominated by a group of scholars in Berlin, most famous among them Ulrich von Wilamowitz-Moellendorff, who approached antiquity with positivist and historicist premises and a strong bias toward textual documents. Kerényi came to feel stifled by the limitations of such a rigid diachronic methodology, which eschewed inquiry into the meaning of artistic and mythical expressions for the people who created them and all too often favored idealized images of the Hellenic gods. His liberation came in 1929 while working as a guide at Greek sites among the material remains, at which time he also met Walter F. Otto.[10] Kerényi later stressed the enduring importance of his realization about the value of material culture for his conception of ancient myth and religion. In the 1967 Foreword to his volume *Auf Spuren des Mythos* (On the Trail of Myth), he reminds his readers that extending philological research by considering the "sinnliche Tradition" (sensory, aesthetic tradition) had already constituted for him a "solution to the crisis of classical philology" before his turn to psychology—a turn that would extend his philological ideas toward an "attempt at a humanistic research of the soul."[11] From this late, retrospective vantage point (he died in 1973), Kerényi insists that such a focus on material culture is justified as a "protection against all kinds of one-dimenionality: both the non-psychological or anti-psychological kind of the philologists, and the panpsychological kind of the psychologists."[12]

The position finally attained in Kerényi's struggle against academic dogmatism receives a new impulse from the far greater challenge of mythology's appropriation by the theorists of fascism. This point will be further developed below. Anticipating somewhat, it can be said that the historical context of scholarly absolutism, resurgent nationalist politics, and incipient fascism formed the crucible in which Kerényi's humanist values evolved. His distinctive style of myth and religion study becomes a reflection of the ethical and scholarly commitments of that maturing humanism.[13]

Methodologically speaking, Kerényi approached myth by trying to grasp the many images and stories of the gods in their particularity and in their *concreteness*—which is to say, not solely their contingent historical unfolding as material and textual records. Each mythic image and each narrative, inasmuch as it can be said to testify to a particular psychical and spiritual situation of men and women at a given point in time, is a trace of human relationship to a complete, complex world (natural, social, spiritual, etc.). In order to get at the foundations of that world's *meaning* for a given culture at a given moment in its history, one must begin from a phenomenological premise: myths, but also the whole material and artistic record that reflects the gods and their stories, must be considered as primary evidence along with any other textual documents. All such traces may be presumed to reflect an intention to intersubjectively communicable meaning. In a fundamental respect, it is this inclusiveness in Kerényi's notion of what constitutes "concrete" evidence that set him apart from the classical scholars of his milieu.[14]

With a retrospective glance, in 1949, at the work of the preceding ten years, Kerényi indicates the enlarged sense in which he conceives of the "material" passed down from ancient times. Mythic narratives, including all of their core thematic variations ("mythologems"), belong just as much to the *Stoff*, the material, of ancient traditions as temples, statues, and artworks:

> The naming of a god is already 'myth' and the elaboration of the myth, the 'mythologem,' even if it goes over into the purely poetic, belongs to the material stock of ancient religion: first as the moving, living material [*Stoff*], the life of the gods in the minds of the people who recognized them as gods (*nomizousi*), and then as written records that give testimony of this life in ever more ossified form.[15]

Mythology, then, as the *movement* of this material, demands for its elucidation an interpretative method that attends to both aspects: the narrowly historical (which must relinquish philological rigidity), and the phenomenological. Insofar as each manifestation of a divine image and all the changing and evolving data intends meaning, it is a record of a human "solution" to a "problem" of human existence which can only be comprehended without prejudice toward perfected, idealized images— of the gods or, for that matter, of Greek or Roman culture. Indeed, Kerényi was often criticized by those clinging to images of "classical" perfection for pointing out the ambivalent and less "humane" features of Greek deities, and on this point he differed, too, from his friend Walter Otto.[16] Practically from the start, he had elected a path that would marginalize him from the mainstream of his field.

II.

By his own self-reckoning, Kerényi's "turning point" and "breakthrough" to his distinctive theoretical position occurred in the period 1938-1939. It is in writings initiated during this period that he first began to use the adjective "primordial" to discuss mythological images of "archaic" provenance and "style." This is reflected in the introduction to his *The Religion of the Greeks and Romans* (1962, original German edition 1940), where he praises that aspect of Jane Ellen Harrison's ritual-focused interpretation of Greek existence that takes the material record as its starting point.[17] Here he characterizes his idea of "cultural style" with brief etymological reflections on the Greek words *bios* and *zoê*, roots of our words zoology and both biology and biography. *Zoê* for Kerényi is "archaic," the impersonal and universal life principle, life in its exuberant, chaotic, indestructible aspect, for which he finds anthropomorphic expression in the figure of Dionysos and his myths. *Bios* is "characterized life," the storied life of the individual, subjectively experienced, and reflects later cultural developments.[18] The extension of this focus on the archaic and primordial beyond morphological studies first comes together in a work on the birth of Helen (1939) and in papers written at that time on the divine child and the *Kore* (or divine maiden); the latter two pieces were published, with psychological commentaries by C. G. Jung, in 1942. Although the word "science" does not appear in the book's original German title as it does in the English versions, Kerényi's letters of this period to Thomas Mann make clear that the works assembled here do attest, in his judgment, to the achievement of an encompassing, "scientific" vision of myth—or as he says, of "the great mythologies."[19]

It should be emphasized that "scientific" for Kerényi now meant hermeneutical with a strong emphasis on the *psychological*. The importance of the "subjective factor" emerges as a key methodological concern in the early 1940s. In his 1944 introduction to the first part of his published correspondence with German novelist Thomas Mann, he presents his idea of method in a simile. Philology, he says, must always remain foremost an interpretive undertaking. At best, the interpreter is like an "organ": both taking in and passing on, both acting and reacting, and these invariably on both conscious and unconscious levels. Her or his whole life, "the structure of his mind, and his own personal experiences constitute an indispensable element of the interpretation, an element that cannot be eliminated but that must be revealed in its fullest clarity."[20] The point, as the letters to Mann and to "young humanists" make clear, is that hermeneutical self-reflexivity must prevail over and serve as corrective to both the narrow positivism of Wilamowitz and the biological determinism of racist Nazi ideology.

There is an affective side to the interpretative engagement with mythic material. Kerényi attributes to this "stuff" an "attractive power" (*Anziehungskraft*), which "forces the interpreter to react, positively or negatively, to it." It is a "subjective reaction, yet one objectively caused by the material."[21] Poets and artists are for Kerényi living examples of this reciprocal dynamic of receptivity and reactivity; the continued, contemporary vitality of myth for poets and novelists—such as Goethe and Hölderlin, D. H. Lawrence and Mann himself—and for thinkers like Friedrich Nietzsche, testifies to myth's *Anziehungskraft*. But this affectivity *works* both ways: that is, it may be worked with consciously, or work upon one unconsciously. That both possibilities exist underscores the necessity of attending to the subjective factor in interpretation.

In this regard, one of the decisive and sustaining impulses for Kerényi's humanism, and for his mature conception of the dynamic vitality of mythic material, was received through the "friendship in letters" with Mann. Exemplary for Kerényi was the novelist's subtle treatment of traditions involving the Greek god Hermes, especially in the novel *Joseph and His Brothers*. Not merely Mann's characterization of the young Joseph himself, but the whole perspective and language of the *Young Joseph* segment, was praised by Kerényi as a "datum of religious history" for what he called its "hermetic" quality. On the evidence of Mann's art and the hermeneutical insight offered through years of correspondence with him, Kerényi went so far as to assign the "hermetic" a mediating position in that antagonistic cultural polarity of the West represented, since Nietzsche, by Apollo and Dionysos.[22]

Moreover, in Kerényi's thinking two contemporaries testify to the actuality of myth's "attractive force": positively in Mann, and negatively, even tragically, in the figure of Nietzsche. The latter case represented for Kerényi the acute danger in the affective attraction which myth can exert upon an individual. It is to Nietzsche that Kerényi pointed when stressing the limits on abstracting any "higher man" within an inflated humanistic impulse. He recognized the "immense tension" between this foreground impulse and the philosopher's "background" fascinations with Dionysos and Ariadne, the collapse of which proved devastating for the man.[23] In this context one may note that, collectively, myth's affective power went on display in the mass seduction of a modern society through the misappropriations of Germanic myth and Romantic folklore—and of Nietzsche's own "Dionysian" philosophy—as carried out by Alfred Rosenberg and the Nazi's propagandists.[24] Myth proved capable of agitating the distressed social conditions of 1930s Germany, stoking the conflagration that Kerényi would later call "typhonic."

Thus, while the example of the artist was probably most illuminating for Kerényi personally, it is clear that he did not confine myth's cotemporary relevance solely to the aesthetic sphere—where, after all, it had always remained vital. Favorably disposed recent commentators have admitted that Kerényi did not sufficiently attend to the historical and sociological aspects of myth's contexts and reception in much of his work. But it has also been recognized that the issue may be related to the pull of the literary impulse in Kerényi's writing, which sometimes eschews the philologist's diachronic sobriety for the narrative realization of a broader, synchronic picture.[25] It is clear that his abiding concern to make myth relevant to modern day people did find one of its persuasive supports in the arena of modern literature, and Mann was one of its luminaries. But more than this, and crucially, Mann was Kerényi's staunch ally in advocating a humanist corrective to the political misuse of myth, that it "be wrested from the hands of the Fascist obscurantists to be 'transmuted' for humane ends."[26]

III.

In his 1945 letter to "young humanists" dealing with the "basic concepts and future opportunities of humanism," Kerényi states that the "rigidity of the old style of humanistic activity . . . must be dissolved" and, henceforth, be "subordinated under a new need: humanity's need for healing." He continues:

282

> The reorientation of all humanistic studies in the widest sense, all
> sciences having to do with human beings, would today be worth
> considering in light of this need: a reorientation in such a way that
> medicine would come to stand at the center of its system of relations.
> A medicine, to be sure, of the *whole* person, encompassing depth
> psychology as much as it does biology and which, aside from its
> practical task of healing people, would have in its sight the
> construction of an anthropology that could serve as the scientific
> foundation for humanism as a philosophical worldview.[27]

The German word "Anthropologie" carries a different meaning than its
English counterpart, suggesting an encompassing, philosophically
articulated '*logos* of the human' rather than the (comparatively) delimited
social science denoted by the English word anthropology. The physician
of the soul offers this new 'anthropological' impulse to humanism because
of the insight he or she has gained into what is missing from the idealized
images and the standard curriculum on the West's cultural heritage: a
sober-eyed view of human nature's "typhonic" undercurrent. This may
sound paradoxical given the place in that heritage of Christian teachings
on evil and the devil. Yet for Kerényi, the historical failure of both
European Christianity and Enlightened humanist education to anticipate
and check the fascist tide strengthened the case for grounding a future
humanism in a psychologically astute 'anthropology.' "To lead a
discordant, indeed, split human race, lying there dismembered, to
humanity is more than an educational problem for grammar school
teachers, more than a task in the style of the old humanists."[28]

Given the arc of his development as a philologist, a conception of
humanism enriched by the insights of the psychologist was a natural, if
not a necessary, outgrowth of Kerényi's evolving sensibility. It was born
from the historical situation he and the humanist tradition faced: a demand
for appropriate tools and absolute candor before the concrete particularity
of the actual *material*—ancient, or modern. Of course, the philologist's
'anthropological' turn also reflects his timely conjunction with C.G. Jung.
This encounter produced the collaborations leading to the 1942
appearance of the first German edition of *Essays on a Science of Mythology*,

as well as Kerényi's involvement with the Eranos circle and the C.G. Jung Institute in Zürich.

A comment in his 1949 overview of the previous ten years of research appears to date to the late 1930s, the period just before the joint work with Jung, Kerényi's having been "forced to acknowledge an axiom that has proven reliable in the practice of depth psychology." No name or ascription is provided, but it is tempting to attribute the observation to a reading of Jung. The "axiom" clearly relates to Kerényi's appreciation of the vitality of mythic material: "there is no thought, no word, no image, and no combination of these . . . which would be meaningless, mere nonsense, an *action gratuite* of the human mind. . . . A non-arbitrary relation . . . of meaning is everywhere to be assumed, even in the most fantastic or primitive of mental constructions." But there follows a significant qualification: "Yet more than this—namely that such a relation is always present—may not be assumed without special reasons. No abstract theory came before the concrete (and, even afterwards, never abstracted) content of mythological images."[29]

In fairness, it must be remembered that the features of Kerényi's conception of myth compatible with Jung's theories had emerged prior to and were the basis for their collaboration, and in works published after Jung's death in 1961, he took pains to differentiate his mythography from Jung's psychology. His idea of "primordial" images, formally similar to Jung's (still evolving) notion of the archetype, predates their contact. Explaining the use of the term "archetypal" in his book on Prometheus, Kerényi points out that the word's prior history in Western ideas was decisive for him, not foremost Jung's usage. He also stresses that his sense of the term is phenomenological and descriptive, not intended as an "explanatory theory."[30] Kerényi remained aloof to many key Jungian concepts, virtually ignoring the central archetypes (Self, Anima/Animus, Wise Old Man, etc.) and such theories as typology and synchronicity, for example. In the Introduction to his *Eleusis*, Kerényi suggests that the relationship with Jung had brought him little that was new theoretically, while Jung thought the mythologist's researches corroborated his own theory of the archetypal configurations of the psyche.[31] In his correspondence with Mann, Kerényi wrote that his greatest satisfaction from the joint work with Jung came from knowing that his contribution to Jung's psychology might assist in the healing of suffering human beings. Consistent with his 1945 letter's advocacy for a future humanism enriched by depth psychology, this statement also situates that advocacy in its broader context of Kerényi's preeminent concerns as a humanist.

IV.

Kerényi continued to promote the value of depth psychology in his late work, and the name most frequently mentioned in such cases was Jung's. But it misrepresents his independence as a scholar, the range of his work, and the precise style of his humanism, to over-hastily identify Kerényi with Jung and the "Jungian" theoretical orbit. Always first a classicist and religious historian steeped in the Greek and Roman sources of Europe's traditions, the horizon of his research remained philological, "occidental," polytheistic, literary—at core, traditionally humanist.[32] Depth psychology represents an 'anthropological' facet of Kerényi's humanism in the sense discussed above: its prospect on the unconscious side of human nature seemed to him to promise a more accurate and sensitive theoretical *logos* of human being.

Karl Kerényi's humanism stands closer to the Enlightenment than to any postmodern deconstruction of the metaphysics and grand narratives of God, history, and self bound up with the West's humanist project.[33] But, fairly evaluated in the context of its time, his humanism is unmistakably preoccupied with issues and aporias pointing beyond modernity. Summarizing, I note four points. One is how deeply impressed he was by the war and the *failure* of traditional humanism. His thought is driven by that failure; he seeks to move beyond, more than to explain it. Another had to do with the pluralism inherent to his vision. Plurality and heterogeneity represent a dimension of lived human experience that Kerényi endeavors, from within his field, to articulate as an abiding feature in the life not only of ancient polytheists, but of contemporary men and women—and not only artists. This, I suspect, was his true advocacy. His hermeneutics, anticipating Gadamer in some respects, insisted upon illuminating the subjectivity behind acts of interpretation and questioned the false 'objectivity' of positivism and historicism.[34] Finally, always concerned with the nuances of the concrete and particular, his perspective resisted the kind of abstraction that fed sterile utilitarian and instrumental modes of thought. These he thought were anathema to a living humanism; carried to extremes, inflated, aloof from human particularities, they became for him part of the theory and the apparatus of an arch-inhumanity.

In the crisis of his age, Kerényi recognized the lack of a heuristic image of humanity that reflected its recrudescent "typhonic" potential, and proposed an anthropological foundation for a humanism that he hoped would legitimize a more heterogeneous self-awareness. The still young 'science' of depth psychology appeared at the time to offer relevant, and badly needed insight to this project. Kerényi's recognition situates him very close to present day concerns, and suggests, in sum, that he be regarded as a humanist thinker prepared to *extend* the framework and the tools of humanism so that it be adequate for the situation of the age. No tragic exemplar of humanism's exhaustion, then, but a partisan, committed to humanism's renewal, exiled at the frontier of the postmodern age by the cataclysmic lapse during his lifetime of humanism's guiding ideals.

Kerényi experienced at close range the intimidation and defamation, the persecution, marginalization, and exile (that is, the ethical demand for a self-imposed exile) that become hallmarks of the *experience* of humanism's failure in the middle and late twentieth century.[35] He sought to confront that failure, at the moment of its distressing civilization-wide manifestation, with the intellectual energy, orientation, and tools of a career coming into its prime—as a classical philologist and historian of religion. The force of the encounter shaped the course of his life and work as a self-designated "itinerant humanist."

V.

David Miller's ardent commitment to education[36] and the humane purpose of his scholarship make him a humanist in the broadest, best sense. Fittingly, he too has been itinerant: between Syracuse and Santa Barbara, Europe, Eranos, Kyoto. So perhaps a last detour, through a metaphor at the heart of modernity's historical and geographical career, is not out of place. The heterogeneous consciousness I've argued was Karl Kerényi's greater advocacy—his humanism at the margin, a stance not so unlike David's—serves humankind in a "post-contact" world. "Contact" here connotes not merely that historical encounter of the West with non-Western cultures, religions, and myths, an encounter that, here in the Americas as elsewhere, and so often before and since, forgot the other in her or his inalienable human dignity. The conduct of these encounters and their far-reaching, indeed, ubiquitous upshot pulses daily in the latest breaking news. Justifiably matters of intense struggle, they also never cease to be reminders of the urgent need to find the terms of a common humanity.

"Post-contact" also means here *post-Freud and Jung*. Surely, we are *after* modernity's encounter with the reality and autonomy of "the Unconscious" as a preoccupation of monadic "selves." Depth psychology today is challenged by medical psychiatry's assertions that we are altogether *after* it as a therapeutic enterprise. Many would share Kerényi's lament as technical rationality comes to pervade even medicine's care for the human being, further marginalizing a healing art that, on the other hand, at its best had always positioned itself at the "margin" in the sense noted early in this paper: subtly attuned to fissures and lacunae in the surfaces of quotidian life, finding the otherness at the heart of 'us'. The *un*-conscious, so like myth in this respect, never ceases to be the site of a conflict of interpretations. David Miller estranges and refracts our gaze upon the place of myth, and of psychology, in the human struggle to circumscribe (at times also to mystify) the *un*-known, the *in*-visible, the *no*-thing—and this he does most humanely.

A final observation from an important recent 'stranger' among us. In perhaps one of his last published enunciations of what he understood by the word humanism, Edward Said, in the Preface to the twenty-fifth anniversary edition of his book *Orientalism*, had several things to say that pulse through the teaching and mentorship of David Miller, things that resonate too with many of Karl Kerényi's concerns. I think, for example, of Said's insistence that the tools of inquiry, which he regarded as a threatened but still available "legacy of humanistic education," are appropriately and necessarily applied to the investigation of human agency in the "world of history made by human beings."[37] In the same place he goes on to say, in words I cannot help but situate in relation to Kerényi's search for a "new" (precise, anthropological, relevant) humanism cognizant of the typhon:

> Humanism is centered upon the agency of human individuality and subjective intuition, rather than on received ideas and approved authority.... [M]ost important, humanism is the only, and I would go so far as to say, the final resistance we have against the inhuman practices and injustices that disfigure human history.

NOTES

[1] Giambattsita Vico, *New Science,* trans. T. Bergin and M. Fisch (Ithaca: Cornell UP, 1976), § 1102-06.

[2] *Strangers to Ourselves,* trans. L.S. Rouiez (New York: Columbia UP, 1991), 1-3, 182, 191-92.

[3] E. Said discusses the centrality of an "estranged" consciousness for Auerbach's idea of humanism in his book *Orientalism* (New York: Vintage, 1979/1994 [2003]), 258-60. Kerényi designates himself as an "itinerant humanist"(wandernden Humanisten) in "Selbstbiographisches,"*Wege und Weggenossen II,* (München: Langen Müller, 1988), 434. Hungarian classical scholar János G. Szilágyi makes note of this moniker and discusses Kerényi's estrangement from his field and his country in a summary of European conferences marking the centennial of Kerényi 's birth. "Kerényi Year 1997" (1997, C3 Center for Culture and Communication, Budapest); >http://www.c3.hu/scripta/books/98/34/kereny.htm< (17 Nov., 2005).

[4] "Lob des Konkreten. Aus einem Brief an einen deutschen Dichterfreund," *Humanistische Seelenforschung* (Stuttgart: Klett-Cotta, 1996), 299.

[5] "Grundbegriffe und Zukunftsmöglichkeiten des Humanismus. Ein Brief an junge Humanisten," *Humanistische Seelenforschung*, 291-92.

[6] "Lob des Konkreten," 301.

[7] *Ibid.*, 300.

[8] *Ibid.*, 298-299.

[9] "Wesen und Gegenwärtigkeit des Mythos," *Wege und Weggenossen I* (München: Langen Müller, 1985), 93. Cf. also the 1957 transcription of a radio lecture bearing the posthumous title "Perspektiven" ("Perspectives") in *Wege und Weggenossen II*, 446-468, esp. 446-51.

[10] Alexander Gelley, trans. and ed., *Mythology and Humanism: The Correspondence of Thomas Mann and Karl Kerényi* (Ithaca, NY: Cornell UP, 1975), 15. Cf. Kerényi's "Bericht über die Arbeiten der Jahren 1939 bis 1948," *Wege und Weggenossen II*, 439-40.

[11] *Auf Spuren des Mythos* (München: Langen-Müller, 1967), 10. The second quotation translates Kerényi's original idea for the title of his *Humanistische Seelenforschung*. See its "Vorwort," 14.

[12] *Auf Spuren des Mythos*, 10.

[13] The ethical dimension of Kerényi's posture toward scholarship has been called his "lasting heritage" (Szilágyi, "Kerényi Year"). Kerényi chafed at the rising nationalism that infected the academy in Hungary at the time he launched his professional career in the '20s. Cf. "Selbstbiographisches," 433-34.

[14] *Mythology and Humanism*, 110-11.

[15] "Bericht," 438. This recognition of the mythic gods as presences to the living *experience* of ancient religion reflects Otto 's greatest, and lasting influence on Kerényi.

[16] *Ibid.*, 439-40. Noting the divergence from Otto here, he stresses his growing regard for the "more difficult and, precisely because of that, probably more genuine" non-classical sources from his 1937 Apollo book forward; cf. also "Grundbegriffe," 294. On criticisms of Kerényi, see *Mythology and Humanism*, 108-113.

[17] *Mythology and Humanism*, 12-13. On Kerényi's "breakthrough" and "turning point," see 85, 95, and cf. "Bericht" 442-43. The 1940 book's

original title is *Die Antike Religion: Eine Grundlegung* (Amsterdam: Pantheon).

[18] The terms are elaborated at length in *Dionysos: Archetypal Image of Indestructible Life*, 1976, trans. Ralph Manheim (Princeton: Princeton UP, 1996), xxxi-xxxvii.

[19] *Mythology and Humanism*, 85-86, 90, 99. C.G. Jung and Karl Kerényi, *Essays on a Science of Mythology*, trans. R.F.C. Hull (Princeton: Princeton UP, 1949/1963), 8-9, 20-21.

[20] *Mythology and Humanism*, 27; "Grundbegriffe," 295-96. In this, Kerényi anticipates aspects of Gadamer's hermeneutics; see note 35 below.

[21] "Bericht," 438.

[22] *Mythology and Humanism*, 9; on Kerényi's praise of *Young Joseph*, 53. It should be mentioned that Kerényi provided Mann with abundant scholarly material in the form of his own essays and monographs, which Mann was keen to receive from his "teacher." Much of Kerényi's work found its way into Mann's fiction. See *ibid.*, 10-15, 166.

[23] "Bachofen—Nietzshce und Ariadne: Zwei Präludien,." in *Wege und Weggenossen II*, 122. Cf. "Lob des Konkreten," 300, on the inflation of the "higher man;" Kerényi notes Wilamowitz-Moellendorff's own inflated idealization of philological science in "Grundbegriffe," 295-296.

[24] For incisive recent comments on the Nazis' manipulations of myth in the broader context of Romantic nationalism and, especially, the academic posterity of Herder's idea of the *Volk*, see Bruce Lincoln, *Theorizing Myth* (Chicago: U Chicago P, 1999), 52-56, 72-75.

[25] See Szilágyi's discussion of "the heart of the 'Kerényi question'" "(Kerenyi Year"). Kerényi addresses the matter, if indirectly, in "Bericht," 439-42, 445; cf. "Vorwort" to *Auf Spuren des Mythos*, 9-12. For another clue, cf. the Preface to his *Heroes of the Greeks*, where he discusses his interest in the fragmented narrative line of Virginia Woolf 's *Orlando* as inspiration for a writerly scholarship appropriate to the fragmentary disposition of myth.

[26] *Mythology and Humanism*, 100.

[27] "Grundbegriffe," 293.

[28] *Ibid.*, 291-93 (quoted passage 293).

[29] "Bericht," 440; cf. also "Kontakte Mit C.G. Jung," a previously unpublished handwritten note penned in 1961 (*Wege und Weggenossen II*), 345-46.

[30] *Prometheus: Archetypal Image of Human Existence*, 1963, trans. Ralph Manheim (Princeton: Princeton UP, 1991/1997), xviii-xix. Kerényi picks up the matter again in the Introduction to *Eleusis* (see next note). The distinction was also emphasized in the 1961-62 fragment "Kontakte," 345-6.

[31] *Eleusis: Archetypal Image of Mother and Daughter*, 1967, trans. Ralph Manheim (Princeton: Princeton UP, 1991), xxiv-xxxiii. Jung's enthusiasm for Kerényi's studies is reflected in letters to him. *C.G. Jung Letters, Volume 1*, ed. G. Adler and A. Jaffe, trans. R.F.C. Hull (Princeton: Princeton UP, 1992). See for example 26 July, 1940, in which Jung suggests writing the commentary for the "Kore" essay; the letters of 18 January and 10 March 1941, which reflect Jung's inspiration to work Kerényi's book on the 'Aegean Festival' scene in Goethe's *Faust* for its alchemical insights; and of 6 July and 1 August, 1944, which request citation of Kerényi's personal communications to Jung regarding Asklepios; these topics found their way into Jung's *Mysterium Coniunctionis*.

[32] Kerényi did of course make forays outside the sphere of Europe's cultural foundations, as evident in the "Kore" essay and, prominently, in his *Labyrinth Studies* (1941). Letters to Mann in America beginning in the late 1930s express his desire to access documents on Native American myth. In *Thomas Mann – Karl Kerényi: Gespräch in Briefen* (Zürich: Insel Verlag, 1960), 85-86, 89.

[33] For one philosophical articulation, see Jacques Derrida, "The Ends of Man" *Margins of Philosophy*, trans. Alan Bass (Chicago, U Chicago P., 1982), especially pp. 114-136.

[34] This point is discussed in a kind assessment of Kerényi by Fritz Graf, historian of ancient religions, in an article in the *Neue Zürcher Zeitung* for the occasion of Kerényi's centenary. "Philologe, Mythologe, Humanist: Vor hundert Jahren wurde Karl Kerényi gestorben." (18 January, 1997), 65. Also mentioned as a conference topic in Szilágyi, "Kerényi Year."

[35] See Szilagyi, "Kerényi Year" on his ostracization by the left in post-War Hungary, largely as a result of his denunciation as a reactionary and irrationalist by György Lucács. Kerényi had returned home in 1947 hoping, fruitlessly, to resume his academic career there. Near the war's end he and his family endured the agonizing loss of contact with his two oldest daughters still in Hungary, one of whom, Grazia, the Nazis had arrested for her outspoken opposition to Hungary's annexation. *Gespräch in Briefen*, 101, 104.

[36] The first three lectures viewable from his website each deal specifically with different aspects of education and testify publicly to this ardor. >http://web.syr.edu/~dlmiller/lectures.htm<

[37] *Orientalism*, xxix. *Margins of Philosophy*, trans. Alan Bass (Chicago, U Chicago P., 1982), especially pp. 114-136.

[34] This point is discussed in a kind assessment of Kerényi by Fritz Graf, historian of ancient religions, in an article in the Neue Zürcher Zeitung for the occasion of Kerényi's centenary. "Philologe, Mythologe, Humanist: Vor hundert Jahren wurde Karl Kerényi gestorben." (18 January, 1997), 65. Also mentioned as a conference topic in Szilágyi, "Kerényi Year."

[35] See Szilagyi, "Kerényi Year" on his ostracization by the left in post-War Hungary, largely as a result of his denunciation as a reactionary and irrationalist by György Lucács. Kerényi had returned home in 1947 hoping, fruitlessly, to resume his academic career there. Near the war's end he and his family endured the agonizing loss of contact with his two oldest daughters still in Hungary, one of whom, Grazia, the Nazis had arrested for her outspoken opposition to Hungary's annexation. Gespräch in Briefen, 101, 104.

[36] The first three lectures viewable from his website each deal specifically with different aspects of education and testify publicly to this ardor. >http://web.syr.edu/~dlmiller/lectures.htm<

[37] *Orientalism*, xxix.

In the Twinkling of His Eye: Homage to David Miller

EDWARD S. CASEY

I.

It is really somewhat uncanny—the way David Miller, the man and his work, keep emerging in my life. I first met the man himself in a full-scale ice storm in Dallas, Texas, in 1976, at the inaugural gathering of archetypal psychologists in North America. Little did I realize that our slipping and sliding together in a van was symbolic of Miller's own elegant evasiveness as a writer, moving from one topic to another with lightning speed and wit, as if navigating the icy surfaces of language and thought: surfaces that conceal the frozen waters underneath. I encountered Miller next in his native habitat of Syracuse when I lectured there at his bidding. I went on for over two hours on that occasion, and David was gracious in his role of host even as he must have fumed under his collar. When he commented briefly upon my diffuse talk, he did so with pithy verve— and a sense of humor which he alone, among archetypalists worldwide, can muster. In fact, he was often chosen to close a major meeting, thanks to his remarkable ability to seize the essence of what had been discussed and to set it into proper perspective—to set it right.

Our most recent meeting was in Santa Barbara, where we were both teaching at Pacifica Graduate Institute: I in my first engagement there, he in his final year of disengagement. We had just discovered that we were both obsessed with the same topic—the edge. As ever, David was far more advanced than I on this subject, and I found myself making many notes on our conversation. We headed pell-mell into comparative edge-work—I the dedicated phenomenologist telling him of my fledgling attempts to describe the edge and to distinguish its primary kinds (rim, verge, brink, border, and boundary); he, much more the scholar, had already mastered an enormous literature on edges in many fields. He had done the hard research which I had put off. But these differences of early approach could not diminish the striking fact that each of us, coming from such different fields (he, from religious studies; I, from philosophy), had settled on the same exact area of research—and an odd one at that, rarely pursued as such in either of our respective specialities.

Something like this totally unexpected convergence had happened to me only very rarely. Half-way through writing a book on imagination, I found out that the wife of the head of the college with which I was affiliated at Oxford University, Mary Warnock, was composing a book at that very moment on the same subject: the two books appeared together in the same year (1976). Then, a decade later, I finished a book on memory, only to learn that Ms. Warnock had just completed her own book on memory: again, the two books were published in the same year (1987). Shortly after, I was sent another book on memory, this one by Paul Connerton of Cambridge University: its approach and conclusions were even more close to my own work than was Warnock's.

Still, Connerton and Warnock were people I had never met, and they were both from England. It was more amazing to me that David Miller, by then a friend and fellow traveler, could converge with me on a subject matter that is as far from the central concerns of philosophy as it is from the core of archetypal psychology. Thus, you can imagine my astonishment when I reflected that our coming to the edge together had been preceded by an earlier, and even more improbable, coincidence: this time around the ostensibly topic of the human glance. It is odd enough for *one* person to write on this apparently marginal moment of vision, which differs from such basic acts as imagination and memory that so many have discussed—but for *two* contemporaries to get into the glance and to find it so richly revealing: this verges on the incredible! How could this have happened?

One can only speculate that David Miller and I were once Siamese twins joined at the brain and separated just after birth by a demonic Cartesian surgeon—so early in life that neither of us can remember our brief moment of interfusion. Or perhaps we are parapsychological brothers who, at some unconscious level, read one another's minds and thus know what the other is thinking at any given moment. This is not, of course, to dismiss the possibility that one, or both, of us is a vampirish plagiarist, cunningly clever in stealing all the original thoughts of the other, including whole directions of research—and then entering into a kryptomnesiacal state wherein one conveniently forgets the act of pilfering itself.

Or maybe more likely, though less interesting theoretically, is the concrete possibility that David Miller and I are just that kind of archetypalist/philosopher who revels in the most far-out phenomena: what I like to call "peri-phenomena." And this is, after all, not wholly unpredictable, given the fascination with the atypical and the odd, the strange and the twisted that has characterized the domain of psychoanalysis since its inception in Freud, whose early axiom was that dreams and symptoms, jokes and parapraxes—each seemingly of such merely passing interest—are "never concerned with trivialities."[1] The same penchant for exploring extremities continued in Jung's passion for the "little people" of imaginal life and for the bizarre multiplicity of feeling-toned complexes; and it is taken still further in Hillman's proclivity for discerning the neglected figures of human fantasy and their counterparts in cultural life.

Nevertheless: to focus on things like the edge and the glance—is this not taking a fascination for the centrifugal beyond the pale? Are we not here pushing the outer envelope of good sense? Indeed, we are: David Miller and myself. We are not moving into nonsense—or so we hope—but we are taking a decided gamble in pursuing such untimely topics.

In this essay, written in homage to David Miller's genius for trivial pursuits that turn out to be decisive explorations of the things that matter most, I will take up our shared passion for the glance in my own terms, rejoining those of Miller only occasionally. In this way, I hope to make a further step toward realizing what seems to be our common destiny of meeting in the midst of the most unlikely conceptual space.[2]

II.

Hermes is an archetypal mediatrix: he brings together not only the gods with one another, but humans with gods (and vice versa). Wherever he is to be found, a matrix of diverse terms arises. We may imagine that the word "mediatrix" combines "medium" and "matrix" in a single word that signifies a Hermetic prowess that, far from merely reconciling existing differences between the terms, brings forth new directions and powers from their emergent connections.

The glance is the main mediatrix of visual perception, a connection-maker between the most disparate things and events. It links very different things in one sweep of the eye, while itself stealing away from view (echoing another aspect of Hermes: his secretiveness, symbolized in classical sculpture by his holding a finger to his lips). Any given glance connects edges and surfaces and whole things and events: people who come face to face, animals encountered in domestic space or in wilderness, basic elements (e.g., water, air, earth, fire), and events of all kinds (e.g., sitting, walking, fighting, pausing, etc.). In every case, the glance acts like a lasso that encircles such items, drawing them into its ambit—only to release them again. Not only does it shoot across a certain space to snare its targets, but it helps to constitute this space itself, making it into a pathway by which subsequent perceptions are carried to their intended objects. This pathway has the special property of being traversible in two directions by the gleam of my glance as it moves out of me ("Out of myself, but wanting to go beyond that ...,"[3] says Rumi) and then, only a moment later, is sent back to me along the same pathway it has itself opened up.

Moving back and forth across this common space, the glance detects what makes up its circumambience; it "picks up information" there, attending to it. But its pathmaking also thickens the space itself by engaging in actions of acknowledgement and recognition, discernment and singularization. Whether as bare apperception or as creative augmentation, the glance makes denser what would otherwise be thin and diaphanous. Its trajectories are not just added to a pre-existing space: they complicate and intensify this space, creating a field wherein connections are made, things happen, and meaning arises. The middle ground thus brought into being is not a neutral meaningless medium but a basis for the emergence of meaning itself. As Merleau-Ponty says:

> We propose ... to consider the order of culture or meaning an original order of *advent*, which should not be derived from that of mere events ... or treated as simply the effect of extraordinary conjunctions. It is characteristic of the human gesture to signify beyond its simple existence in fact, to inaugurate a meaning ....
> Each [such gesture] is both a beginning and a continuation which ... points to a [further] continuation or recommencement. ...
> Advent is a promise of events.[4]

A glance can be considered the eye's gesture toward the advent of meaning in the visual world—toward a "coming-to" (as "ad-vent" literally means) that signifies something more than bare existence or mere contiguity or conjunction. Going beyond the level of spatio-temporal location (where its pinpointing powers are already at play), it opens onto a level of meaning or visual significance (e.g., historicity of structure, presentation of sense) that promises further insights in subsequent acts of glancing and eventual acts of informed judgment. This, too, is thickening: enriching the present with meaning and with what is to come.[5]

In short, *the action is in the interaction*, and the glance as a mediatrix puts us into the midst of things and events, creating from their momentary interfusion an advent of meaning that exceeds their "simple presence."[6] The glance connects the otherwise unconnected across a space common to the glancer and the glanced-at; it brings them together in a place they share that is more than simple location. It is a genuine interplace in the literal sense of this term: a place of the between as well as between places. As such, it is a scene of what Jankélévitch calls *entrevision*, "intervision," literally "seing between."[7] Linking things in the visual field is the specific work of the glance, whose probative force transforms what it apprehends into a meaningful spectacle.

This means that the glance as mediatrix is part of the action itself. It is not in a purely spectatorial position, as an oculocentric interpretation would maintain. Instead, it is engaged in its own outgoing venture—its *advent*ure—as a full participant in the crisscrossing betweenness of the visual world. Only in this fashion can it create common ground and realize a new level of vision, an altered state of seeing that envisions new forms of meaning.

Such a basic transformation occurs, for example, when my glance interacts with that of another person: "Suddenly a gleam appeared, a little bit below and out in front of [her] eyes; [her] glance is raised and comes to fasten on the very things I am seeing."[8] Merleau-Ponty is here speaking of another person, whose glance I am myself seeing; I cannot but be struck by its forwardness as it rushes out of the other's eyes and attaches itself to some particular thing in a visual environment I share with this other. Our glances intersect at a place in the visual field where they encounter each other, reminding us that Hermes was also the god of crossroads.

In this particular circumstance, my glance not only notices the other's but rejoins it as both of our looks converge on a commonly beheld item: each noting something set forth between us. The result is a dialectic of lookings that, even short of a direct exchange (as when two lovers glance at each other[9]), engage in a conjoint action of crossed looks that takes place in its own shared space, that constituted by simultaneous glancing. In this delicate but often fateful drama, two trajectories are opened across the same visual space, one of which is directed entirely onto the thing seen and the other (my own) onto this same thing as well as the other's looking at it, my own glance crossing as well as rejoining the other's. And when more than two people engage in glancing at something in common, other combinations, bringing still further complications, emerge. This is not the place to trace out the ramifying interpersonal matrix of the glance —nor that of the different kind of complexity that ensues when other animals and inanimate objects are involved. Suffice it to say that in every such instance Hermetic connections occur, common space emerges, advent of meaning arises, and the plot of intervision thickens—all of this thanks to the glance as mediatrix.

III.

Another attribute of Hermes is his celebrated speed. This, too, accrues to the glance and is one of its major positive features. But speed in what sense? Clearly, we are not speaking of measurable velocity: who could clock a glance? Who would try? Nor are we speaking of the extremities of speed—zero or infinite speed. These alternatives belong to the ancient conception of the perfect cosmic circle, which can be considered to be wholly at rest or moving at a literally in-finite speed (i.e., a speed that cannot be computed by any finite number).[10] But the conception of time as "the moving image of eternity" (in the formula of the *Timaeus*), according to which time returns upon itself in perfect circularity, does not obtain for the glance, which if anything traces out a more elliptical path whose two epicenters are provided by the eye and the glanced-at thing or event.

The epicenters themselves, temporally rather than spatially regarded, embody the two beats of the time of the glance. These beats are not the successive tick-tock members of J.M. McTaggert's celebrated A series in which each would have a separate status; nor do they represent anything like the past/present/future of the B series.[11] Instead, they are quasi-simultaneous moments of time: so close to simultaneous that we cannot separate them in experience even if we can distinguish them in theory. They are convergent moments: no sooner does my glance go out than it is returned to me in some form—mimetically in the case of a mirror, as a response in the case of other humans who take in my glance, and as a trace in the instance of inanimate objects. In each case, the glancer has the impression of a virtually immediate return of the look, as if it leapt back from the target in the same moment in which it reached this target.

The interleaving of the outbound and the return trajectories of the glance, though not perfectly circular, is so intimate that we are not even aware of them as distinct phases of the same experience: I look at myself in the mirror and my image comes back to me right away, with such dazzling speed that one would be hard put to classify the circumstance as involving duration. Instead of unfolding—the *déroulement* with which Bergson characterizes duration[12]—time here happens at a kind of *absolute speed* that is not to be confused with infinite speed. Absolute speed is not simply a lot of speed, not even a very great lot of it (as with infinite speed, which is still measurable in principle even if no number can be affixed to it). It is, rather, speed that happens *all at once, totum simul.* It happens not just in a highly compressed state (as "simultaneous" and "instantaneous" both signify) but with sudden effect as an event that takes place—as "at a single stroke" (*tout d'un coup*) implies. The absolute speed of the glance is that of an advent, a heightened event that occurs in a flash, not unlike lightning—whose flash also occurs with absolute speed. This flash or stroke of happening is comparable to the moment of "sudden awakening" to which Walter Benjamin pointed, or to the *Augenblick* that combines time with eternity in a single event on Kierkegaard's conception —or to the *Augenblick* that closes off presence on Derrida's deconstructive reading of the same term in Husserl's *Logical Investigations.*

We are not talking of the speed of light—which has a numerical value, however vast—even if light is a material condition of the glance itself. It is a matter of *the absolute speed of advention.* Advention or "coming-to," which is the progenitor of coming-to-*be*, occurs in a flash. This flash need not be as dramatic as a stroke of lightning. It can be as inconspicuous as the twinkling of an eye. In contrast with the blink that closes the eye, a twinkle is not terminated by a moment of closure. Where closure ends an event—hence allows for its possible measurement—non-closure lets time emerge as ab-solute: not to be dissolved in numbers or minutes, not to be counted as such but rather sheerly to happen: just to be, or rather *to be as becoming.* In the twinkling of an eye, with absolute speed, an event comes to be as an advent; it becomes existent, all at once and in a single stroke.

The Biblical phrase "in the twinkling of an eye" (*en rhipó opthalmou*) comes paired with the equally significant phrase "in a moment" (*en atomé*) to yield the celebrated claim of the New Testament: "In a moment, in the twinkling of an eye, we shall all be transformed" (1 *Corinthians* 15, 51-2; *RSV*).[13] The absolute speed of advention is here at stake. The moment of transformation is that of the advention of the divine into the human realm, resulting in an instantaneous transformation that might be called an "advant," a word that combines *avant* ("before"), "to" (*ad-*), and more prosaically "advantage." Advants happen, however, not only in the moment of the incursion of the divine into the human domain but also between human beings in epiphanic moments: e.g., that of the "face to face," a phrase that Levinas borrows from theological discourse, wherein it describes the human encounter with the divine (evident in phrases like "now I see my savior face to face"). Whichever exact faces are at stake, in the absolute advant of the glance, something transformative occurs: as David Miller says laconically, "the twinkle changes things."[14] Something advenes within the ordinary world of perception and interpersonal communication. This something, the advant, stands out upon the surface of the most mundane setting, giving to the glancer the advantage of a special leverage upon the visual world. This is the visual equivalent of the Archimedian principle: "give me [the right place] and I will move the whole world." Just so: the world is seen anew in the twinkling of an eye, and in the intense illumination of this epiphanic moment the seeing subject is also renewed. One transformation not only calls for the other but induces the other to intervene—immediately, without delay. Both transformations occur at (almost) the same time: in the moment of the glance that is enacted with absolute speed.

Am I advocating a dromocentrism of the glance? "Dromocentrism," a coinage of Paul Virilio's, means being wholly centered on speed—the fascination, and the fate, of Western civilization according to Virilio.[15] Whatever the ultimate truth of Virilio's claim, there is an undeniable dromocentric dimension of the glance, a "good dromocentrism" as we might call it, which is allied with the visuocentrism which I would contrast with oculocentrism. Just as the glance is irrecusably visuocentric (it is oculocentric only when appropriated for determinate scientific, social, or political purposes), so it does indeed prize speed. Not speed for its own sake (i.e., the target of Virilio's caustic critique) but for the sake of the change that the luminescence of the look can bring. Or let us say: for the *enantiodromia* it effects—in Heraclitus's word for "sudden reversal into the opposite" (where "sudden" translates *dromia*, itself derived from *dromein*, "to run").

In the twinkling of an eye, in the absolute speed of the glance, a transformation of self and world alike takes place, a sudden reversal occurs, and all becomes different. This is what the transformative speed of the glance promises—and very often enacts. The change wrought by its advant is subtle but sweeping.[16] It is just here that the habituality of the glance, its inherent tacit knowledge, is suspended if not overcome; for at this moment of its history the glance, despite the sedimented history of antecedent acts of looking, is capable of bringing about the radically new, what is coming and to come, what is going to *be* something visually extraordinary standing out from the dense ground of its own becoming.

IV.

To glance is to be open to surprise. It is to enter a disclosure space where surprise is not only possible but highly probable. Why else would we glance unless we were willing to be surprised? (This is so even when we are fearful, furtively glancing at precisely what we fear the most.) Were we not willing to be surprised, we would restrict the field of vision to what is already fully known—to what we can expect to be the case. Rather than looking *out*, we would look *in*: either inside the perimeter of the familiar or inside ourselves, where we think we know the way. (It is revealing that we rarely speak of "glancing inside ourselves.") The characteristic vector of the glance is outward. Which is just what Husserl's preferred term "visual ray" (*Blickstrahl*) connotes: the eye's ray moves from the retina into the world—a world full of surprise, whether on the streets of Paris or in a mall in Fairfield, California.

Despite the many ways in which it occurs, in glancing we move into an arena of open possibility where, as Heraclitus put it, "Unless you expect the unexpected you will never find [truth], for it is hard to discover and hard to attain."[17] It is the unexpected, or at least the not fully known,

302

that we take in with the glance: to this reverse directionality from the world to us there corresponds the *Weltstrahlen* posited in Husserl's later writings (though already present in Greek theories of vision as intromissionist). By our glance we are drawn—or more exactly, we draw ourselves—into a region where many things can happen and thus where we are likely to be surprised: where we will have to take in what we did not expect to encounter. If a mere glance can take in so much, this is only because we have risked something to begin with: if nothing is ventured in vision, nothing is gained in sight. The venture, the adventure, of the glance is to go out into a domain of the unfamiliar and unknown, whether hoped for or feared, and to witness what happens there—come what may.

To venture out in this way is to be *curious* as to what lies outside of direct vision. In contrast with Heidegger's caustic and dismissive analysis of curiosity as on a par with gossip—both being forms of everyday fallenness—the curiosity at stake in the glance is a positive epistemic matter.[18] It is not a question of being cognitively "nosy" or seeking the new for the sheer sake of the new, as in "idle curiosity." The glancer is genuinely curious as to what may be the case around her, and wants to find out even at the expense of being disappointed or shocked by what meets the glance. (One thinks of Plato's example in the *Republic* of being overcome by spirit, by *thumos*, when a person is impelled to glance at a corpse on the roadside even though his reason tells him not to. The morbid, as well as the erotic, are virtually irresistible objects of the glance.) On the other hand, the curiosity in question is not to be assimilated to *wonder*, that prototypical philosophical emotion.[19] Wonder implies a sense of awe or mystery that is missing in the curiosity appropriate to the glance. Wonder may be induced by glancing, especially in "the now of recognizability" as specified by Benjamin, but once aroused from the sudden and surprising it calls for a slow, contemplative looking that is more akin to the gaze than to the glance and that includes an element of longing: *pothos* ("longing") and *thaumazein* ("to wonder") are closely affine in early Greek thinking. The longing is to know the ultimate truth of the way things *are*—the metaphysical truth of being, as Aristotle holds—

whereas glancing is content to know the truth of what happens on the surface of things: that is, what is first in the order of seeming rather than in the order of being. The glancer reverses the counsel of Wallace Stevens's emperor of ice cream: not "let be be finale of seem" but rather "let seem be the content of be."[20]

The active curiosity of glancing is expressed in the simple desire to know *what is going on in my circumambient world.* To enact this curiosity in a glance I cannot be visually cautious — or else I will close myself to what the glance reveals. I must be willing to expose myself to what my glance itself exposes. I must be, in every sense of the word, *open-eyed* to what I do not yet know for sure is the case—to what is concealed from the glance as it starts to send its ray outward. And it is just because the world conceals so much of itself—gives itself only by partial profiles, as Husserl insists—that the glance is drawn to discover what I do not yet know about my physical or social surroundings, my overall layout. I take in the world at a glance only because the world itself withdraws so radically from full revelation. It does not give itself all at once, but for this very reason the glance is inspired to light on appearances that present themselves to me here and now—even if these appearances, and their status as being apperceived together, cannot claim to deliver the ultimate truth of things.

The price of this gift of the world's seeming—this discovery of what appears to be the case in terms of the presented surfaces of particular places—is comparatively small. The price is simply surprise. To glance into the world is to let oneself be surprised by the world. "Surprise" is regarded by theorists of emotion as one of the seven basic emotions (happiness, fear, anger, sadness, disgust/contempt, and interest being the other ones).[21] According to one leading researcher, the aim of surprise, especially in its primitive form of "startle," is "to help prepare the individual to deal effectively with [a] new or sudden event and with the consequences of this event."[22] Beyond its sheer utility, however, surprise is the emotional *response* to the discovery of the unexpected, and it is the constant companion of glancing. To glance is to expose oneself to surprise, and it is to do so in the mode of the sudden.

The importance of the sudden was brought to late modern attention by Kierkegaard, for whom it represented the exception to the Hegelian System, that which forever evades this System—in which nothing happens suddenly but only according to the slow labor of the negative.[23] The sudden interrupts and disrupts the Juggernaut of continual dialectical synthesis. Like the instant, it is a factor of discontinuity. Hence its disconcerting character: human beings generally, and not only logocrats such as Hegel, prefer the continuous and predictable. But they also know that all is not continuous and predictable. Thus they glance out around themselves in order to anticipate the sudden so that it will not arrive wholly unbidden, blindsiding them.

The sudden cuts into the customary, arriving seemingly from nowhere. To meet it half-way, rather than being its mere victim, is to beat it at its own game. Thus we go out to meet the sudden—in a glance, often defined as "a hurried [or quick] look."[24] Our glance's characteristic celerity, its dartingness, matches that of the sudden it is prepared to confront: one swiftness calls for another. This is why it is never too soon to glance (except in the tragic case of Orpheus, who couldn't prevent himself from glancing backward at Eurydice too early). The more quickly we glance the more adequate we are to the world's waywardness, its quirky happening, its effervescent eventfulness. In the face of this cosmic uncertainty, we are saved by a glance—by something transitory that matters greatly in the larger scheme of things.

Kierkegaard, speaking out of the temporocentrism that kept him tied to Hegel despite his animadversions against the System, considered the sudden to be a temporal category—thus allied exclusively with the present moment (*Augenblick*). But if the sudden is a truly radical interruption *of time itself*, then it cannot be just another temporal notion —something to be swallowed and surpassed by the Saturnic succession of time. On the contrary: part of being sudden is to resist temporal, indeed causal, analysis: to appear, not just from nowhere but more particularly from *nowhen*. Moreover, the sudden characterizes our experience of place as well as time. This is a lesson we learn from Benjamin's

Arcades Project, which traces the sudden and the surprising alike as they arose in city life in late nineteenth-century Paris.

Typically, we experience the sudden as attaching to a given scene of action: "the forest is aflame!" we say, pinning the sudden on a patch of fuming woods that constitutes a concrete place. Although we can certainly have sudden thoughts or memories, the suddenness belonging to the glance seeks material exemplification—and thus a place in which to appear (as well as edged surfaces in which to be manifest). This follows from the fact that we glance from here to there, that is, *from one place to_another.* This transplacement happens in an *Augenblick,* literally 'look of the eyes' and not merely 'moment' as the German word is often translated into English; and it is a look that happens immediately (as *augenblicklich* colloquially connotes), "in the blink of an eye," a close cousin of the twinkle. The action of the glance is an immediate look (outward) of the eyes—a look that is equal to the sudden way the world of places, the place-world, emerges differently from what we had expected, thereby surprising us.[25]

It is not because of time-consciousness, then, that we must "admit the other into the self-identity of the *Augenblick*; nonpresence and nonevidence ... into the *blink of an instant.*"[26] These words of Derrida's —intended to deconstruct Husserl's phrase "*im selben Augenblick*" ('at the same time', 'simultaneously') as employed in the latter's *Logical Investigations*—could also apply to the glance. For it is by the glance that what is other to/other than what we had expected is allowed to interrupt our self-certainty and self-presence—that the non-present and the non-evident emerge for us as lifelong lookers.

The glance allows us to savor the world as a surprising affair—as something that happens suddenly, somewhere. It lets us see the world on a slender sleeve of seeming whose surface surprises us in the sudden unexpectedness of its appearances. It lets us see so much in so little—so much surface and place, so little time and space. If the poetic image is, according to Bachelard, "a sudden salience on the surface of the psyche,"[27] the content of the glance is an equally sudden salience on the surface of things. The source of this content is a place-world that, surprising us, is itself surprised in a glance.

V.

The glance possesses a final positive power: a special gift for undoing divisive dyads of various sorts—especially traditional binaries that pit one metaphysical term or set of terms over against another. This may seem paradoxical, given my earlier emphasis on the two-way, in-and-out dialectic of the glance, as well as on its two-beat and two-space character. But the paradox is only apparent; it dissolves when we consider the connective strength of glancing and its laying out of the shared ground of intimate relationship between disparate items. Here we return to the first of its Hermetic virtues—linkage across shared space. Indeed, the glance can be said to be the apperceptual equivalent of the imagination conceived as "the link of links"(Bruno). It is thanks to its chiasmatic power of crossing-over in the midst of a common space that the glance comes into its own, and it does so by disowning dichotomies that threaten to divide this space into incompatible oppositions.

I have in mind such binary terms as mind vs. matter, self vs. other, spirit vs. soul, sky vs. earth. Each of these dyads suggests a forced choice between one or the other of the two terms, rather than their mutual affirmation or complex collocation. In Derrida's elegant formulation: it is a matter of "neither/nor, that is, *simultaneously* either *or*."[28] Instead of exclusionary choices, or third options, we should recognize the choice between members of a given dyad as something "undecidable" that vacillates between extremes, choosing neither alone ("neither/nor") while respecting both ("*simultaneously* either *or*").[29] This logic is not only *like* that of the glance; it describes its own proclivity for moving fitfully but forcefully between carefully articulated terms—between points on a surface in acts of apperceptive transfer that affirm the entire field of vision in its epiphenomenal displays. Not only across this field but within it—along the faultlines on its surface—the glance adroitly connects the disconnected, solders the split, undoes the dichotomized. As David Miller says pointedly:

how can there be divisive dualisms—heaven over against hell, divine over against human, male over against female, reality over against representations—when there is a twinkle in the perspectival eye, a riffling-ruffling-rippling (*rhipō*) perspective of the human and the cosmic, when everything is a mirror: mirrors mirroring mirrors, up and down and in and out? And everything *is* a mirror when it is reflected upon, for in the reflections the world twinkles back at us.[30]

Miller here emphasizes the mirror as a basis for understanding the dynamics of the glance in its ritornelle movement. But more than mirroring is at stake: also operative is the sense that the world at which we glance somehow looks back at us: it does not just return our own image but its own, quite different visage. This sense has been articulated by painters such as Klee and elaborated by Merleau-Ponty; it is given express formulation by Lacan: "the pre-existence of a look—I see only from one point, but in my existence I am looked at from all sides."[31] If ordinary things and not only literal mirror images return our glance—if there is a more complex order of visual exchange in the perceptual world than is captured in any model of one-way looking—then the traditional dyad that puts the human on one side and everything non-human on the other is no longer viable. For glancing will occur in many circumstances in which such a dichotomy does not obtain. In these circumstances of lively intervision—wherein looks of many beings crisscross in every which way—the glance will be a primary prompter, catalyzing the most diverse and unlikely collaborations. No longer to be regarded as subservient to the sobriety of the gaze, it will be recognized as the major interanimating force in the world of vision: a world that is taken in at a glance.

VI.

In this essay I have been pursuing the inner logic of the glance—its penchant for intermediacy, its alliance with the sudden and the surprising, its deconstruction of dyads. There is much more to be said about the character and fate of the glance. Here, I have invoked only a few aspects of its Hermetic genius, and I do so in a spirit of drawing closer to the seminal thought of David Miller: to honor this thought for its premonitory insight. Long before I wandered into the topic—mainly from an acute sense of the neglect of the glance in previous philosophical discussions of visual perception—Miller had clearly discerned its more encompassing significance as it forms part of that comportment called "the twinkling of the eye."

True to his learned origins, Miller took off from a famous Biblical passage—an ancient precursory text—and explored the farther reaches of this peculiar visual act. I began my own work from a phenomenological base of the description of human experience in its perceptual origins. But we meet in the middle—in a shared excitement at discovering the unsuspected power of a supposedly marginal phase of vision. Both the glance and the twinkling of the eye are characteristically dismissed as inconsequential or superficial—as "just looking." Both Miller and I acknowledge the ec-centric status of glancing and twinkling, but consider this very eccentricity an epistemic virtue that is found in no other visual behavior. Not only an epistemic virtue but also ethical, religious, and cosmic virtues as well. For both of us, the peri-phenomenon proves to be the phenomenon itself. Just as the glance is often the first look onto a scene, so the twinkling of the eye can open up an ambiance of confident and trusting affirmation, with a twist of humor intimated in its very unrehearsed spontaneity. Moreover, each visual act takes us very deeply into a given circumstance—much more deeply than we are led to believe when it is claimed that such acts are merely trivial. But nothing is trivial in the enactment of a glance or a twinkle—no more than in a dream or a symptom. From each we learn much about the place-worlds in which we have no choice but to participate.

I point here to two convergent paths edging on each other, both dedicated to the pursuit of the unobvious in the context of the everyday, the extraordinary in the ordinary. But David Miller, as always, is in the lead position—out there first, skiing skillfully down the most precipitous slope, inspiring others with his wit and his wisdom, first among equals. We are fortunate to have him as our friend and teacher, our intrepid guide, our *spiritus rector*, our mercurial mentor: himself Hermetic in his fleet-footed forays into the crossroads of the unexpected and the novel.

His appreciative readers and students not only benefit from encountering him at these crossroads; they are transformed by the trail he blazes and by his incomparable presence throughout: at once rigorous and hilarious, athletic and scholarly, reserved and warmly personal. We grasp all of this in one glance at his trajectory, catching a glimpse of his mind and body alike; we see it in the twinkling of his eye as it takes us in, and our own twinkling back at him in turn, grateful and transfigured as we are for having him in our shared sight.

NOTES

[1] Sigmund Freud, *The Interpretation of Dreams*, tr. J. Strachey (New York: Avon, 1969), 215: "Dreams are never concerned with trivialities; we do not allow our sleep to be disturbed by trifles."

[2] Several of the following pages have been adapted, in altered form, from the Epilogue to my forthcoming book, *The World at a Glance* (Indiana University Press, 2006).

[3] Rumi, "What I See in Your Eyes," from *The Glance: Songs of Soul-Meeting*, tr. Coleman Barks (New York: Penguin Compass, 1999), 52.

[4] M. Merleau-Ponty, "Indirect Language and the Voices of Silence," tr. R. McCleary and reprinted from *Signs* in G.A. Johnson, ed. *The Merleau-Ponty Aesthetics Reader: Philosophy and Painting* (Evanston: Northwestern University Press, 1993), 105-6; his italics.

[5] On the emergence of visual significance, see especially Rudolf Arnheim, *Visual Thinking* (Berkeley: University of California Press, 1969).

[6] "Its value exceeds its simple presence" ("Indirect Language and the Voices of Silence," 105). What Merleau-Ponty here says of "gesture" is all the more true of the glance.

[7] See Vladimir Jankélévitch, *Philosophie Première: Introduction à une philosophie du 'presque'* (Paris: Presses Universitaires de France, 1954), Introduction.

[8] Merleau-Ponty, "The Philosopher and his Shadow," tr. R. McCleary in *Signs* (Evanston: Northwestern University Press, 1964), 169. This statement should be set beside that of Wittgenstein: "The ear receives;

the eye looks. (It casts glances, it flashes, radiates, gleams.)" (*Zettel.*, tr. G.E.M. Anscombe & G.H. von Wright [Berkeley: University of California Press, 1976], 40)

⁹ Popular songs do not fail to refer to this circumstance: "He won't leave my sight for a glance" (line from "The Music that Makes Me Dance," as sung by Shirley Horne on the album *You Won't Forget Me*; "Strangers in the night/ exchanging glances" from the song "Strangers in the Night"; "You and your glance make this love," from *Finian's Rainbow.*)

¹⁰ It is this circumstance to which Derrida alludes when he employs the phrase "at the zero or infinite speed of the circle." (Jacques Derrida, *Given Time I: Counterfeit Money*, tr. P. Kamuf [Chicago: University of Chicago Press, 1992], 24). He is discussing the idea of the gift as belonging to a circular exchange that suggests the ancient paradigm.

¹¹ Regarding these two series, see J.M. McTaggert, "Time," chapter 33 of Book V of his *The Nature of Existence*, Vol. 2 (Cambridge: Cambridge University Press, 1927); as reprinted in R.M. Gale, *The Philosophy of Time* (New York: Humanities Press, 1978).

¹² On *déroulement*, which can also mean "spreading out," see *Time and Free Will: An Essay on the Immediate Data of Consciousness*, tr. F.L. Pogson (New York: Dover, 2001), 73-4: "we shall now have to inquire what the multiplicity of our inner states becomes, what form duration assumes, when the space in which it unfolds (*déroule*) is eliminated."

¹³ For a remarkable treatment of this dictum, see David L. Miller, "Through the Looking-Glass – The World as Enigma," in R. Ritsema, ed. *Spiegelung in Mensch und Cosmos* (Insel Verlag, 1986), 401 ff. As will be seen in what follows, I am much indebted to Miller for his far-ranging yet acute analysis in this essay.

¹⁴ *Ibid.*, 401.

¹⁵ Paul Virilio, *Speed and Politics*, tr. M. Polizzotti (New York: Semiotexte, 1986) as well as "La Dromoscopie et la lumière de la vitesse," *Critiques* (1978).

¹⁶ "Sweeping" is another meaning of *rhipé*, and it is certainly striking that we speak unselfconsciously of a "sweeping glance." Still further senses of *rhipé* include swinging and rushing—the former suggesting the

swinging back and forth in the glance's two-beat rhythm, the latter the rapidity of the glance.

[17] Heraclitus, Fragment #18 (Diels-Kranz), translation of P. Wheelwright in his book *Heraclitus* (New York: Atheneum, 1968), 20.

[18] For Heidegger's analysis of curiosity, see *Being and Time*, tr. J. Macquarrie & E. Robinson (New York: Harper & Row, 1962), section 36, 214 -19.

[19] In Aristotle's words: "It is owing to their wonder that men both now begin and at first began to philosophize." (Aristotle, *Metaphysics* A, 982 b 12-13; in the W.D. Ross translation as revised by J. Barnes; as cited in J.L. Ackrill, ed. *A New Aristotle Reader* [Princeton: Princeton University Press, 1982], 258.)

[20] The line "Let be be finale of seem" comes from "The Emperor of Ice-Cream," first published in 1922 and found in *The Collected Poems of Wallace Stevens* (New York: Knopf, 1954).

[21] On the seven basic emotions, see Paul Ekman, ed. *Emotion in the Human Face* (New York: Cambridge, 1982; 2nd ed.), esp. chapter three.

[22] Carroll Izard, *Human Emotions* (New York: Plenum 1977), 281. I owe this reference and that in the previous footnote to Jenefer Robinson, "Startle," *Journal of Philosophy* (1995), Vol. 92 (Feb., 1995), 53-74. Robinson makes it clear that startle is also closely related to fear: startle is "a developmentally early form of two emotions in particular, namely, fear and surprise"(57).

[23] Søren Kierkegaard, "Interlude," *Philosophical Fragments* (tr. D. Swenson & H. Hong (Princeton: Princeton University Press, 1962), 89-110.

[24] "Hurried look" is from the *Oxford English Dictionary*; "brief look" is given in the *American Heritage Dictionary*.

[25] For discussion of several points in this paragraph, and for reflections on the importance of the bodily "here," I am grateful to Irene Klaver in conversation.

[26] Jacques Derrida, *Speech and Phenomena*, tr. D. Allison (Evanston: Northwestern University Press, 1973), p. 65; his italics.

²⁷ Bachelard, *The Poetics of Space*, tr. M. Jolas (New York: Orion, 1964), xi.

²⁸ Jacques Derrida, *Positions*, tr. A. Bass (Chicago: University of Chicago Press, 1981), 43; his italics.

²⁹ On the logic of undecidability, see *ibid.*, 42 ff.

³⁰ Miller, "Through a Looking-Glass—the World as Enigma," 401-2; his italics.

³¹ Jacques Lacan, *The Four Fundamental Concepts of Psychoanalysis*, tr. A. Sheridan (New York: Norton, 1977), 72. I have changed "gaze" to the more neutral verb "look," since the French word, *le regard*, can mean either gaze or glance. For Lacan's revised discussion of the mirror—beyond his earlier "mirror stage"—see *ibid.*, 80 ff,. in which the situation of "seeing myself seeing" is analyzed. In "Eye and Mind" Merleau-Ponty cites André Marchand on the forest looking at me rather than the reverse—"it was not I who was looking at the forest … I felt that the trees were looking at me" ("Eye and Mind," tr. M.B. Smith in *The Merleau-Ponty Aesthetics Reader*, 129)—and he elaborates on this theme in *The Visible and the Invisible*, tr. A. Lingis (Evanston: Northwestern University Press, 1968), chapter four, esp. 154-5: "As soon as I see, it is necessary that the vision … be doubled with a complementary vision or with another vision: myself seen from without … he who sees cannot possess the visible unless he is possessed by it, unless he *is of it*, unless, by principle, according to what is required by the articulation of the look with the things, he is one of the visibles, capable, by a singular reversal, of seeing them …" (his italics).

CONTRIBUTORS

J. HEATH ATCHLEY is Senior Lecturer in Philosophy and Religion at Western New England College. He is completing a book entitled *The Immanent Secular: Philosophical Encounters in Religion and Culture.*

EDWARD S. CASEY is Distinguished Professor at the State University of New York at Stony Brook, where he teaches as well as at the New School for Social Research and at Pacifica Graduate Institute. His books include *Spirit and Soul: Essays in Philosophical Psychology; Imagining; Remembering; Getting Back into Place; Representing Place in Landscape Painting and Maps;* and (most recently) *Earth-Mapping: Artists Reshaping Landscape.*

CHRISTINE DOWNING was a graduate school colleague of David Miller's at Drew University and decades later taught with him at Pacifica Graduate Institute. Her thirteen books include, most recently, *The Luxury of Afterwards* and *Preludes* (for which David wrote a Foreword.)

WILLIAM DRAKE operates a grain business in central Illinois and is also an architect practicing in Chicago and New Mexico. He studied mythology at Pacifica Graduate Institute with David Miller who served as teacher, mentor, friend, and adviser on his doctoral dissertation.

TED ESTESS, Dean of The Honors College and Professor of English at the University of Houston, where he also holds the Jane Morin Cizik Chair, was David Miller's student at Syracuse University in the late 1960s and early 70s. Author of a book on Elie Wiesel, Estess has published literary critical articles on writers such as Samuel Beckett (the subject of his dissertation, directed by David Miller), Walker Percy, Mary Gordon, William Kennedy, and more recently, several pieces of creative non-fiction.

VICTOR FAESSEL, who studied with David Miller at Pacifica Graduate Institute, is Assistant Editor of English-language publications at the Center for Interdisciplinary Study of Monotheistic Religions (CISMOR),

Doshisha University, Kyoto, Japan. He is currently completing a translation of works on the labyrinth and related topics by Karl Kerényi.

ELIZABETH FERGUS-JEAN is an artist and a professor of mythological studies. Her solo-exhibitions, lectures, and teaching involve memory, creativity, image understanding, and visual voice. Her artwork has frequently appeared on the covers of numerous international journals.

WOLFGANG GIEGERICH is a Jungian psychoanalyst in private practice near Münich, Germany. He is the author of numerous books and articles in many languages. His most recent books are *Dialectics & Analytical Psychology* (with David Miller and Greg Mogenson), *The Neurosis of Psychology: Primary Papers Towards a Critical Psychology* (both Spring Journal Books), and *La Fine del Senso e la Nascita dell' Uomo* (Milano: La biblioteca di Vivarium, 2005).

JEAN GRAYBEAL studied with David Miller in the Religion Department at Syracuse University, where she completed her Ph.D. in 1986. She is Associate Professor at the Gallatin School of Individualized Study, New York University, and the author of *Language and "the Feminine" in Nietzsche and Heidegger.*

SOPHIA HELLER received her Ph.D. in Mythological Studies from Pacifica Graduate Institute in 2003. She is the author of *The Absence of Myth* (SUNY, 2006).

JAMES HILLMAN, writer, psychoanalyst, citizen, is author of, among many other books, *ReVisioning Psychology* and *The Dream and the Underworld,* and is happy to consider himself a long-term friend of David Miller. "We met at Lago Maggiore in the late 1960s; he has always been a gracious and generous intellectual and emotional giver."

STANLEY ROMAINE HOPPER was Dean of the Graduate School at Drew University when David Miller, Jim Wiggins, and Christine Downing were students there and served as David's *"Doktor-Vater;"* later he and David were for many years faculty colleagues at Syracuse University. His books include *Spiritual Problems in Contemporary Literature* and the anthology, *Interpretation: The Poetry of Meaning*, co-edited by David.

PAUL KUGLER is a Jungian analyst in private practice in East Aurora, New York. He is past President of the Inter-Regional Society of Jungian Analysts and a past member of the Executive Committee of the International Association of Analytical Psychologists. The author of numerous publications, including *Supervision: Jungian Perspectives on Clinical Supervision* (Daimon Verlag, 1995) and *The Alchemy of Discourse: Image, Sound and Psyche* (Revised edition, Daimon Verlag, 2002), his new book *Raids on the Unthinkable: Freudian and Jungian Psychoanalyses* (Spring Journal Books) was released in Spring of 2005.

JAN MARLAN is a Jungian analyst in private practice in Pittsburgh, PA, where she resides with her husband and 134 stuffed wolves.

STAN MARLAN is a Jungian analyst, an Adjunct Clinical Professor of Psychology at Duquesne University, and the author of *The Black Sun: The Alchemy and Art of Darkness*.

PATRICIA COX MILLER is W. Earl Ledden Professor of Religion at Syracuse University. She is the author, most recently, of *Women in Early Christianity: Translations from Greek Texts* (2005). She has been married to David L. Miller since 1984.

GREG MOGENSON is a Jungian analyst practicing in London, Ontario, Canada. The author of many articles in the field of analytical psychology, his books include *A Most Accursed Religion, The Dove in the Consulting Room, Northern Gnosis, Greeting the Angels,* and *Dialectics & Analytical Psychology* (with Wolfgang Giegerich and David L. Miller). His essay in the present volume pays tribute to David Miller's generous colleagueship and seminal contribution to archetypal psychology.

THOMAS MOORE is the author of *Care of the Soul* and over a dozen other books on themes in religion, depth psychology, and the arts. He has a Ph.D. in religion from Syracuse University and degrees in music and theology. He has lived in a religious order and has been a psychotherapist for over twenty-five years.

GINETTE PARIS is a member of the core faculty at Pacifica Graduate Institute, where she teaches depth psychology in the Mythological Studies Program. She is the author of *Pagan Grace* (Spring Publications, 1990) and *Pagan Meditations* (Spring Publications, 1986).

ROBERT D. ROMANYSHYN, a Senior Core Faculty Member at Pacifica Graduate Institute and an Affiliate Member of The Inter-Regional Society of Jungian Analysts, is the author of five books and is currently finishing another, *The Wounded Researcher*. He has known David as a colleague and friend since the early 70s and most admires how his scholarship blends irony, humor, and the sense of serious light heartedness.

SUSAN L. SCHWARTZ is Associate Professor and Chair of the Department of Religion Studies, Muhlenberg College, Allentown, PA. She is author of *Rasa: Performing the Divine in India* and co-author of *Religions of Star Trek*. She studied with David Miller at Syracuse University; he served as her dissertation advisor and she served as his teaching assistant.

LYNDA SEXSON is the author of *Ordinarily Sacred, Margaret of the Imperfections*, and *Hamlet's Planets*. She looks forward to celebrating David Miller's centennial with thirty more fragments for him.

GLEN SLATER teaches at Pacifica Graduate Institute in the departments of Mythological Studies and Depth Psychology. He has written a number of articles for various depth psychological publications, including the *Spring* and *Salt* journals. He recently edited and introduced the third volume of the *Uniform Edition* of James Hillman's writings. Glen has known David Miller for many years, as student, sidekick and colleague.

ERNEST WALLWORK is Professor of Religion at Syracuse University (where he has been a colleague of David Miller for 23 years) and a psychoanalyst in private practice in Washington, D.C. and Syracuse, New York. He is the author of *Psychoanalysis and Ethics* (New Haven, Ct.: Yale University

CONTRIBUTORS

Press, 1991) and *Durkheim: Morality and Milieu* (Cambridge, Mass.: Harvard University Press, 1972) and co-author of *Critical Issues in Modern Religion* (Englewood Cliffs, N.J.: Prentice Hall, 1973, second edition, 1991).

JIM WIGGINS is Eliphalet Remington Professor of Religion Emeritus, at Syracuse University. He served as Executive Director of the American Academy of Religion from 1982-1991 and since 2002 has been the Executive Director of the InterReligious Council of Central New York. Among his books are *Religion as Story* and *In Praise of Religious Diversity.*